Global Values in a Changing World

Global Values in a Changing World

Sonja Zweegers & Afke de Groot (eds.)

KIT Publishers – Amsterdam

Global Values in a Changing World
Sonja Zweegers and Afke de Groot (eds.)

KIT Publishers
Mauritskade 63
P.O. Box 95001
1090 HA Amsterdam
The Netherlands
E-mail: publishers@kit.nl
www.kit.nl/publishers

This publication was supported by the Society for International Development (SID).
Global Values in a Changing World is also the title of the 2010-2011 lecture series organised
by SID NL in partnership with the NCDO and the VU University.

Editing: Sonja Zweegers, Amsterdam, the Netherlands
Coordination: Afke de Groot (SID NL)
Design: Ad van Helmond, Amsterdam, the Netherlands
Cover design: Ronald Boiten, Amersfoort, the Netherlands
Printing: Bariet, Ruinen, the Netherlands

ISBN 978 94 6022 210 8
NUR 754

Contents

Preface   *7*
  René Grotenhuis

Introduction and Acknowledgements   *9*
  Afke de Groot

Part I: Global Values in a Changing World

'Country ownership' without a social contract:
towards a realistic perspective   *19*
  David Booth

Disconnected societies: rich versus poor in the development debate   *35*
  Gary Dymski

The migration and development pendulum: a critical view
on research and policy   *62*
  Hein de Haas

The role of external interventions redefined   *101*
  Paul Collier

Social responsibility in a context of change: from corporate and
organisational, to networks, markets and territories   *121*
  Patricia Almeida Ashley

Meeting global challenges: regaining sovereignty   *151*
  Inge Kaul

China's complexity in addressing 'global' security challenges   *170*
     Shi Yinhong

We are citizens of the world?   *182*
     Kate Nash

Part II: Challenging Universality

The universalisation of human rights: reflections on obstacles
and the way forward   *205*
     Willem van Genugten

SID NL Annual Conference 2011
     Global values in a changing world: challenging universality   *238*

The universality of values: a historical perspective   *240*
     Jack Donnelly

Universality of values in practice: dealing with new global realities   *248*
     Meghna Abraham

Different approaches towards universality   *257*
     *Panel Discussion with Meghna Abraham, David Forsythe,
     Seth Kaplan, and Tom Zwart*

Challenging universality: conclusions and summary   *273*
     Concluding words by Lionel Veer and Eduard Nazarski
     Conference summary by Roeland Muskens, Wereld in Woorden

Contributors   *290*

Preface

Ever since the Universal Declaration on Human Rights was adopted in 1949, by the newly established United Nations, a steadily developing body of conventions on international norms and rights has been established. That could give the impression that our world is moving into a clear direction, where globally accepted values are the basis of the rights of people and of the interaction between states. But over the years the reality of implementation of these international norms and rights was, to say the least, piecemeal. Nation-states stressed their sovereignty in implementing and interpreting these universal declarations and conventions.

The geopolitical shift that started in the first decade of the 21st century has its implications for the debate on universality of rights, norms and values. New emerging powers in the geopolitical arena and developing countries are taking a more self-confident position and sometimes question the basis of these universal rights and values as being too much based on western thinking and its system of liberal democracy. The multi-polarity of the world nowadays requires a new understanding of global values and norms, with greater and more shared ownership of the international community.

The Society for International Development Netherlands Chapter is convinced that global values are important and increasingly so in a globalising world. In the interconnectedness of our world, relations between individuals, communities and states need the basis of shared values. A rule-based international community needs shared underlying values to make sure that our mutual relations and our communications are based on a shared understanding of human dignity and on respect for one another. As the concept of Global Citizenship is taking hold in the globalising world, and increasingly people are looking at global citizenship as complementary (not opposed) to their national citizenship, the need for global values that are underpinning that global citizenship is becoming important. At the same time the reality of the nation-state is still there. We are far away from a global government with global jurisdiction. The process of building global values, universal rights and norms will remain hard work as it implies harmonising very diverse national realities in the direction of more and more common understanding and practice.

With the 2010-2011 lecture series, "Global Values in a Changing World. Synergy of State and Society in a Globalised World", SID-Netherlands has contributed to this process of reflection on the need for global values that could provide a strong foundation for global interaction between citizens and states in the world of today and tomorrow.

René Grotenhuis

President
Society for International Development
Netherlands Chapter

Introduction and Acknowledgements

In the 2010-2011 academic year the Dutch chapter of the Society for International Development (SID) focused in its annual lecture series on the connection between internationally agreed norms and values, and the way they are a practical reality in a changing world, which is both globalised and localised.

International treaties, conventions, and declarations have been developed in an attempt to establish a world in which people's basic rights and needs are provided for. An increasing number of states, including those in the South, have ratified these agreements and incorporated them into national legislation, but many of them are slow in implementing them in reality. These documents are relevant for international development, as they provide a necessary framework of underlying principles and values for citizens, enabling them to live together peacefully in a globalising world. The discrepancy between theory and practice, and conflicts between values and interests result in the debate on whether such norms and values are truly universal.

But states are no longer the only actors that shape global developments, and private actors and civil society also have important roles to play. Implementation of these agreements seems to come about mainly where social contracts are established within states; where communities and societies as a whole decide to adopt these globally agreed norms and systems, and translate them into concrete rules, regulations and enforcement mechanisms.

Speakers were invited to address challenges and opportunities for such social contracts in a globalised world, and their implications for international development. Part I of this book presents the lectures of eight international experts, and the ensuing discussions with a diverse audience representing students and academics, policy makers, NGOs, consultants and others. Part II presents the outcome of the conference organised in September 2011 to mark the closure of the lecture series.

The lectures

The first chapters of the book deal with the significance of social contracts for the 'traditional' development agenda of poverty reduction. *Ownership* is, since the Paris Declaration for Aid Effectiveness (2005) and the Accra Agenda for Action (2008), the norm for development effectiveness. David Booth, of the *Overseas Development Institute*, did extensive research on this 'new global value' of 'country ownership' of aid-supported development efforts. In his lecture Booth argues that the values behind these international agreements are not entirely realistic. The idea of good governance as a key for development is highly controversial, as democracy has different effects in different countries. Booth concludes that the two main instruments devised to get around the problem of deficient endogenous commitment ('good governance' and 'democratic ownership') are not effective at all. He argues that development cannot be achieved without endogenous drivers. In order to shape more effective development assistance, the concept of country ownership needs to be linked to a realistic perspective on the likely political drivers of development efforts in poor countries.

Donors should be careful when presuming that social contracts exist in targeting countries. An increasing challenge to such social contracts is the increasing gap between rich and poor within societies. The problem of these 'disconnected societies' was addressed by Gary Dymski of the California University, Riverside. He argues that economic reforms, such as the deregulation of finance, has produced a state of disconnect between elites able to exploit the opportunities offered by global capital mobility and a lower middle and working class that is increasingly excluded from the market. If states fail to address the increasing inequality between rich and poor, social cohesion is seriously under threat and compromises development strategies. Dymski argues that equity must be restored as an explicit goal of state policy. The elites have to be made more accountable and become more integrated in national development processes so that development is truly seen as a collective endeavour, whereas the poor need mechanisms to ensure their full economic and political inclusion so as to partake as equal citizens in the development process.

Central here is the role of the state. States cannot be absolved from their responsibility to the foundations for a development process in which everyone can participate. This was also put forward by Hein de Haas, senior fellow at the International Migration Institute of the University of Oxford. He warned for over-emphasising the role of migrants as agents of change at the expense of a critical focus on the role of nation-states in development.

If societies and people themselves increasingly develop by their own authentic way, then what are the implications of external interventions? When is foreign assistance 'facilitating', when is it even 'stimulating', and what are worst practices of external interventions: spoiling own initiatives of civil society and states? Paul Collier first of all warns that the mantra of 'ownership, not donorship' does not automatically imply that beneficial outcomes are produced when local actors are empowered. He then continues to describe two 'rather detrimental', so he argues, forms of international interventions: 'policy conditionality', when developing countries need to adopt certain policies prescribed by the donor if they want to receive aid, and 'budget support' in those cases when it is not applied effectively. Both undermine the link between government and citizens, and destroy the accountability of governments to their citizens. Collier calls for more 'politically intelligent efforts' to support development. He emphasises the importance of an informed citizenry to the functioning of institutions and the fostering of economic growth, and introduces 'governance conditionality', which helps a government to enforce its own laws. A second way to support development efforts is to improve the integrity of multinational companies.

When it comes to the private sector and development, the debate has mainly centred around the concept of corporate social responsibility (CSR), with an emphasis on seeking innovations in business models and management tools in order to come to sustainable development solutions. In her lecture on social responsibility, Patricia Almeida Ashley claims that the mainstream of global perspectives on CSR is still very much focused on a corporate or organisational level of social responsibility, relying on businesses to act as agents of change. She argues that it should be approached within a broader scope of social networks and institutional fields. She presents a conceptual framework, the 'MASTER'-model of multi-actor and multilevel social responsibility in a territorial scope, connecting layers of stakeholders' social responsibilities towards development and equity goals. In this model social responsibility is still based on the conception of organisations, but as 'dots' that are part of a larger institutional context.

We are living in a world of real interdependency. In previous SID-lecture series[1] it has already been addressed that securing the global common goods (fresh water, clean air, food, energy, etcetera) have been accepted as part of the agenda of international cooperation. Traditional 'donor' countries bear to a great deal (but not exclusively) the responsibility for solving the global crises on energy, climate change, and food security. Also with regards to migration there is a clear shared responsibility of donor and developing countries. Inge Kaul, former director of the UNDP's *Human Development Report Office*, argues that political thinking has not caught up to this global reality of today. States think too much in terms of zero-sum, rather than recognising the fact that global cooperation is really the best strategy for realising all our national interests. The world needs better cooperation between states. Instead, decisions are often based on the need to protect our 'own' needs, failing to understand that global issues affect everyone. In her lecture 'Meeting global challenges: regaining sovereignty', Inge Kaul introduces the concept 'Responsible Sovereignty' as key to structuring and organising a next World Order, whereby respect for each other's freedoms coupled with accountability of one's actions, creates a norm of interaction that fosters social cohesiveness and peace.

Shi Yinhong, Professor of International Relations at the Renmin University of China, was invited to clarify China's point of view. He explains that China faces a constant dialectical tension between its particularistic and universalistic impulses. In his lecture he uses the example of global security to illustrate his point. China is engaged in a much broader and deeper international cooperation compared to the past.

1   See Berendsen, B. (ed.) *Emerging Global Scarcities and Power Shifts,* KIT Publishers, 2009; and Berendsen, B. (ed.) *Common Goods in a Divided World,* KIT Publishers, 2011

China deals with global security challenges with increasing responsiveness and even takes the initiative to assume greater international responsibility. However, there is a remarkable complexity and sophistication embedded in China's attitude, positions and policies in the area of global challenges and corresponding multilateral cooperation. China's response to global security challenges and norms is coloured by its complexity. Shi concludes that China does accept international cooperation and is more and more open for cooperation with Western countries, but it will remain tied to particularistic interests driven by its own unique philosophy and way of thinking.

The question remains of how and by whom global norms and values are to be advanced. Many speakers emphasised the need to harness the strength of civil society actors and build on what they can create from below. Paul Collier refers to the importance of an informed citizenry to the functioning institutions and the fostering of economic growth. In addition, both Inge Kaul and Willem van Genugten stress the importance of a bottom-up process of *universalisation* rather than *universality*, in which local views are taken into account, and where the politically and legally responsible are confronted from below with the obligation to uphold internationally agreed standards. Is the idea of global citizenship the answer to make global values really rooted in societies and is global citizenship the best guarantee for the global common goods?

Part I of this volume concludes with a chapter on global citizenship. Kate Nash argues in her lecture that that the idea of 'global citizenship' is close, but still utopian. The understanding of 'global citizenship' as it currently stands, mediated through national structures, is insufficient. Nash argues there are two types of practices that encourage people to imagine ourselves as 'world citizens'. The first is the global digital media, which is changing our daily experience of being part of humanity. We are world citizens in that we daily respond to images and stories of suffering elsewhere in the world. The second type is the structures of human rights, which embed us in obligations to people in other countries through our *national* citizenship. We are also world citizens in that we have indirect political obligations to those people, through our states of which we are nationals, insofar as they have signed up to international human agreements. In this sense, world citizenship is strangely exercised as national citizenship, oriented towards our own governments. An appeal to citizens' solidarity is necessary if we are to truly share in a global community of fate.

The conference

Part II covers the conference 'Global Values in a Changing World: Challenging Universality', which was organised in September 2011 in The Hague to mark the closing of the lecture series. Part II starts with the lecture series' inaugural lecture delivered a year earlier by Professor Willem van Genugten, which presents a clear introduction to the subject of the conference. The lecture by Van Genugten gives a historic overview, and issues four warnings concerning the supposed 'universality' of human rights. First of all, it would be too simple to label the numerous international conventions 'universally accepted' just because they have a UN-label. Van Genugten furthermore warns that universality does not mean that local contexts should not be taken into consideration: universality does *not* imply uniformity. Third, many states accept agreements and standards, but at the same time refuse to accept external control or criticism. It is finally important to note, Van Genugten argues, that there are frictions between international legal obligations and national (constitutional) legal characteristics of states. Discussions on the universality of human rights are not only relevant between states and international law, but more so within sovereign states, and between national governments and local communities.

In his keynote speech at the conference, 'Challenging Universality', Jack Donnelly, Professor at the University of Denver, concludes that universality is limited. When referring to human rights he prefers to use the term 'relative universality'. Human rights can be considered universal in the sense that they are deeply rooted in international legal consensus, and that they have become overriding social and political goals and practices as a result of the rise of modern states and modern markets. Donnelly argues that there is consensus about the broad conception of human rights and its related values, but that the implementation greatly varies. Local differences and particularities are hardly culturally defined. According to Donnelly, the more a society is enmeshed between markets and states, the more its members will view human rights as universal. The differences are not between East and West, or North and South.

Meghna Abraham, affiliated to the International Secretariat of Amnesty International, agrees with Donnelly that at the levels of interpretation and implementation there are significant challenges. She identifies the greatest challenge being how to ensure the universal applicability and implementation of human rights. It is in particular the people who live in poverty, and who face discrimination, who receive insufficient attention. The link between human rights and poverty is insufficiently made. Another challenge is ensuring the accountability of new actors, such as private companies and International Financial Institutions.

In the panel discussion that follows, Seth Kaplan links human rights to social stability. In countries with much social stability there is usually more room for free speech than in countries with social unrest. What is necessary is to build capacity within states, to strengthen institutions that are crucial to improve basic rule of law. Kaplan also critically notes that the discussions during the conference are not so much on 'challenging universality', but rather on 'promoting universality'. Kaplan argues that many parts of the globe are offended by the way the West tries to promote human rights. Professor Tom Zwart, who introduced the receptor-approach, then emphasises that in many cases it would be not effective to try and impose western systems onto local, traditional circumstances.

Abraham contends by stating that the fact that all rights are applicable to all people everywhere is not open to debate. She stresses that the main instrument, a legal framework rooted in international rules and regulations, must have practical meaning on local level, in order to make progress in implementation.

Acknowledgements

The 2010-2011 lecture series would not have been possible without the support of the NCDO, a Dutch expertise and advisory centre for citizenship and international cooperation, and the VU University in Amsterdam, where the lectures have been held for many years now. On behalf of the Netherlands Chapter of the Society for International

Development (SID NL), I would like to thank them for these partnerships.

I am very grateful to the Dutch Section of Amnesty International, Eduard Nazarski, Wilco de Jonge, and Lars van Troost in particular, for their advisory role in the preparation of the conference. I would also like to thank the Worldconnectors Roundtable and PwC for making the conference possible.

At the Secretariat of SID NL we owe much gratitude to the members of the SID NL Advisory Council and the SID NL Board. I would like to mention Bernard Berendsen in particular. He has edited the previous four volumes, and has been a great advisor on the realisation of this volume as well.

Much appreciation goes out to my colleagues at the Secretariat of SID NL; Tom Bakker, Wilma Bakker, Frida van der Graaf, Ladan Hakimi, Sylvia Kay, Iem Roos, and Anne-Marie Slaa have all participated in making the lectures and the conference a success. Anne-Marie, Sylvia, Ladan and Tom also contributed to transferring spoken word to paper by making excellent summary reports and transcriptions when necessary.

Last but not least, SID NL thanks Sonja Zweegers for the wonderful job she did in editing all the texts, and Ron Smit and his team at KIT Publishers for their confidence. This is yet another volume that can be added to the SID-series published at KIT, which now comprises five books giving a good overview of how the debate on international cooperation has been developed over the last six years.

At SID we continue the discussion on a wide range of issues of national and international development. We will dedicate our attention to the role of different actors such as the state, civil society actors, and the private sector. We will look back and evaluate, but more so look forward to new forms of international cooperation, and discuss ways to shape our global future.

I thank you, the reader, for showing interest in SID, and I hope this volume will inspire you to move the debate forward.

Afke de Groot

Coordinator Society for International Development
Netherlands Chapter

PART I

Global Values in a Changing World

'Country ownership' without a social contract: towards a realistic perspective

David Booth

About 15 years ago,[1] the development assistance business invented a new global value – country ownership of aid-supported development efforts. I think this was an important and positive step. Of course, from a social scientific point of view 'country ownership' is a vulgar term, but by the standards usually applied to the practical concepts that guide international policies, it does a reasonably good job – it captures well the main implications of a large body of research and practical experience.

I have in mind here the experience that built up in the 1990s in support of two propositions: 1) that poor countries cannot achieve development solely on the basis of external support – there need to be endogenous drivers; and 2) that the two main devices that aid donors have devised to get around the problem of deficient endogenous commitment do not work well. The second proposition refers to the use of project funding as a means of deliberately *by-passing country institutions*, and the attachment of policy conditionalities to grants and soft loans with the intention of *'buying reform'*.

The evidence on these points – that project modalities do institutional harm and that conditionalities do not work – was already substantial in 1999. It has not become less compelling since then. 1999 was a key date because it was in that year that a substantial international consensus built up on the need to bring development assistance into line with the critique of by-passing and conditionality. Since that time, 'ownership' has been a recurrent theme in international policy. The original discussion was around Enhanced HIPC

---

1   Readers are requested to bear in mind that this lecture was delivered in December 2010. It addresses the international discussion on country ownership and aid effectiveness a year ahead of the 4th High Level Forum held in Busan, 29 Nov-1 Dec 2011.

debt relief and Poverty Reduction Strategy Papers (PRSPs). This then strongly influenced the 2005 Paris Declaration on Aid Effectiveness. In 2011, country ownership will again be the central theme at the 4th High Level Forum on Aid Effectiveness to be held in Busan, Korea.

All this is positive in my view. However, a major problem remains. In order to be useful in shaping more effective development assistance, the concept of country ownership needs to be linked to a realistic perspective on the likely political drivers of development effort in poor countries. I believe that too much of the current approach to aid effectiveness is based on wishful thinking. Most of the time, we choose to ignore the knowledge and understanding we have about politics and development. We do this because we find it comfortable – and our leaders find it politically convenient – to derive policy approaches directly from our ideological values.

To be clear, my argument is not that values have no place in development and poverty reduction. I am not against 'global values', and do not see anything fundamentally wrong with the aspirations articulated in such places as the UN charter. My dispute is with *policy approaches that are driven by values without the intermediation of evidence* from either research or practical experience.

My contention in relation to country ownership is therefore this: if we were really serious about it, our next step would be to ask what is known about the conditions under which it has been achieved, historically and in more recent times. We have tended not to do that. Instead, we have given 'ownership' the status of a global value and then piled on top of it a series of other conventional standards and judgements about how countries *ought* to be governed – making the implicit assumption that 'all good things go together'. This is unhelpful, because it is not evidence-based.

I will argue that it is particularly unhelpful in regard to values concerning democratic governance and the rule of law. And I would include here the idea that governance is 'good' – good for country-owned development – only when state-society relationships are underpinned by a 'social contract'.

That is my proposition. I want to support it with reference to two particular topics: 1) the current debate about what to do with the Paris Declaration at the High Level Forum in Busan; and 2) the light shed on 'ownership' by current research on governance and development in sub-Saharan Africa.

Country ownership and the Paris Declaration

What is wrong with the Paris Declaration? Two things in my view. First, the ownership commitments are placed at the front, but their effect has been diluted (even by comparison with the earlier Rome Declaration) by the addition of commitments under several other headings – not just aid alignment and harmonisation, but 'management for results' and a multi-stranded 'mutual accountability'. There is an implication that the additional commitments are all conducive to country ownership, so that the whole forms a coherent package. However, the evidence for this is weak.

The alignment commitments, and to a lesser extent the harmonisation ones, are on the whole desirable. Their main limitation is that they relate to the technocratic level of aid management and provide no answers to the question of what donors should do if, in spite of everything, governments or other country actors do not assume leadership of development efforts in their territory. It is worse with 'results management': the evidence that 'results-oriented reporting and assessment frameworks' provide a good point of entry for support to country ownership is quite unconvincing. Finally, the key commitment under mutual accountability is about accountability within developing countries and calls for a strengthening of parliamentary oversight and participatory processes around national development strategies. The prominence given to these issues is also not evidence-based – which brings me to my second criticism.

The second thing wrong with the Paris Declaration is that it does not reflect very much of the learning that has been produced around the last attempt to use aid and debt relief directly to engineer greater country ownership – the Poverty Reduction Strategy Paper initiative. I have been associated with the view that, at the time, PRSPs were a worthwhile experiment, given the lack of well supported alternatives. But from the very first studies and evaluations, it was clear that the best that would be achieved through the PRSP initiative was greater efficiency at the technocratic level. The crucial political levers would hardly be touched, *unless* the politicians discovered their own reasons for increasing the effectiveness of development efforts (Booth, 2003; Dijkstra, 2005).

After the first review of PRSP experience, the IMF and the World Bank drew the conclusion that the original guidelines had under-emphasised parliamentary involvement. International NGOs, for their part, continued to press the interests of 'civil society'. They, and others with strong institutional commitments to building Monitoring and Evaluation systems, pushed for more attention to M&E. This is how the Paris Declaration came to have the shape and content that it did. But it was not what the serious studies were saying and recommending.

These were not mere mistakes. Nor were they just the reflection of vested interests in the aid business (although those exist too). Rather, many well-intentioned people find it natural to suppose that institutional arrangements that have proven their worth in highly industrialised Northern countries cannot fail to have something important to contribute to the development of poor countries. Over the past twenty years, this basic impulse has been one of the driving forces behind the idea – now deeply entrenched in developing as well as donor countries – that the key to successful development is 'good governance'. Good governance is usually taken to mean democratic governance and the institutional 'best practices' now established in advanced market economies.

The relationship between democratisation and development has never been a simple question, but we know some basic things about it. We know, for example, that institutions like parliaments and elections have very different effects in different social and economic settings. This is one of the themes of the important 2009 book by Douglass North and others (North et al., 2009). More recently (2010), Jörg Faust of the German Development Institute has addressed more specifically the notion that aid effectiveness might be enhanced by being linked to democratisation – with 'ownership' being replaced by 'democratic ownership'. Faust shows that this is based on a fundamental misunderstanding of how democracy works, in the long run, to generate social benefits.

There is indeed some danger that HLF4 will be the occasion for new efforts to merge the aid effectiveness agenda with good governance understood in this way. Already at the Accra review meeting in 2008 there were signs of this, limited only by the fact that the World Bank and other key supporters have difficulty with taking positions on 'politics'. The fact that the Koreans and delegates of other countries that are in transition from beneficiaries to donors know full well that their development breakthroughs were achieved without 'good governance', ought to help, but it may not. The capacity of economically successful countries to ignore their own history and 'kick away the ladder' by which they climbed to development (Chang, 2002) should not be underestimated.

Country ownership for African development

My argument so far has been that allowing development assistance to be driven by global values rooted in Northern experience without the intervention of evidence-based arguments is a bad thing. It is particularly bad in the context of low-income Africa, both because development challenges are especially great there, and because the brunt of the international community's mistakes tends to be borne by Africa.

What does experience and evidence tell us about the conditions under which country-owned development efforts are likely to be effective in Africa? It certainly does not tell us that one of the requirements is a full adoption by African countries of the governance arrangements that are now enjoyed in most advanced industrial countries – in other words, the institutional underpinnings of a liberal-democratic 'social contract' and a fully capitalist property-rights regime.

For certain, recent research and experience does support strongly the proposition that *peaceful* development calls for a political settlement or 'elite bargain'. The major elements of the country's elite must reach a binding agreement on the terms under which they will compete for power without taking up arms (Di John and Putzel, 2009; Parks and Cole, 2010). However, the *elite* in the phrase 'elite bargain' is to be taken seriously. The necessary bargain may well have to embrace all significant identity groups and involve the elites of neighbouring powers (as, for example, in Afghanistan and DRC); but the idea that it has to be inclusive of the broad masses or be socially progressive is not empirically grounded. A political settlement, in this context, is *not* a social contract.

In fact, I would suggest, it is quite unrealistic to expect poor developing countries to institute a social contract in the normal, post-Enlightenment sense of that term. If country-owned development efforts depend on the prior establishment of an effective political or social democracy, the prospects are not good. But that is not all. The efforts of ideological entrepreneurs and aid donors to promote democratic governance and other 'best practices' have been highly successful in changing opinions around the world. But the corresponding ratcheting-up of expectations has probably done more harm than good to the prospects for development in the poorest countries.

A very significant body of research and some of the most recognised practitioner-researchers now agree with Brian Levy of the World Bank in declaring the 'best-practice' approach bankrupt (2010). Highlights on the economics side include Dani Rodrik's (2007) recognition that – after China's development breakthrough – we do not really know what are the right institutions for inducing sustained improvements in economic and social welfare in very poor countries. They also include Mustaq Khan's argument that states need the freedom and the means to oversee a process of 'primitive accumulation', in which rents and rent-seeking are used to finance the costly learning processes involved in getting capitalism started (Gray and Khan, 2010).

Focusing more directly on politics, we have the invitation from Merilee Grindle (2007) to think more seriously about which governance reforms might be 'good enough' to get development started. We have Mick Moore and Sue Unsworth urging us to pay more attention to what exists, and can be built upon, in country governance arrangements and less to 'gap filling' – that is, trying to supply what those arrangements seem to lack by comparison with typical OECD member states (Future State, 2010).

Current research focused on Africa, with the experience of Southeast Asia in the background, is helping to flesh out this point of view. For example, an excellent Dutch research project (van Donge et al., 2012) has shown that the dramatic differences in development performance between African and comparable Southeast Asian states is at one level not about governance at all, but about policy. All of the Southeast Asian countries included in the study, but none of the African ones, targeted investment at the rural smallholder sector during their early growth processes.

We still have to be concerned, of course, about *why* African leaders persist in pursuing the wrong policies. Researchers focusing on this question are beginning to generate specific propositions about the development potentialities of different types of regime. For example, a research stream of the Africa Power & Politics Programme led by Tim Kelsall has been discovering several important things about the most likely institutional form of 'country owned development efforts' in Africa today (Kelsall, 2011).

According to this research, a precondition for country ownership is that the country's ruling elite come to an agreement that their interests lie in enlarging the national economic 'pie' and not just in competing with each other for a larger slice of the pie. Such an agreement seems more likely if the rulers are sufficiently secure in power that they are able to take the long view. It seems less likely if they do not. But they need the means as well as the desire to impose discipline on themselves and on at least key sections of the administration. This involves the issue of the generation and utilisation of *rents*.

For the reasons given by Mushtaq Khan (and in a different way by North and company) the key question in the early stage of capitalist development is not whether markets are free and property rights are generally protected. The key question is what happens to *rents* and control of key productive *assets*. The majority of successful developers in Africa are likely to be of a broadly neo-patrimonial type, as they have been in Asia and indeed were in early modern Europe.[2] But they will be distinguished from other neo-patrimonial states by their attainment of a centralised management of rents and the long time horizon of their rulers.

On the basis of a survey of past and current experience, Kelsall and his team think it would be unwise to dismiss the possibility of a

---

2   That is, there will be a systematic blurring of the distinction between the wealth of the state and the personal wealth of the ruler or rulers, leading to some degree of institutionalised acceptance of rent-seeking on the part of the political leadership.

developmental (neo)patrimonialism. In fact, that is the kind of country ownership that seems most likely to be both effective and feasible. We think this has important implications for donors and for the wider community of people who care about development and Africa. The examples supporting this argument include phases in the history of Botswana, Côte d'Ivoire, Kenya and Malawi. Currently, we are looking at Tanzania, where CCM seems to enjoy a number of the preconditions for a long-horizon disciplining of rent generation and management, but somehow fails to get it together (Cooksey and Kelsall, 2011). And we are examining closely the contrasts between Uganda and Rwanda, where ex-guerrilla regimes have shown an increasingly divergent ability to manage rents for development purposes.

The three East African cases illustrate an important aspect of the argument. All three could be described as imperfect democracies. In accord with the conventional, value-driven, 'gap filling' doctrine, aid-funded governance and human rights work concentrates on trying to remove the imperfections by means of 'deepening democracy' programmes and governance monitoring exercises. Arguably, these activities are harmless even if rather ineffectual so long as the basic political incentive structure remains as it typically is in 'young democracies' (Keefer and Khemani, 2005; Keefer, 2007). But in at least two situations, they can be harmful. One is where instigating elections destroys the political settlement that has sustained the peace, without putting a new one in its place (Putzel, 2010). The other is where the elite is moving towards a developmental rent-utilisation regime and is hindered in doing so by donor disapproval or local ideologies appealing to 'global values' based on today's institutions in the North.

Our leading instance here is Rwanda under Paul Kagame's RPF. With due respect to Paul Collier's views (2009: 182-183), we are not convinced that Uganda remained for very long on a pathway towards a developmental rent-utilisation regime after Museveni's take-over. So the combined internal and external pressure that led to the abandonment of the 'no-party' Movement system cannot be held responsible for the free-wheeling clientelism that now prevails in that country. On the other hand, Rwanda *does* seem to be on a developmental-patrimonial path (Booth and Golooba-Mutebi, 2011).

No doubt, this is for very special reasons, and I would not want to propose emulating all aspects of Kagame's rule – any more than one would wish to emulate Houphouët-Boigny, Kamuzu Banda, Suharto or Mahathir Mohamed. But a key point is that some of the things about which even Kagame's closest donor friends have reservations are those that most clearly belong to the toolkit of centralised rent management as analysed by Khan and Kelsall. I refer particularly to the way a holding company fully owned by the ruling party has been used to channel rents of various kinds into productive and infra-structural investments. The donors express concern about this – they worry about the 'levelness of the playing field' for private entrepre-neurs, applying the yardstick that is generally seen as appropriate for business-politics linkages in their own countries. However, our examination of the story of Tri-Star Investments (now rebranded as Crystal Ventures Ltd.) suggests that crowding out of private firms has been minimal. In fact, we find significant crowding-in as well as a range of other beneficial effects.

In assessing this conclusion, proper account needs to be taken of three things: the extreme weakness of the domestic private sec-tor post-genocide; the country's small, landlocked market; and the unwillingness of firms of any origin to take on the risks and learn-ing costs associated with pioneering investment even in such poten-tially lucrative sectors as mobile phones. Given this context, we think the Tri-Star/Crystal Ventures story fits well with the relevant theory, whether one prefers the 19th century concept of 'primitive accumu-lation' in the manner of Khan, or the modern idea preferred by the firm's current Chief Executive, 'early-stage venture capitalism' .

This is what the 'country ownership' question should be about. Country ownership is and *should* be a global value, but we must be serious about what this means. It commits us to seeking out and rec-ognising the most likely drivers of development effort in poor coun-tries. On current evidence, these seem most likely to be found in a leadership with a long-term development vision and some kind of machinery for managing well the rent generation and utilisation, which are central to all early development processes.

I am aware that for the development cooperation business this is a lot to take on board in one go. We have at least several decades of high-minded rhetoric to unlearn before we can handle the messages emerging from the research I have been discussing. Drawing out the full implications for policy dialogue around ownership and effective aid is going to be hard, at both global and country levels. I do think, however, that we should begin to do this now.

References

Booth, David and Frederick Golooba-Mutebi (2011) *Developmental Patrimonialism? The Case of Rwanda.* Working Paper 16. London: Africa Power and Politics Programme.

Booth, David (ed.) (2003) *Fighting Poverty in Africa: Are PRSPs Making a Difference?* London: Overseas Development Institute.

Chang, Ha-Joon (2002) *Kicking Away the Ladder: Development Strategy in Historical Perspective.* London: Anthem Press.

Collier, Paul (2009) *Wars, Guns and Votes: Democracy in Dangerous Places.* London: Bodley Head.

Cooksey, Brian and Tim Kelsall (2011) *The Political Economy of the Investment Climate in Tanzania.* Research Report 01. London: Africa Power and Politics Programme.

Di John, Jonathan and James Putzel (2009) *Political Settlements: Issues Paper.* Birmingham: Governance and Social Development Resource Cente.

Dijkstra, Geske (2005) 'The PRSP Approach and the Illusion of Improved Aid Effectiveness: Lessons from Bolivia, Honduras and Nicaragua', *Development Policy Review* 23(4): 443-464.

Faust, Jörg (2010) 'Policy Experiments, Democratic Ownership and Development Assistance', *Development Policy Review* 28(5): 515-534.

Future State, Centre for the (2010) *An Upside Down View of Governance.* Brighton: Institute of Development Studies.

Gray, Hazel and Mushtaq Khan (2010) 'Good Governance and Growth in Africa: What Can We Learn from Tanzania?' in V. Padayachee (ed.) *The Political Economy of Africa.* London: Routledge: 339-356.

Grindle, Merilee (2007) 'Good Enough Governance Revisited', *Development Policy Review* 25(5): 553-574.

Keefer, Philip (2007) 'Clientelism, Credibility, and the Policy Choices of Young Democracies', *American Journal of Political Science* 51(4): 804-821.

Keefer, Philip and Stuti Khemani (2005) 'Democracy, Public Expenditures, and the Poor: Understanding Political Incentives for Providing Public Services', *World Bank Research Observer* 20(1): 1-27.

Kelsall, Tim (2011) 'Rethinking the Relationship Between Neo-Patrimonialism and Economic Development in Africa', *IDS Bulletin* 42(2).

Levy, Brian (2010) *Development Trajectories: An Evolutionary Approach to Integrating Governance and Growth*. Economic Premise 15. Washington, DC: World Bank.

North, Douglass C., John J. Wallis and Barry R. Weingast (2009) *Violence and Social Orders: A Conceptual Framework for Interpreting Recorded Human History*. Cambridge: Cambridge University Press.

Parks, Thomas and William Cole (2010) *Political Settlements: Implications for International Development Policy and Practice*. Occasional Paper 2. Bangkok: The Asia Foundation.

Putzel, James (2010) *Do No Harm: International Support for Statebuilding*. Paris: OECD DAC Fragile State Group.

Rodrik, Dani (2007) *One Economics, Many Recipes: Globalization, Institutions, and Economic Growth*. Princeton, NJ: Princeton University Press.

Van Donge, Jan Kees, David Henley and Peter Lewis (2012) 'Tracking Development in Southeast Asia and sub-Saharan Africa: The Primacy of Policy', *Development Policy Review* 30(S1): s5-s24.

Summary

According to Booth, creating a greater degree of country ownership is an important step towards generating greater aid effectiveness in developing countries. Using development projects to bypass the institutions of the countries in which these projects take place has proven harmful. This was recognised in the Paris Declaration in 2005, which placed country ownership high on the agenda. However, according to Booth, the Paris Declaration, and renewed versions of it, are not realistic about the conditions under which country-owned development happens. They are based on ideologically based wishful thinking, instead of focusing on the knowledge that we have. Western donors often presume that social contracts exist in targeted countries, but this is certainly not always the case. The manner in which the aid effectiveness discussion has evolved following the Paris Declaration is problematic for two reasons.

First, ownership commitments are placed at the forefront, but their effect has been diluted by the addition of supplementary commitments under several headings, such as aid harmonisation and results-based management. The presumption is that these additional commitments are all conducive to country ownership, but the evidence for this is weak.

Second, the consensus does not reflect any learning from earlier initiatives such as the Poverty Reduction Strategy Papers (PRSPs). Apart from that, the idea of good governance as a key for development, which comes into the Paris Declaration's concept of 'mutual accountability', is questionable; democracy and other institutional 'best practices' have very different effects in different countries.

In discussing the policies for development cooperation of Western donor countries, Booth argues that values need to be supported by evidence on what works. Booth pointed to the differential success rates in the development of Southeast Asia compared to many African countries as evidence that it is not so much the quality of governance as it is the adoption of specific policies that makes a difference for development. When it comes to governance, we should recognise that the best-practice approach is bankrupt; we do not know the key institutional factors that cause development. Instead, we should be more realistic in our approach and support governance arrangements that are 'good enough' to produce development results, building on the structures that exist.

Booth argues for a focus on governments that deliver development instead of focusing on governments that perfectly meet our standards of good governance. Peaceful development needs to be underpinned by an elite bargain. Sustained economic growth calls for a particular kind of elite bargain in which elites agree to work towards creating a larger pie for the whole country through a productive use of the rents in the country rather than only seeking their own enrichment. Focusing on this elite agreement could thus be an important strategy for development policy.

You will read below that, in the discussion after the lecture, the question was raised of how we view the concept of democracy, especially since democratisation seems to create a slow, but stable form of growth. Booth acknowledges that development and democracy are often seen as correlated, as is even supported by empirical evidence. However, this relation is only true in general terms because the theory breaks down when applied to the progress of very poor countries. Here, democracy does not seem to make much of a difference for growth in the country. Another question from the audience asked Booth's opinion on the current popularity of results-based management. Booth commented that results-based management based on, for example, monitoring and evaluation mechanisms, does not seem to automatically generate incentives for policy-makers.

Discussion

Questions from the audience:
Can you react to the development of democratic countries? (i.e., they have a less rapid, but more stable development.)
Can you explain the success of Bangladesh, which has no elite bargain, but has seen enormous economic growth?
Can you say more about the values and dangers of results-based management?

Response by David Booth
Research on the relationship between democratisation and development has been going on for a long time and new layers are added to it every five years or so. Much of it has been broadly supportive of the idea that development and democratisation go together. But it is particularly supportive if your method is to pool all of the country data that you have on all of the countries of the world and to then carry out a regression analysis. That does indeed produce the result that development is associated with high levels of democratisation. But questions remain about the implications of this relationship at the global level. Mushtaq Khan's argument, which I am very persuaded by, is to ask what the relationship is between these variables when just looking at the very poor countries and the countries that are a little less poor. In other words, just consider sub-Saharan Africa, India, China and the countries in Southeast Asia, which have made it into the Middle Income category. The relevant question is: How do you get from being a very poor country to being one that is not so poor? How

can Africa achieve what Vietnam, Malaysia or Thailand are achieving? Khan shows that the democracy/development correlation breaks down if you ask that question.

Bangladesh is an exception. Brian Levy, whose name I mentioned, who is actively developing some of these ideas at the World Bank, is very interested in the Bangladesh exception – particularly in the idea that you can have islands of success, within countries that are otherwise (especially in regard to governance) completely disastrous – as is the case with Bangladesh. It is a very different case than Southeast Asia. As Paul Collier always emphasises, it depends a lot on the fact that Bangladesh is a coastal state and its export industries have very low transport costs, which is not the case for a number of the African countries that we are interested in.

Results-based management is indeed extremely fashionable along with the principle of closely monitoring progress towards the Millennium Development Goals. The question is whether it helps to strengthen country ownership of development efforts. During the early years of Poverty Reduction Strategy Papers in Africa, I was involved in a number of consultancy exercises, concerning the monitoring of Poverty Reduction Strategy Papers. We tried very hard to think of ways in which the monitoring system could be used to trigger political responses that would improve the overall efforts that countries were making – but we found very little evidence to support that idea. So, monitoring at the global level around the Millennium Development Goals has an influence at the global level, and it has some influence on politicians at the national level, but I would not overrate it. Fundamentally, politicians within poor countries are responding to other kinds of incentives and unless we can address ways of changing those incentives, we are not going to get the country-owned development efforts that we need.

Questions from the audience:
Could you clarify the concept of social contract in your title? Should there not be a sort of consensus between the elite and the population about rent?

Can good governance still have a value if we change the definition? What sense does it make to use the concept of 'country'? Why not give ownership to 'subject groups'?

Response by David Booth:
In the Khan model of a developmental elite bargain, as we are interpreting it in our research, the elite or the ruling organisation – take, for example, the CCM in Tanzania – does need to reach an agreement about how it is going to invest and how it is going to stop a free-for-all of self-enrichment by particular groups of politicians. But I do not think it is useful to use the term social contract in that way. You could also argue that the sort of clientelist relationship that particular big men have with their followers in a typical African political system involves a kind of contract. But it is not the kind of contract that Rousseau and Tom Paine and people like that wrote about in the 18th century European context; it is not a democratic pact.

If we were to redefine 'good governance' in terms of people having a degree of control over the factors that are determining their own lives, would it make a difference to the argument? It could do. I am tempted to redefine good governance as what works to improve the conditions for the mass of ordinary people in all of the important dimensions, including self-respect and empowerment, and so forth. But I am wary of redefinitions that make the argument completely circular. It is important to base policies on empirical research; we need to discover the facts about what things work to produce the kind of outcomes that we think are important. We should not be solving that problem by definition.

And yes, there is a problem with the concept of 'country'. Clearly, one of the preconditions for a developmental form of neopatrimonialism is that there is a group that sees itself as, first and foremost, the leadership of a country. One of the reasons that things are, from this point of view, easier in Rwanda, is that Rwanda has a history of being a real country. It has been a country for a long time, well before the colonial state was established, which is not the case for Tanzania or Uganda. Actually, thanks to the kind of leadership that Nyerere developed in Tanzania, it has become a country in certain important respects, which means that if CCM, the ruling party, had a mind to build on the nationalist elements in the Nyerere legacy, they would be quite well-placed to do so. So yes, the idea of ownership by countries, as opposed to groups within countries, is problematic — more in places like Kenya, less so in Tanzania. The answer has to be country-specific.

Disconnected societies: rich versus poor in the development debate

Gary A. Dymski [3]

Much of the world is still recovering from a cataclysmic dual financial and macroeconomic crisis whose roots were in the globalisation of finance. Empirical evidence suggests that globalisation has also increased income inequality (Mayer-Foulkes, 2009). Some economists argue that inequality fuelled the crisis (Rajan 2010); and while comprehensive post-crisis data are not yet available, in many nations the rise in unemployment and in foreclosures has surely increased income and wealth inequality. There are more poor and richer rich than before the current wave financial globalisation took hold three decades ago (Milanovic 2003, 2010).

To be accurate, this assessment must be carefully framed. As profound as it has been over nearly five years, the global economic crisis has concentrated its fury on upper-income 'global North' nations. Some of the nations with the largest shares of global population – in particular, China, India, Brazil, and Russia – have been relatively unaffected; and their economic growth has been restored. Indeed, it can be argued that insofar as these BRICS, and some others with large shares of global population (such as Indonesia), have grown faster than virtually all global-North nations, the global crisis has reduced global inequality.

The question examined in this chapter is this: How does the current state of global inequality matter for the future of global development? As the global-crisis example readily shows, this question can be answered in very different ways. One approach focuses on the fact that global inequality, when measured on a population-adjusted

---

3   The author's affiliation was Department of Economics, University of California, Riverside when this lecture was delivered. His affiliation with the Economics Division at the Leeds University Business School began 1 April 2012.

nation-by-nation basis, is being systematically reduced because lower-income countries have generated a faster pace of growth than upper-income countries for a number of years (including the recent crisis years). In this view, the focus of attention for those interested in global development should be on the rising average circumstances of residents of the global South, as the centre of gravity of global economic growth shifts toward the emerging economies. For reasons explored in the next section, that approach is not taken here. We instead prefer a second approach, which emphasises the rise or decline of inequality within each nation. And the available evidence suggests that within almost every nation – in most of the developed world, and in the developing world as well – inequality is worsening. In particular, the gap between rich and poor is widening.

We focus here on the growing gap between the rich and the rest of society, with special attention to how this gap affects and is affected by the financial deregulations and innovations that have characterised the neoliberal (post-1980) era.[4] We argue that the deregulation of finance has facilitated institutional developments in financial markets that have produced a state of disconnect between elites, able to exploit the opportunities offered by global capital mobility, and lower middle and working classes that are increasingly squeezed and excluded from mainstream markets. This 'disconnection' played a part in the emergence of subprime mortgages and other forms of predatory lending, and in the erosion of public services – including housing. It was the collapse of governmental commitment to supplying public or subsidised housing construction, after all, combined with lagging income growth, which made so many people so desperate to jump into unaffordable mortgages. While their incomes were stuck in neutral, they relied on the hope that the value of the homes they were buying would continue to escalate at astronomical rates.

This disconnection process, which in globalised capitalism is linked to specialised circuits of goods/services and capital, is advancing in the global South. In almost all developing countries we see

---

4   The lecture on which this chapter is based was delivered before the 'Occupy' movement emerged, with its emphasis on the 'one percent'. Coincidentally, some of the empirical data used here focuses on the income level of the top one percent.

a rapid increase of the elite and higher middle class strata – and a parallel growth of an urbanised lower-income segment. Data on the division of wealth in these countries points to an increasing gap between rich and poor. These elites are increasingly more connected to the consumption norms, investment patterns, and cultural values of prosperous global North countries, and ever more disconnected from their own societies. This trend threatens the basis of development as a national 'mission.' For these elites and higher middle classes no longer view themselves as responsible for national development; instead, their needs have to be appeased. The poor are seen as peripheral to the development problem; they may pose demands that must be accommodated, but their needs are not coterminous with national developmental targets. This implies that development no longer represents a project embraced by all layers of societies emerging from the shadows of colonialism or neo-colonialism; consequently, the goals and instruments of development policy must be rethought.

The economic growth trajectory associated with neoliberalism therefore jeopardises rather than bolsters the search for an equitable and sustainable global development strategy. These institutional developments must be addressed by what might be termed 'countervailing' policy reactions; if they are not, perverse interactions between short-termism in finance, the erosion of public capacity, and deteriorating income levels will undercut the possibility of sustainable growth. Among the fundamental changes in the current economic system that can reduce this disconnect are these: the greater accountability of global elites; shifts from orthodox to heterodox economic policies; the enactment of redistributionist measures; and efforts to increase the political and economic participation of the poor.

Two ways of looking at the evolution of global inequality

In 1955, Simon Kuznets found what appeared to be a trans-national, trans-historical, non-linear relationship between economic growth and inequality, wherein greater inequality accompanied nations' transition from a low- to a middle-income income level – with the possibility of that inequality being reduced as income levels grew even higher. Kuznets' article launched a debate that remains unresolved a half-century later. Many economists take it as a premise that increasing income inequality is necessary to accelerate economic development in lower-income countries (Aghion, Caroli, and Garcia-Peñalosa 1999). This 'Kuznets curve' relationship has remained a stylised fact even while most recent evidence has found little relationship between economic growth and inequality (see, for example, Barro 2000).[5] Either conclusion would lead many economists to conclude that having increasing numbers of rich and poor is irrelevant for growth, and hence for development.

The debate among economists focuses on how inequality affects the pace of income growth per se. Some authors are beginning to go further by talking about structural consequences of this gap; for example, Kumhof and Rancière (2010) argue that the wealth gap will cause large-scale borrowing of the savings of rich households by non-rich households, a development that is not sustainable.[6]

Our exploration will not wade into the ongoing debate about the impact of inequality on economic growth. We instead focus on how the growing gap between the rich and the rest of society affect and are affected by economic reforms undertaken in the neoliberal era, particularly in finance. To set the stage, we first review some of the relevant evidence. This review is necessarily fragmentary; but it establishes an empirical basis for our analysis.

An overview of general global trends with respect to inequality must acknowledge, first of all, that there are two ways of understanding what is happening. One approach is to examine the average levels of income on a nation-by-nation basis. The World Bank's annual World Development Reports includes statistics and graphics on per-capita GDP per global region, which utilises this approach; its 2002 version suggested precisely the global 'catch-up' of low-income portions of the world. Figure 1, which is taken from Milanovic (2002), provides a snapshot of this approach; it shows levels of national aver-

---

5   In addition to Barro's paper, portions of the vast literature on this topic are discussed in
     Acemoglu and Robinson (2002) and in Foellmi and Zweimüller (2003).

6   These authors' assertion assumes the exogeneity of money. In a Keynesian approach, this
     savings-based argument would be modified by lenders' endogenous money creation.

age income across the world in 1993 on the basis of household-survey data. Significantly, China and India are divided into rural and urban areas. Most people could be considered relatively poor; but because of their weight in global population, the progress of China and India in average income levels leads to the tentative conclusion that average prosperity has been rising globally. In particular, this appears to reflect the coming-of-age of the emerging BRICS economies.

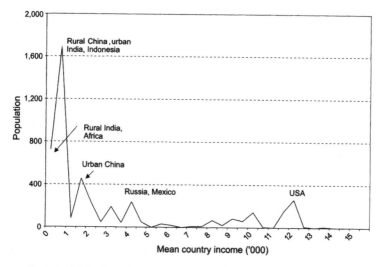

Figure 1: Distribution of population (in millions). According to average per capital income of country where they live (in '000 $PPP per year)

Source: Figure 6 in Milanovic (2002), p. 80.

There is another way of looking at global inequality, however. Rather than averaging national (or sub-national) experience across individuals, one can instead examine inequality within nations, regions, and cities. Here, evidence suggests a polarisation between rich and poor within these geographic areas – or more precisely, between the elite and upper middle class, on one side, the working class and the marginalised poor on the other.

This polarisation is dramatically illustrated in a 2010 study by Edward Wolff. The author shows that between 1983 and 2004, the number of households in the US is up a third, but the number of millionaires is up by 168 percent and the number of millionaires with a net worth over $10 billion is up over 400 percent. So there are now more rich; and the rich have a greater share of the total income.

One immediate explanation for this remarkable shift is financialisation. Throughout the neoliberal era, financial flows have comprised an increasingly dominant share of all economic activity (Palley 2007). While this is occurring, wages are falling as a percentage share of total income. A 2008 report by the International Labour Office (ILO) shows that in 51 of 73 countries for which data are available, the share of wages in total income declined over the past decade. The ILO study found that the largest decline in wage share occurred in Latin America (a 13 percent decline), followed by the Asia/Pacific region (10 percent) and the advanced economies (9 percent). Since non-wage income primarily includes profits or interest, the wage-share decrease, financialisation, and explosion in the millionaire population are interconnected.

So profits and interest, rather than wages, are driving much economic growth. This implies that the elite strata in many nations are increasing their share of national income. The well-known study by Piketty and Saez (2003), measuring the income shares of the wealthiest households from 1913 to the present shows that income shares for those in the top 10 percent, but below the top 1 percent, have grown very slightly from the 1970s to the present. However, the top 1 percent households, after a relatively steady decline from the Great Depression to 1978, have seen an explosive growth in their income share (to nearly 25 percent as of 2007); see Figure 2.

Piketty and Saez, with Facundo Alvaredo and Tony Atkinson, have established a 'World Top Income Database' (at http://g-mond. parisschoolofeconomics.eu/topincomes/), which contains data for many nations parallel to that shown in Figure 2 for the United States. The striking V-shaped pattern in the historical evolution of elite incomes found there for the US emerges in the data for most European countries for which data are available; the share of total national income accruing to the top 10 percent earners declines in the post-war period, reaches a low in the mid-1970s, and then steadily

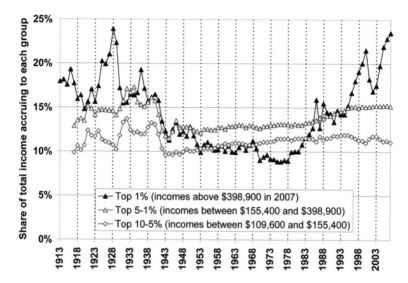

Figure 2: Decomposing the top decile US income share into 3 groups, 1913–2007
Source: Saez (2009, page 6).

rises again from the early 1980s onwards.[7] Two European countries are outliers: Germany and the Netherlands.[8]

In the countries of the global South, a similar phenomenon emerges. In particular, India and China both show an increase in the income share of the wealthy in the last few decades. The percentages are lower, but the rising income of the elite is clearly evident. The global picture thus seems to be that after a period of decreasing inequality in the post-war period, inequality has again been on the rise in the neoliberal era.

---

7   In the SID-NL lecture in March 2011, this historical V-shaped pattern was demonstrated for the following countries: United Kingdom, 1948-2005, top 1 percent; France, 1948-2006, top 1 percent; Italy, 1974-2004, top 1 percent; Portugal, 1976-2005, top 1 percent; Spain, 1981-2005, top 1 percent.

8   The Netherlands' pattern differs entirely from that found elsewhere in Europe. Whereas the Dutch top 1 percent and the 1-5 percent groups have seen a decrease in income shares from 1948 to 1999, the familiar V-shape appears for the top 10-5 percent group in this time-frame.

The neoliberal era: the rise of financial speculation and financial power

Why does this V-shape pattern emerge in so many countries? The downward tilt of the V-shape pattern until the 1970s is readily explained. The immediate post-War years through the early 1970s have been termed the "golden age of capitalism" (Marglin and Schor 1992). A capital-labour 'accord' assuring shop-floor peace in exchange for income security, together with Keynesian stimulus policies, provided the basis for stable profits. The spread of prosperity across the middle class (a 'Fordist' regime wherein Ford workers could buy the cars they made) validated Verdoorn's law, wherein increases in productivity due to increased returns broadened the consumer markets in which increasingly prosperous workers were participating. The Bretton Woods regime of fixed exchange rates assured that little financial speculation troubled the waters of these accumulation processes. Banking was closely regulated, with strict limits on geographic and product-line competition. While minorities and women were only marginally included, this period qualified as a 'golden' age compared to what had come before in economies driven by capitalist firms.[9]

So wealth and income were more evenly distributed, and workers more prosperous. What went wrong? The 1970s witnessed a long goodbye to the post-WWII order. In 1971 the US pulled out of the Bretton Woods system; then 1973 brought a stock-market crash and the first of two oil-price shocks. After some years of 'stagflation,' inflation was strangled by the aggressive high-interest rate regime of Paul Volcker; the combination of high interest rates and recession that followed both, tamed oil prices and then triggered the Latin American debt crisis. In 1985, the Plaza Accord struck between the US and Japan, at a time when Japan was perceived as a threat to the global economic dominance of the US, led to a Japanese asset bubble that, once punctured in 1990, generated a period stagnation from which Japan has not yet fully escaped. These policy moves, from the

---

9   In the developing world, the term 'golden age' does not apply to this time period. These
     were, in many cases, years of escape from colonial status or from occupation.

dollar devaluation in 1971 onward, represented a shift on the part of the United States from being a global hegemon to taking care of its own interests, including its use and protection of what Eichengreen has called the US's 'exorbitant privilege' of issuing the preferred reserve currency of the global economy.

While the 1970s was a decade of transition, the 1980s marked the beginning of the neo-liberal era. Both the US and the UK had newly-elected leaders – Ronald Reagan and Margaret Thatcher. Their regimes were committed to deregulation and a reduced role for government in the economy, and whose first acts included assaults on organised labour – air traffic controllers, in the US, and mineworkers, in the UK. The 'capital-labour accord' was ended.

Crises in the global South in the neoliberal era led to privatisation, cuts in public expenditure, and market-opening there as well, especially when the International Monetary Fund was brought in to restore national solvency after debt crisis. The opening of overseas markets, and the end of pattern bargaining with unions, led to widespread de-industrialisation by global-North manufacturers; the rebasing of production and assembly operations in global-South countries whose wage levels and environmental-protection standards were lower than in home markets. Meanwhile, the combination of volatile exchange- and interest-rate environments with the step-by-step deregulation of financial intermediaries and financial markets created a brave new world both for innovative and interlinked financial risk-management and risk-taking activities. For example, derivative instruments simultaneously offered insurance against loss to one party to the transaction while providing opportunities for speculation to the other.

The US took advantage of its post-hegemonic hegemony (Dymski 2010a) to run 'twin deficits' in both its public fisc and its trade balance. Running systematically large deficits on current account implies a surplus on the capital account. Consequently, money that flowed out to support trade deficits flowed back in on capital account. This was convenient for financing the government deficit, and indeed for creating a securitised market for mortgage finance; but overall, it transformed the US into a global liquidity sink.

These shifts both invited and required strategic adaptations. One notable implication is the emergence of Wall Street as a dominant force in global finance. Figure 3 illustrates this development by contrasting the total market value (as of the end of May) of financial firms listed as among the Business Week 'Global 1000,' by region, for the period 1989-2004. Four points in time are shown, permitting an evaluation of the impact of the bursting of the Japanese asset bubble, the outbreak of the Asian financial crisis, and the 11 September 2001 attacks. What is notable here is the decline of the Japan/Hong Kong/Singapore total (due mostly to shifts in Japanese banks' values), the modest rise in UK and European banks' values, and the dramatic rise in the value of US financial firms. Figure 3 illustrates the impact of systematic capital-account inflows on asset value. Most of these flows were channelled into government securities, mortgage-backed securities, and eventually subprime and other investment instruments.

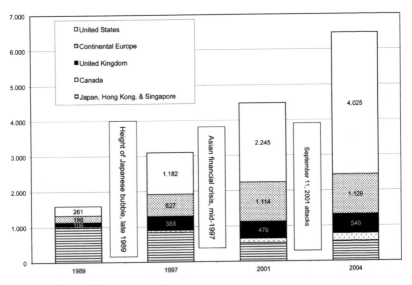

Figure 3: Market Value of Financial Firms Listed in Business Week 1000, by Global Areas, 1989-2004 (in US $B)

Source: Business Week magazine issues in May for the years shown. Note that only publicly-listed companies' market value is included: so privately-held and government-owned firms are excluded. Firms included are in the banking, insurance, broker/dealer, and diversified financial company categories. Data were compiled by the author.

This brings us to the question of how specifically the upward-sloping portion of the top-one-percent V began rising so steeply after the mid-1970s. This involved a set of interlocking factors; but this rise began with – and was defined by – the rise in top-level financial incomes.

The rise of Wall Street, and of the wave of financial innovations and of new financial markets that emerged in the neoliberal era, has been a dominant factor in rising financial-sector incomes. And Piketty and Saez (2003) have shown that the explosion of financial-sector incomes is the primary driver of the share of top-one-percent income-earners in US income. The spread of new practices across global financial sectors and competition for market share have boosted financial incomes in many countries. To cite just two recent studies, Bell and Van Reenenb (2010) show that rising financial incomes are behind the explosion in income inequality in the United Kingdom; and Godechot (2011) demonstrates this for France. But beyond the fact that bankers are richer, these shifts have a further implication; together with widespread financial deregulation, they validate the growth in the power of finance to discipline governments and people throughout the world. This power has not been shared tranquilly by the high and mighty; throughout the neoliberal era, large banking firms used acquisitions and regulatory arbitrage to fight over market share (Dymski 2012). The financial crisis of 2007-08, of course, would demonstrate that beyond market share, the largest banking firms in the US and in other high-income nations had become too big to fail (Dymski 2011a).

Strategic adaptations to the rise of finance and the inversion of Verdoorn's law

The increasing dominance of financial firms, eased by deregulation and backed by ever-freer financial flows, necessitated strategic adaptations at the regional, national, firm, and household levels. In many cases, these adaptations increased inequality – typically, not just for the top one percent, but across the income spectrum. In this era of capital mobility, governments competed for capital investment by creating conditions advantageous to high and stable returns to capital. National industries also worried about market share, as the global factory spread. Since the US was no longer providing global coordination, regional groupings emerged as institutional vehicles for attracting investment and stabilising markets. These neoliberal mechanism designs (Dymski 2011b) included the trilateral North American Free Trade Agreement (NAFTA) pact. The participation of the US in this arrangement, and its pursuit of other bilateral arrangements, signalled its effective retreat from any responsibility for coordinating multilateral trade.

Europe, in turn, experienced the fall of the Berlin Wall and the reunification of Germany; it enhanced internal policy coordination via the European Monetary Union, and ultimately created the Euro as a common currency in January 1999. Nations joining the Eurozone agreed to operate their budgets and macroeconomic policies under a strict set of rules emphasising fiscal and monetary discipline. These rules did not explicitly outlaw Keynesian policy, but clearly did restrict the scope for applying it. The Eurozone mechanism illustrated the dominant view within Europe that it must compete for footloose capital like every other region. Recurring financial crises in global-South nations during the years of creating these mechanism designs – Mexico 1994, East Asia 1997, Brazil/ Russia/Turkey 1998, Argentina 2001- provided reminders, were any needed, of the dominance of stateless mega-finance

At the microeconomic level, employment was characterised by flexibilisation and the loss of security. This pattern had profound consequences in the global North. Buchanan *et al.* (2011) demonstrate this for the UK, the US, and Australia. In the UK, employment grew very little between 1979 and 1990 – that is, during the period of Tory government; and in that period, as one might expect, private-sector job growth outpaced public-sector job growth. But in the 1990s, under a Labour government that championed industrial policy, private sector employment growth was less than that in the public sector. Jobs for women grew primarily in the state and parastatal sectors. In the United States, the neoliberal era played out similarly; predictably, the supply-side-focused Reagan administration cut public sector jobs, and presided over a flexibilisation of private-sector employment. But the Democratic administration that took over in the

1990s pursued an economic policy that saw employment growth in the private sector became increasingly pro-cyclical and eventually stop altogether. Public sector employment growth picked up some but not all of the slack. Australian employment experience was similar to that in the US.

These trends demonstrate an ironic twist in these (and other global-North nations') economic policies in the last decade of the 20th century (and the first in the 21st); most sustained job growth was generated in the public sector, but it was precisely public-sector services and expenditures that were under sustained attack as a sustainable basis for employment growth. So even pro-working class political parties largely abandoned the broad embrace of Fordist economic policies. Mass consumption based on mass production was no longer consistent with the global economic conditions that neoliberalism had created.

The end of Fordism as a production strategy did not signal the end of mass consumption; the embrace of the global-factory system pushed down costs on many consumption goods even as wages fell. The gap between consumption expectations – and the need for housing – and household income was filled by another set of financial innovations, beginning in the 1990s, that targeted lower-income and working-class households. US housing finance had been rescued in the 1980s by the increased use of securitisation, which permitted non-bank financial funds to provide finance and took mortgage loans off bank (and thrift) lenders' books. While the low-risk, mortgage-backed securities of the 1980s were backed largely by the federal housing enterprises (Fannie Mae and Freddie Mac), securitisation in the 1990s expanded to include riskier credit contracts, both housing related and non-housing related, backed by private-market guarantors (and derivatives markets based on these guarantees). This marked the birth of the subprime lending market; lenders made risky mortgage loans that they could sell off to structured investment vehicles (SIVs) along with other risky paper. Financing these SIVs created a huge draw on short-term money markets, but the US's global liquidity sink status made this finance readily available.

While subprime mortgage loans were available for those who sought housing, other innovative financial instruments – including payday loans and tax-anticipation loans – were available for the working and even non-working poor. So the working class and the poor became new strategic targets in the emerging financialised growth model that replaced Fordism. And as documented elsewhere, this occurred in a racially disparate fashion. Areas in which minorities concentrated, which had in the past been subject to redlining and discrimination in lending practices, were targeted for subprime lending. In effect, those who had experienced financial exclusion were especially likely to be subjected to predatory financial inclusion (Dymski 2010b).

These trends implied, first, that the wealthy no longer regarded Keynesian stimulus policies or robust public-sector spending as the basis of their own high incomes. Their incomes increasingly were derived from high profits, interest income, and non-interest financial-sector income (fees). That is, their welfare was steadily disconnected from the welfare of the political economy in which they vote.[10] Second, financial-sector profits per se – which, as noted, are intimately linked with the incomes of very rich households – no longer depended on successful high-wage Keynesian policies.[11] These factors, in turn, crucially affected economic dynamics.

The exploitation of profit making possibilities by those in the commanding heights of every nation's income distribution, on a globalised basis, increasingly shaped corporate strategies – with little or no resistance (indeed, often with assistance) from those nations' elected officials. These post-Fordist strategies were not, of course, framed explicitly as pro-rich economic policies. Of course, the availability of low-cost consumer goods together with the increasingly democratic access to credit made life bearable for the mass of the population. It is also true that with the increasing role of pension funds in corporate share ownership, workers who had had access to secure employment had a stake in rising financial-sector income

---

10 Battle (2012) describes the paradoxical implications of elite income growth in an overall landscape of stagnation on the art and real-estate markets.

11 As one illustration of this behaviour, Folkman, Froud et al. (2009) show that private equity takeovers of firms involve the extraction of large rewards by senior intermediaries, at the expense of the funds available for managing ongoing firm operations (and at the expense of those operations' coherence).

flows. But in the main, those who were positioned to make profits, fees, and interest from the growth of financialisation, the globalisation of production, and the deregulation of finance were those at the very top of the income/wealth pyramid. These trends were not explicitly understood as a set of pro-one-percent economic policies. They were understood as policies that would reduce the tyranny of government regulation and liberate entrepreneurship (indeed, they still are). However, their impacts, as the empirical section above demonstrated, was asymmetric across the income spectrum.

There were several important implications of these developments for the global South. Most obviously, the increasing volume of low-wage labour in global-South export sectors, together with the opening of many global-South economies in the wake of financial crises, transformed global-South development strategies. Instead of the infant-industry-led, protected-markets, regulated-finance approach that accompanied the Golden Age, developing economies shifted to export-oriented production with open markets and technology transfer. Policies insuring relatively flat income distributions were also relaxed; new members of the wealthy elite emerged in many countries.

This did lead to a middle class bulge (Ravallion 2009), in that the export-linked jobs created generated incomes that qualified as middle-class in economies whose baseline incomes were far lower than in the global-North nations with which they traded. At the same time, this middle-class surge was and is vulnerable, as Ravallion (2009) points out. This vulnerability is both structural and cyclical. On one hand, global-factory, least-cost-seeking production puts into motion a kind of inverse Verdoorn's law: lower wage manufacturing feeds demand for low-cost goods and spurs on low-wage job growth in global North and South alike. Cyclical downturns then threaten income/payment gaps of the sort that invite predatory, unsustainable short-term credit surges. Indeed, high-rate (and implicitly high-risk) lending instruments aimed at the 'new middle classes' of BRICS nations – who often have monetary incomes similar to those in the lower reaches of the US working class – have grown at astronomical rates in many countries in the global South. High interest-rate payments commitments can only be met so long as growth is sustained.

When this picture for the global South is put together, a key conclusion from our analysis of global-North trends emerges for the global South as well: many countries have wealthy elites who are well positioned to make money based on their participation in financialisation and trade activities that do not depend on robust macroeconomic growth; indeed, these elites will not resist policies that retreat from Keynesian stimulus. In effect, the forces pushing economic policies toward stagnation in the global North are increasingly mimicked in the global South.

The subprime crisis and its aftermath

The forces dividing the interests of a rich global elite ever further from those of the broad mass of working people in many societies have implications for governmental reactions to economic disasters or crises. Before discussing the subprime crisis itself, we might note the seismic shift in thinking that has occurred in the transition from the Fordist to the neoliberal eras. Thinking about public finance was dominated by the text of Musgrave (1959), which affirmed redistribution from wealthy to poor via tax and budgetary expenditures as a key component of fiscal policy. As the neoliberal era emerged, the ideas of public-choice theorists such as Buchanan and Tullock (1962) gained influence. The public-choice perspective took the Pareto welfare criterion as the guiding principle for fiscal policy: income redistribution can be justified only if it increases the welfare of those from whom income is taken.

Anti-poverty and disaster-response policies in the Fordist and neoliberal eras have reflected these differing conceptual starting points. For example, President Lyndon Johnson launched a 'war on poverty' as a national initiative in the 1960s; and even President Nixon's proposal for welfare reform in 1972 was based on a redistributivist proposal for a negative income tax. In the neoliberal era, however, anti-poverty policies have been reduced in scope and ambition. Further, anti-poverty strategy has shifted from redistributing wealth from the rich to the poor, toward identifying mechanisms for stimulating the poor to create their own means of advancing. An example is micro-finance, which is a form of financing from below.

Shocks highlighting the challenges posed by inequality evoke a very different response in this era than in the past. For example, the US 'War on Poverty' was spurred in part because of urban riots and disturbances in the 1960s; one component of this 'War' was a serious effort to increase the stock of low-income affordable housing via public and subsidised housing programmes. By the 1980s, public-sector housing production was largely replaced by the provision of vouchers so that low-income households could bid for private-sector housing units; and public housing units were privatised. Then, when Los Angeles exploded in a widespread riot in 1992, the only federal public-policy response was the creation of a community-development financial institution fund, which selectively supported a number of bank-lending demonstration projects – not including Los Angeles (Dymski 2009).

This helps explain the tepid response to the financial crisis of 2008. This crisis represented a conjuncture of three elements: first, speculation and overleveraging by Wall Street megabanks; second, boom euphoria in housing markets; third, the desperation of people who saw their safety nets collapsing, and who got into housing they could not afford unless prices continued to rise indefinitely. The most forceful response to the crisis involved public guarantees and subsidies for firms in the financial sector, especially for those megabanks judged "too big to fail" (Dymski 2011a). These policies, of course, underwrote the financial resources and incomes of the rich.

Corrective actions to rein in excesses by megabanks and the bloated financial sector – such as size restrictions or bonus limitations on megabanks, reporting requirements on hedge funds, and so on – have been ruled off the table. Instead, these same market players are even now challenging sovereign government's debt levels. This pre-supposes not only the opposition of 'financial markets' and 'states,' but the prerogative of those whose wealth is globally mobile to escape permanent association with the nations whose workers and borrowers gave rise to their wealth. The hyper-rich and the funds they control, even after the 2007-8 near-meltdown of the financial system, are not only demonstrating their ability to seek hyper-optimised gains via overleveraged position-taking that puts national and global pools of liquidity at risk, they are asserting this as their right.

Below this lofty income level, the middle class grows more desperate. Their wealth is often linked to homes they cannot afford to sell, financed by mortgages they struggle to pay. They are losing employment and security. Both ashamed and afraid, they increasingly blame government for abandoning them, and working class and poor borrowers (and often, former homeowners) for the end of the housing boom on which all their hopes for escaping their permanent condition of falling behind came to depend. Solidarity decimated, society divides into those who seek to escape, those who blame, and those who are blamed for worsening crisis conditions that each party lacks either the incentive or the means to address.

Final considerations

At this moment in historical time, the prospects for effective Keynesian policy or renewed Verdoornian growth in higher income countries are bleak at best. Like dominoes lined up in advance, reactionary politics in one country after another are taking on – and sometimes destroying – social contracts in OECD countries. These are the very countries that have served (by accommodating exports) as engines of growth for nations in the global South. Now some nations (or groups of nations) with larger economies are becoming the locomotives that pull global economic growth in their wake. Thus far, these nations' growth has blocked a global depression, but they are exhibiting cracks as the slowdown made inevitable by the policy stances of global-North nations proceeds.

But these new potential global-locomotive nations are under pressure from growing inequality. In China, a wealthy elite is accruing ever-more national income. India's IT revolution has led to the rise of a new elite; in Brazil, mineral riches and financial innovations lie behind rising inequality. In these three nations, several years of steady growth have generated lifestyle expectations on the part of middle classes that are usually linked to credit growth. The growing prosperity of some members of economically marginal classes is jeopardised by the still-more-rapid growth of their expectations and by the ready availability of high-cost credit.

In sum, the disconnect between the rich and the rest of society is moving forcefully from global North to South. This disconnect may pose four potential problems for the future of economic development in the global South. First, while China, India and Brazil, in particular, have sufficiently integrated production to support Keynesian stimulus policies, these nations' rich elites, who are very important in these nations' governments, depend ever less on domestic spending-led growth. To earn mega-profits, they don't need a mass consumption society in any of these three countries. Indeed, Brazil and India are under foreign financial market pressure to maintain orthodox policies. In other words, if the global North will not lead, maybe these countries are not in a position to do it either.

The second problem is home ownership. The expansion of home ownership, especially in Brazil and India, is problematic because so much informal housing is being built. The validation of informal-housing ownership claims requires vigilant real-time governance – in nations whose urban governance structures are already overwhelmed and fragile. Taxation is already an issue and it is the middle class that is precariously hanging on to home ownership, that is not able to afford the lifestyle it once could, and that is being called on to pay the taxes that would expand this governance. So, bringing *favelas* and lower-income enclaves into components of integrated cities poses a real – and as yet unmet – challenge.

The third problem derived from the rich-poor disconnect is that while financial institutions can help span the rich-poor divide, banks in India and Brazil have been more inclined to make no loans or predatory loans – not productive loans – to members of lower-income communities. In China, the situation is more opaque; there, it appears that modest lending by official banks is sometimes offset (or more than offset) by predatory credit contracts offered by informal lenders.

The final problem exists at the level of global macro-economic policy: OECD nations are pulling away from fiscal stimulus, even though these middle class-bulge (and other global-South) nations rely indirectly on global-North fiscal stimulus policies. Further, in a world of unregulated global currency markets and global financial movements, some global South countries are targeted for speculation by financial funds engaging in the carry trade.[12] This both inhibits global-South growth and raises financial fragility in global North and South alike – all while compromising the pool of available global liquidity.

How do we connect again? The rich must be made accountable to the economic policies and practices that have provided the basis of their wealth. While they may want to be mobile, they must pay their fair share. Working class and poor communities require political and economic inclusion, two conditions that feed off one another. Moving in this direction will require reducing financial exploitation and creating mechanisms that assure ownership rights and access to resources in poor and informal communities. The gain-sharing needed from the globally-mobile rich and the rights- and opportunity-expansion needed by the poor and marginalised will be more readily achieved in a growth-oriented global economy than in one whose nation-states are pre-committed to stagnationist policies. The struggles against the growing rich-poor disconnect in every nation, and the global stagnation that threatens the growth capacity of all nations, are interlinked. A prosperous global economy requires less, not more, inequality – and a lower, not a higher, income share for the richest households – within every nation.

References

Acemoglu, D. and James A. Robinson (2002) 'The Political Economy of the Kuznets Curve,' *Review of Development Economics* 6(2), pages 183-203.

Aghion, P., E. Caroli, and C. García-Peñalosa (1999) 'Inequality and Economic Growth: The Perspective of the New Growth Theories,' *Journal of Economic Literature* 37(4), December 1999, pages 1615-1660.

Barro, Robert (2000) 'Inequality and Growth in a Panel of Countries,' *Journal of Economic Growth* 5, March 2000, pages 5-32.

Battle, Laura (2012) 'Estate of the Art,' *Financial Times*, April 15, 2012

---

12 The 'carry trade' is the name given to an investment strategy wherein financial investors borrow funds in countries with low interest rates and invest them in maturity-matched, relatively-riskless investment vehicles in countries with substantially higher interest rates.

Bell, B. and John Van Reenenb (2010) 'Bankers' Pay and Extreme Wage Inequality in the UK,' Centre for Economic Performance, London School of Economics, April 2010.

Buchanan, J., G. Dymski, J. Froud, S. Johal and Karel Williams (2011) 'Labour after the Great Complacence: Unsustainable employment portfolios in the USA, the UK and Australia,' Paper prepared for Work after Fordism: A workshop on theorising organisational diversity and dominant trends in contemporary capitalism. Queen Mary University of London, 12 – 13 May 2011

Buchanan, James M., and Gordon Tullock (1962) The Calculus of Consent: Logical Foundations of Constitutional Democracy. Ann Arbor: University of Michigan

Dymski, Gary A. (2009) 'Financing Community Development in the U.S.: A Comparison of "War on Poverty" and 1990s Approaches,' Review of Black Political Economy 36(3-4), September/December 2009, pages 245-73.

Dymski, Gary A. (2010a) 'The Global Crisis and the Governance of Power in Finance,' in The Financial Crisis: Origins and Implications, edited by Philip Arestis, Rogério Sobreira, and José Luís Oreiro, London: Palgrave-Macmillan, pages 63-86.

Dymski, Gary A. (2010b) 'Development as Social Inclusion: Reflections on the US subprime crisis,' Development 53(3), pages 368-75.

Dymski, Gary A. (2011a) 'Genie out of the Bottle: The Evolution of Too-Big-to-Fail Policy and Banking Strategy in the US,' mimeo, University of California, Riverside, June 2011.

Dymski, Gary A. (2011b) 'Limits of Policy Intervention in a World of Neoliberal Mechanism Designs: Paradoxes of the Global Crisis,' Panoeconomicus 58(3), September 2011, pages 285-308.

Dymski, Gary A. (2012) 'Financial Mergers and Acquisitions: From Regulation to Strategic Repositioning to Geo-Economics,' Chapter 22 in The Oxford Handbook of Mergers & Acquisitions (Oxford University Press), co-edited by David Faulkner, Satu Teerikangas, and Richard Joseph. Forthcoming 2012.

Eichengreen, Barry (2011) Exorbitant Privilege: The Rise and Fall of the Dollar and the Future of the International Monetary System. New York: Oxford University Press.

Foellmi, R. and Josef Zweimüller (2003) 'Inequality and Economic Growth European versus U.S. Experiences,' Working Paper No. 158, Institute for Empirical Research in Economics, University of Zurich, June 2003.

Folkman, P., J. Froud, S. Johal and K. Williams (2007) 'Working for Themselves? Capital Market Intermediaries and Present Day Capitalism,' *Business History* 49(4), July 2007, pages 552-72.

Godechot, Olivier (2011) 'Finance and the rise in inequalities in France,' Working Paper No. 2011-13, Paris School of Economics, April 2011.

International Labor Office (ILO) (2008) *World of Work Report 2008: Income inequalities in the age of financial globalization,* International Institute for Labour Studies. Geneva: International Labour Office.

Kumhof, M. and Romain Rancière (2010) 'Leveraging Inequality,' *Finance and Development,* December 2010, Washington, DC: International Monetary Fund, pages 28-31.

Kuznets, Simon (1955) 'Economic Growth and Income Inequality,' *American Economic Review* 65, pages 1-28.

Marglin, S.A. and Juliet B. Schor (eds.) (1992) *The Golden Age of Capitalism: Reinterpreting the Postwar Experience.* Oxford: Oxford University Press.

Mayer-Foulkes, David A. (2009) 'Long-Term Fundamentals of the 2008 Economic Crisis,'*Global Economy Journal* 9(4), Article 6.

Milanovic, Branko (2002) 'True World Income Distribution, 1988 and 1993: First Calculation Based on Household Surveys Alone,' *Economic Journal* 112, No. 476, January 2002, pages 51-92.

Milanovic, Branko (2003) 'The Two Faces of Globalization: Against Globalization as We Know It,' *World Development* 31(4), pages 667-83.

Milanovic, Branko (2010) 'More or Less: Income inequality has risen over the past quarter-century instead of falling as expected,' *Finance and Development,* September 2010, Washington, DC: International Monetary Fund, pages 6-11.

Milanovic, Branko (2011) 'Global Inequality: From Class to Location, from Proletarians to Migrants,' *Policy Research Working Paper 5820,* Washington, DC: The World Bank, September 2011.

Musgrave, Richard A. (1959) *The Theory of Public Finance: A Study in Public Economy.* New York: McGraw-Hill.

Palley, Thomas I. (2007) 'Financializaiton: What it is and why it matters,' *Working Paper No. 525,* Annandale-on-Hudson, NY: Levy Economics Institute of Bard College, December 2007.

Piketty, T. and Emmanuel Saez (2003) 'Income Inequality in the United States, 1913-1998,' *Quarterly Journal of Economics* 118(1), pages 1-39.

Rajan, Raghuram (2010) 'How Inequality Fueled the Crisis,' Project Syndicate blog-post, July 9, 2010. Accessed at http://www.project-syndicate.org/commentary/how-inequality-fueled-the-crisis on April 8, 2012.

Ravallion, Martin (2009) 'The Developing World's Bulging (but Vulnerable) 'Middle Class',' Policy Research Working Paper 4816, Washington, DC: The World Bank, Development Research Group, January 2009.

Saez, Emmanuel (2009) 'Striking it Richer: The Evolution of Top Incomes in the United States,' Working Paper, Institute for Research on Labor and Employment, Berkeley: University of California, Berkeley, 5 August 2009.

Williamson, Jeffrey G. (1997) 'Globalization and Inequality, Past and Present,' *The World Bank Research Observer* 12(2), August 1997, pages 117-35.

Wolff, Edward N. (2010) 'Recent Trends in Household Wealth in the United States: Rising Debt and the Middle-Class Squeeze–an Update to 2007,' *Working Paper No. 589*, Annandale-on-Hudson, NY: Levy Economics Institute of Bard College, March 2010.

Summary

Dymski presented an incisive and critical analysis of the current state of global inequality. He argued that the economic reforms undertaken in the neoliberal era, in particular the deregulation of finance, had produced a state of disconnect between elites able to exploit the opportunities offered by global capital mobility and a middle/working class who are increasingly squeezed and excluded from the market. The economic growth trajectory associated with neoliberalism is one which therefore jeopardises rather than bolsters the search for an equitable and sustainable global development strategy. To achieve such a goal, Dymski proposed a number of fundamental changes in the current economic system including: greater accountability of global elites; a shift away from orthodox to heterodox economic policies; the enactment of redistributionist measures; and efforts to increase the political and economic participation of the poor.

Dymski began his lecture by giving an overview of the general global trend with respect to inequality. He noted that while GDP per capita is rising overall, wages are falling as a percentage share of total income. In other words, profits rather than wages are driving much of the growth. Who is responsible for this global rise in non-wage income? Dymski turned here to look at changes over time in the economic activity of the elite strata. He pointed to a striking V shaped pattern that can be seen across many OECD countries in which the share of total national income accruing to the top 10 percent earners declines in the post-war period, reaching a low in the mid-1970s, and then steadily rises again from the early 1980s onwards. In the countries of the Global South we also see a somewhat similar phenomenon with India and China both showing an increase in the income share of the wealthy in the last few decades. The global picture thus seems to be that after a period of decreasing inequality in the post-war period, inequality has again been on the rise in the neoliberal era.

How are we to understand these developments? Dymski argued that neoliberal reforms, especially financial reforms, have undercut the basis for equitable growth. In the Global North, we have witnessed the collapse of the Bretton Woods system of fixed exchange rates, capital controls and Keynesian fiscal policy grounded in the social welfare state. With the implementation of neoliberal reforms in the 1980s, processes of liberalisation, privatisation and deregulation have eroded social safety nets at the same time as they have produced increased job insecurity with the flexibilisation of work and the outsourcing of production by TNCs to low-wage economies. This has adversely affected the position of the middle and especially the working class as they have suffered from the effects of deindustrialisation and the retreat of Keynesian macro-economic policy. The rich by contrast have been able to take advantage of these transformations.

Dymski saw the emergence of global finance as particularly implicated in this story. As the financial sector has become increasingly delinked from the real economy, the wealthy have been able to derive their income from profits made in the financial sector rather than through wage labour or Keynesian stimulus policies upon which the middle and working class are more dependent. Furthermore, financial instruments have been used to exploit the poor and disadvantaged through, for example, the emergence of the subprime lending market where high risk mortgages are issued to largely poorer families in ethnically excluded areas looking to get on the housing ladder. The repercussions of this type of financial activity are by now well known in the wake of the economic crisis it has wrought.

The Global South has also experienced the effects of neoliberal policies. Countries of the Global South have, generally speaking, shifted from a state-led, import substitution model of development towards the neoclassical economic model. While this has produced economic growth and led to the creation of a (fragile) middle class, Dymski argued that this type of growth was unlikely to be sustainable given that it is primarily based on low wage manufacturing, which only stimulates low-wage job growth. Dymski argued that in the neo-liberal era, virtuous circles of economic growth based on Verdoorn's law in which higher growth leads to higher productivity, which produces higher wages, are no longer possible. The wealthy elite in the Global South have prospered, but Dymski saw the prospects for the middle class and poor as much bleaker.

This is especially so given the types of anti-poverty strategies that are now being pursued. Dymski believed that policies of wealth redistribution are now seen as politically unviable by many governments who subscribe to a Pareto-optimal allocation of resources. Instead of redistribution, poverty is to be tackled by treating the poor as entrepreneurs, not employees, whereby they become new targets of financialised growth. The growth in micro-finance projects is a prominent example of this type of strategy. Dymski was sceptical of these sort of initiatives and argued for a much stronger emphasis to be placed on income redistribution.

In the aftermath of the global financial crisis, Dymski summed up the outlook of the different groups as follows. The rich have learned that they are in fact beyond regulation since they are 'too big to fail'. In a world of footloose finance, the rich are able to escape scrutiny and economic belt-tightening . This is not the case for the middle classes who are becoming increasingly desperate in the face of the foreclosure crisis and rising job insecurity. The poor meanwhile are in dire straits, risking social disappearance as welfare state policies are deemed too expensive and increasingly abandoned.

Dymski concluded his lecture by reflecting on the prospects for equitable global growth. He identified four 'problems of disconnection' that threaten to undermine the social contract upon which such a strategy is predicated. Firstly, Dymski saw the role of elites in the development process as deeply troubling given that they derive their wealth in large part from foreign capital markets and not from the creation of a domestic mass consumption society. Development is hereby no longer seen as a national project. Secondly, both the North and the South face the problem of expanding home ownership. In the South, rapid urbanisation and growing populations put an inordinate amount of pressure on housing provision. Unmet demand for housing leads to the emergence of squatter settlements, whose informal nature often deprives people of their full citizenship rights. In the North, the collapse of the housing market has placed whole groups of people in a new condition of insecurity, unable to afford to maintain their current lifestyle. Thirdly, access to credit is highly unequal with the credit needs of the poor in many developing countries either completely ignored or exploited through the issuing of predatory loans. Lastly, in the realm of global macro-economic policies, unregulated financial movements mean that that the global economy remains inherently unstable and crisis prone.

In order for these problems of disconnection to be overcome and to renew the possibility of equitable global growth, Dymski advanced the following solutions. The rich have to be made more accountable and become more integrated in national development processes so that development is truly seen as a collective endeavour. The middle class needs to ally with the poor to push for a fair taxation system and to confront the vested interests of the elite. Finally, the poor require mechanisms to ensure their full economic and political inclusion so as to partake as equal citizens in the development process.

The lecture was followed by a discussion in which audience members were invited to provide comments and ask questions. A recurring theme here was the belief that Dymski had been too pessimistic in his portrait of global inequality. According to World Bank statistics for instance, global inequality has been decreasing, helped in large part by the economic successes of India and China in lifting thousands of people out of poverty. Dymski acknowledged this fact, but remained unswerving in his pessimism. He could not see where the leadership for a global development strategy could come from. The uncontrolled global elite who had been wounded, but who ultimately emerged victorious from the global financial crisis is a major problem, which has yet to be addressed.

Another recurring theme during the discussion was the role that non-economic factors play in explaining trends in global inequality. What about the impact of technology or culture on patterns of stratification? Dymski recognised the importance of both of these factors. He noted for instance that in Brazil there was more of a culture of care and concern compared to the US, while in India there is a drive to increase the financial inclusion of the poor. Technological acquisition meanwhile is crucial for the upgrading of the skill set of the population that, in the move from manufacturing to service economies, is increasingly valued. It is those with low levels of skills and education who are losing out.

The final words were given to the moderator, Paul van Seters (Tilburg University), to provide a closing statement. Van Seters saw two opposing forces at work when it comes to global economic growth and inequality. On the one hand, we have globalisation from above in the form of a global economy which does at times resemble a form of casino capitalism. On the other hand, we also have globalisation from below in the shape of social movements. Here we may find a source of cautious optimism as reform minded activists strive to make the global economic system more equitable.

The migration and development pendulum: a critical view on research and policy[13]

Hein de Haas

Over the past decade, the issue of migration and development has been at the centre of attention of research and development policies. This has coincided with a striking, rather sudden turnaround of views, from pessimist 'brain drain' views, which dominated thinking on the issue before the 2000s, to optimistic 'brain gain' views on the same issue a few years later. In many ways, migration and remittances seem to have become the new 'development mantra' (cf. Kapur, 2003).

How can we explain this surge in interest in the issue alongside the shift towards optimistic views? In part, this has to do with the spectacular surge in global remittances. According to official World Bank statistics, in 1990 migrants sent back the equivalent of US$24 billion to lower- and middle-income countries: this amount had more than doubled to US$59 billion in 2000 and reached a spectacular US$243 in 2008. Although a significant part of this increase should be attributed to the better measurement of remittances by central banks – itself a consequence of the increasing attention being paid to the issue – there is little doubt that there has also been a real increase.

Real remittances are estimated to be at least twice as high, because many remittances are sent through informal channels or taken as cash payments (de Haas and Plug, 2006; Pieke et al., 2005). Remittances have also overtaken the amount of official development assistance (ODA) provided to low- and middle-income countries. In 1990, with US$55 billion, ODA was still more than twice the amount of remittances. In 2000, ODA had stagnated at US$53 billion and grew to US$126 billion in 2008 (see Figure 1).

The rapid growth of remittances has contributed to the increas-

---

13   This lecture was based on the text of this article, which was originally published in June 2012 in *International Migration, Volume 50, Issue 3, pp. 8-25*

ing attention being paid to migration as a potential development resource by – mainly European – governments, development agencies and organizations such as the United Nations (UN) and the European Union (EU), financial institutions such as the World Bank (WB) and the International Monetary Fund (IMF), as well as other international organizations such as the International Labour Office (ILO), the International Organization for Migration (IOM) and the UNDP (IOM, 2006; Skeldon, 2008; UNDP, 2009; World Bank, 2007).

While surging migrant remittances can partly explain the increasing attention being paid to migration and development, it cannot entirely explain the rapid shift from pessimistic to optimistic views. In fact, remittances have increasingly come to be seen as a rather ideal 'bottom up' source of development finance. The argument is that remittances are a safety net for relatively poor areas and countries, and remittances are freer from political barriers and controls than either product or other capital flows. Remittances appear to be a more effective instrument for income redistribution than large, bureaucratic development programmes or development aid. This 'private' foreign aid seems to flow directly to the people who really need it, does not require a costly bureaucracy on the sending side, and far less of it is likely to be siphoned off into the pockets of corrupt government officials (Kapur, 2003).

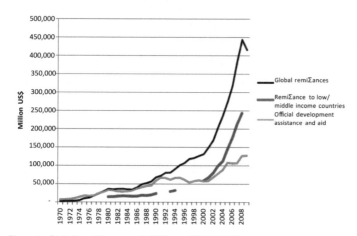

Figure 1: Global remittance and aid flows, 1970–2009
Source: World Development Indicators database, World Bank.

As part of the same shift, there is also growing optimism about the potential role of 'migrant diasporas' in contributing to social, economic and political development. Additionally, the argument that migration would lead to remittance dependency and 'brain drain' is increasingly being countered by the argument that migration can lead to significant gains through a counter-flow of remittances, investments, trade relations, new knowledge, innovations, attitudes and information (Lowell and Findlay, 2002; Stark et al., 1997).

On the basis of an analysis of the evolution of the migration and development debate, in this paper I challenge the above views. First of all, I show that migration and development is anything but a new topic, and that the recent wave of optimism largely tastes like old wine in new bottles. In fact, in post-war Europe, the debate on migration and development has swung back and forth like a pendulum between optimistic and pessimistic views.

Second, in this paper I argue that shifts in the migration and development debate have been part of more general shifts in development theory, which, in their turn, largely reflect ideological shifts. Over the past decade, national governments of European countries such as the United Kingdom, the Netherlands, France and Belgium have attempted to formulate policies to link migration and development issues. Policies have particularly focused on attempts to facilitate remittances and to engage migrants and so-called 'diaspora organizations' in development cooperation, but have turned out to be very difficult to implement. The extent to which the stated priority for this issue has been turned into concrete action has been very limited (de Haas, 2006), and there seems to be an increasing feeling of disappointment with the issue, somehow similar to the early stage of 1970s pessimism.

Third, in this paper I argue that empirical evidence on the mixed and strongly context- dependent development impacts of migration should warn against overly optimistic views that somehow portray migration as a silver bullet development 'fix', as well as against overly pessimistic views that put the blame for underdevelopment on migration, and that undervalue the real, day-to-day contributions migrants make to improve well-being, living standards and economic conditions in origin countries.

Despite its considerable benefits for individuals and communities, migration alone cannot remove more structural development constraints. In fact, if lessons from past experiences and research are not taken on board, there looms a huge danger of naïve optimism, which overlooks the fact that much 'neo-optimism' on migration and development reflects neoliberal views in which migrants and markets, not states, become responsible for bringing about development. This leads to the following two questions:

1. What is the impact of migration in development processes in origin countries? and, on the basis of these insights
2. What role can public policies (in sending and receiving countries) realistically play to enhance this impact?

In the remainder of this paper, I aim to answer these questions through a review of research and policy evidence.

The migration and development pendulum

Migration and development is anything but a new topic. In the entire post-war period, the issue has been at the core of the migration policy debate, particularly in Europe. The policy and research debate on migration and development has swung back and forth like a pendulum, from optimism in the 1950s and 1960s, to pessimism, scepticism and relative neglect since the early 1970s, and towards more optimistic views since 2000. These rather sudden mood swings are the most striking character of this debate, and demand further explanation. In the post-war decades of rebuilding and rapid economic growth in North-West European countries, migration from Southern Europe, North Africa and other countries on the European periphery, such as Turkey, Ireland and Finland, was generally seen as a process that benefited both destination and origin countries. While migration of surplus labour from poor countries provided the industries of wealthy countries with much-needed labour, the expectation was that remittances – and, more broadly, the experience, skills and knowledge that migrants acquired before returning – would greatly help developing countries in their economic take-off. So, in this view, migration simultaneously stimulates growth in origin and destination countries (Adler, 1981; Kindleberger, 1965; Penninx, 1982). In this 'developmentalism' era, states were ascribed a crucial role in development planning. Hence, both sending and receiving states aimed to 'manage' migration, often through concluding bilateral recruitment agreements.

After the oil crisis of 1973, Europe experienced a massive economic downturn, industrial restructuring and increasing unemployment. This more or less coincided with a turning point in thinking on migration and development issues. As of the late 1960s, prevalent optimistic views on migration and development were increasingly challenged by views of migration as a mechanism that was provoking not only a 'brain drain' but also dependency of emigration regions and countries on migrant remittances, thus aggravating problems of underdevelopment. It was increasingly believed that migrants would tend to fritter remittances away on 'conspicuous consumption' and that they would mainly invest their money in 'non-productive' enterprises such as housing (cf. Almeida, 1973; Lipton, 1980; Reichert, 1981; Rhoades, 1979). Also, the sociocultural effects of migration were increasingly placed in a negative light. Exposure to the relative wealth and success of migrants, combined with changing tastes and expanding material aspirations, were thought to make the way of life in migrant-sending regions and countries less appealing. A 'culture of migration' would subsequently perpetuate a vicious circle of ongoing out-migration and aggravated underdevelopment.

It should be noted that this shift partly reflected a general paradigm shift in social sciences towards neo-Marxist views and particularly, in development theory, from 'developmentalist' towards dependency theory. This coincided with increasing critique on the assumed benefits of capitalist growth for poor societies, in which migration was increasingly seen as a exploitation mechanism. In European policy circles, the attention being paid to the issue was rapidly disappearing as well. This was partly because of growing disillusion with policies linking return migration and development through departure bonuses, training programmes before return and investment programmes for return migrants (Entzinger, 1985; Penninx, 1982). At the same time, some research programmes concluded that unfavourable economic and political conditions in origin countries such as Turkey and Morocco explained why relatively few migrants were willing to return and invest (De Mas, 1978; Hamdouch et al., 1979).

There was concurrently an increasing awareness that many supposedly 'temporary migrants' or 'guest workers' from Mediterranean countries were there to stay. This shifted the attention of policy and of (government-funded) research to issues around migrant integration. In addition, in the 1970s and early 1980s it was widely assumed that the great age of migration had ended. Consequently, the origin country and development perspective was quickly lost from sight. In the development policy field, a high degree of scepticism on the issue of migration and development persisted until the late 1990s. Against the background of a long period of pessimism and near-neglect, the sudden 'rediscovery' of the migration and development issue, and the rapid shift from pessimistic to optimistic views of 'migration and development' among multilateral organizations, governments and development agencies since 2000, are remarkable phenomena.

My key argument is that, in order to develop a more nuanced view on migration and development, and to think of more sensible and realistic policy responses, it is crucial to move beyond the 'negative versus positive', 'brain drain versus brain gain', 'consumption versus investment' type of debates. In the following sections, I will further elaborate this argument by analysing the key arguments and assumptions of the 'optimistic' and 'pessimistic' views on migration and development, and by discussing ways to bridge these views.

Two radically opposed migration and development paradigms

Migration and development has been the subject of continuous and sometimes heated debate in the social sciences for over half a century at least (Bauer and Zimmermann, 1998; de Haas, 2010a; Russell, 1992). In this debate, one can broadly distinguish two opposed approaches; that is, the 'balanced growth' theory versus the critical 'asymmetric development' theory. Alternatively, one might call them 'migration optimists' and 'migration pessimists'. The migration optimists are generally inspired by neoclassical migration economy and/or 'developmentalist' modernization theories (see de Haas, 2010a for an elaboration on the theoretical foundations and assumptions of these theories). Notwithstanding significant differences between neo-classical and developmentalist views – particularly the different roles that they attribute to the state – they both believe that migration has generally had a positive impact on the development process in sending areas.

Most migration pessimists are affiliated to what I dub here as 'structuralist' social theory, which encompasses neo-Marxist, dependency and world systems theory (Frank, 1966, 1969; Wallerstein, 1974, 1980). In general, structuralist approaches towards migration and development tend to treat migration as a negative phenomenon, contributing to the further underdevelopment of the economies of the sending countries and to the undermining of their sociocultural cohesion (Hayes, 1991). Table 1 summarizes the main arguments of both migration and development paradigms.

Table 1: Opposed paradigms on migration and development

Migration pessimists		Migration optimists
"Structuralist" social theory	↔	Functionalist social theory
Dependency theory	↔	Neoclassical theory
Disintegration / uprooting	↔	Modernization
Net South–North transfer	↔	Net South–North transfer
Brain drain	↔	Brain gain
More inequality	↔	Less inequality
Remittance consumption	↔	Remittance investment
Dependency	↔	Development
Divergence	↔	Convergence

Source: Adapted from de Haas (2010a).

Basically, migration pessimists generally view migration as an outflow of larger processes of capitalist expansion, which undermine traditional livelihoods, uproot rural populations and leave them no choice but to join the urban proletariat in order to survive. Situated within the broader paradigm of (historical) structuralism, migration pessimists postulate that economic and political power is unequally distributed among wealthy and poor countries, that people have unequal access to resources, and that capitalist expansion has the tendency to reinforce these inequalities. Instead of modernizing and gradually progressing towards economic development, underdeveloped countries are trapped in their disadvantaged position within the global geopolitical structure. Within this view, the process of international migration further undermines local and regional economies through depriving them of their most valuable human resources.

Because migrants are assumed to be among the 'best and brightest' and most entrepreneurial spirits, migration goes along with 'brain drain', which systematically undermines development efforts by states and educational investments in particular. Because international migrants are seldom among the poorest sections of communities, remittances are believed to reinforce income inequality in origin communities. Remittances provide only a temporary, unreliable and external source of income, which is rarely invested 'productively' but, rather, spent on (often conspicuous) consumption of consumer goods (for which the spread of consumerist capitalist ideologies is creating an insatiable need), which have to be imported from abroad, thereby further increasing the dependency on remittances and undermining local or domestic production.

So, the pessimists view migration not just as detrimental to the economies of underdeveloped countries, but also as one of the very causes of underdevelopment. According to these perspectives, migration ruins stable peasant societies, undermines their economies and uproots their populations, further fuelling out-migration. In this way, communities and entire societies get caught up in a structural dependency on migration which, despite its contribution to the survival of migrants and their families, constantly undermines processes of sustained development. The migration optimists turn this analysis completely upside down. Neoclassical and developmentalist approaches evaluate the movement of people from labour-abundant to labour-scarce regions and countries – along with a presumed transfer of capital in the opposite direction – as a process contributing to a more optimal allocation of production factors, higher productivity and, hence, better outcomes for all. Additionally, through counter-flows of knowledge and/or through return, migrants are seen as active agents of economic growth. Migration optimists tend to counter the 'brain drain' argument by arguing that the productivity of labour in sending areas is low and that unemployment and underemployment are often high. Migration enables people to increase the returns on their skills and their 'human capital', which is to their own benefit as well as to the benefit of the economies as a whole. It also enables the labour of those left behind to become more productive and to increase their earnings.

Migration optimists counter the argument that remittances encourage consumption and that this is negative by pointing out that many migrants do invest and that consumption always consumes the major part of household expenditure, that consumption enables people to improve their living standards and that, last but not least, consumption can have positive multiplier effects as long as goods and services are mainly bought locally or domestically. This view also casts so-called 'non-productive investments' in a much more positive light. For instance, migrants have often been castigated for massively investing in housing. However, besides the argument that decent housing contributes to basic well-being, health and safety, and that denying migrants' rights to proper housing would be to apply different standards to migrants than policymakers and researchers would probably apply to themselves, investment in construction in migrant-sending areas can create significant employment and income for the often poorer non-migrants (de Haas, 2007).

This 'trickling down' also explains why migration and remittances indirectly contribute to increasing incomes and decreasing poverty of all members of sending communities, including non-migrants. Because increasing incomes and the expansion of networks further remove poverty constraints, migration becomes accessible for increasingly large sections of the population. In this view large-scale, largely free migration is highly beneficial for development, and obstacles to migration will severely limit these poverty- and inequality-reducing effects.

So, while migration optimists and migration pessimists both see migration as an intrinsic part of capitalist expansion, economic growth and urbanization, they have radically opposed views on the outcome of this process. However, they share the fundamental view that migration is the outcome of development failure and assume a negative correlation between development levels and rates of out-migration. While it is important to observe that this is a problematic assumption in view of evidence that aspiration- and capabilities-increasing development processes tend to increase migration propensities, and that highly developed societies tend to have structurally higher levels of mobility and migration (de Haas, 2010b), this issue lies beyond the scope of this paper.

For the purpose of this paper, the more relevant issue is to understand how such radically different views on migration and development can coexist. In fact, both paradigms provide such different accounts of migration both in its causes and consequences, that it leads one to wonder to what extent these views can be reconciled. I will argue that, to a certain extent, this is possible if we see these accounts as two extremes, or ideal types, of a diverse continuum of possible migration impacts, in which the specific conditions under which migration occurs also largely determine the nature of its development impacts.

In brief, my key argument here runs as follows. The more unfavourable and constrained local development contexts are, the more restricted the access of the poor to social security, public services and markets, and the more structural are the socio-economic and power inequalities and authoritarianism that are ingrained into societies; and the more difficult the access of the poor to non-exploitative forms of (labour) migration is, the higher is the probability that the impacts will fit within the predictions of the migration pessimists, particularly with regard to the potential contributions of migration to sustainable, macro-level development processes. In these situations, migration might even function to reinforce pre-existing inequalities by mainly serving the material interests of the already well-off and by maintaining the (often authoritarian) political status quo.

On the other hand, in environments where positive development conditions prevail, where structural inequalities are relatively low or decreasing, and also the relatively poor have access to basic education, health and markets, migration is more likely to play the positive role predicted by the migration optimists. This is related to the core critique on neoclassical views: they tend to be rather blind to power inequalities that make the poor structurally disadvantaged and severely constrain their access to markets and information, as well as their ability to reap benefits from their inclusion in the capitalist economy. Rather, such conditions are likely to trap them in situations of structural exploitation and might make them even worse off. In fact, this is the situation prevailing in many countries characterized by high levels of inequality, corruption and sluggish economic growth.

A second way to bridge apparently irreconcilable views is by distinguishing different levels of analysis when assessing migration impacts. For instance, when the focus is on micro-level indicators such as the role of migration in sustaining, securing and improving the livelihoods of individuals, families and communities (which has been the focus of many surveys and much statistical analysis), one is much more likely to draw positive conclusions than if the focus is on a concept of 'national development', or the contribution of migration to structural reform or decreasing inequalities. In fact, 'national development' was the focus of the 'developmentalist' paradigm of the 1950s and 1960s, and, with the benefit of hindsight, it can therefore not be surprising that those who believed that migration would do the 'development trick' were bound to become disappointed. Empirical researchers, to the contrary, tend to base their views on analysis of household survey data and generally conclude that migration does contribute to household income, living standards and investment. However, such household comparisons cannot be used as an argument that migration 'thus' contributes to more general processes of national development and structural reform.

This is obviously related to the hugely different ways in which 'development' tends to be seen and (mostly implicitly) defined by different paradigms, social science disciplines (ranging from economics to anthropology) and political ideologies. This is why some of the apparently 'fundamental' differences can in fact be rather spurious, as they reflect implicit definitions of what 'development' actually entails, as well as widely diverging epistemological view- points on which empirical and analytical tools are valid means to measure a complex, multidimensional concept such as 'development'.

The latter observation brings me to the third way in which conceptual confusion can be reduced and apparently opposed views can be partly bridged. Besides the clearly distinguishing different levels of analysis (micro–meso–macro), it is equally important to unpack the analysis of migration impacts along the multiple dimensions of development. This includes aspects such as income levels, socio-economic inequalities, social security, living standards, physical and socio-psychological health, education, gender roles, cultural change and political reform. In practice, migration impacts are generally mixed across these different dimensions. This is another reason why the extremely positive or negative accounts or ideal types on migration development presented in Table 1 are less likely to occur in reality.

Migration rarely has a uniform impact across these dimensions, and this reveals the fundamental ambiguities involved in weighing these different dimensions. For instance, how should we judge a situation in which migration remittances have led to an overall increase in incomes, but have significantly increased inequality in a sending community? How does this affect our evaluations of migration impacts on the aggregate level? Does it mean that migration had a positive or negative impact on migration? Such an exercise will inevitably partly reflect value judgements, in particular with regard to the weight attached to distributional versus mean income objectives (see also Stark et al., 1988). Another example is the concept of 'dependency'. Structuralist views see dependency on global capitalism as inherently detrimental to the economic sustainability and sociocultural cohesion of communities and nations, whereas functionalist views would rather interpret dependency as a sign of spatial 'connectivity', which facilitates economic exchanges and increases productivity.

It is crucial to observe that definitions and the relative importance attached to different dimensions of development, as well as the related methodological choices, partly reflect deep-seated preferences and value judgements. This also partly explains why ideological shifts have had such a profound influence on social scientific views on migration and development. However, before further discussing the large role of value judgements and ideologies in shaping views on migration and development, it seems useful to have a closer look at the empirical evidence on the highly diverse impacts of migration.

Empirical evidence on migration impacts

Since the 2000s, there has been a rapid increase of the number of research papers on migration and development and remittances. While their tone on migration and development is generally upbeat, this somehow obscures a substantial research literature that has developed over the 1980s and 1990s, which has allowed for a much more nuanced view, and which has moved the academic debate on migration and development well beyond a simplistic opposition between optimistic and pessimistic views. This particularly happened under the influence of the new economics of labour migration (NELM) (Stark, 1991; Taylor, 1999) and related 'livelihood perspectives' in other social science disciplines (de Haan, 2002), which challenged the then dominant pessimistic views on migration impacts and offered a more subtle view, in which both positive and negative development responses were possible, depending on the degree to which sending countries and regions provided attractive environments in which to invest and to which to return (de Haas, 2010a). A growing number of studies have countered overly pessimistic views on migration and development. Several reviews of the research literature (Agunias, 2006; de Haas, 2007; Katseli et al., 2006; Özden and Schiff, 2005; Taylor et al., 1996a, b; UNDP, 2009) have pointed to the potentially positive role of migrants and remittances in social, economic and political transformation processes in societies and communities of origin.

These reviews of empirical evidence also support the view that migration is a rather deliberate attempt by migrants and their families to spread income risks, and that migration can often been seen as a livelihood strategy and an investment pursued by a household to improve its social and economic status in the longer term. In this way, both internal and international migration can have a crucial insurance function in protecting people from the destabilizing and exclusionary effects of absent or ill-functioning markets, high inequality, corruption and authoritarianism, failing state policies and a lack of state-provided social security and basic public services such as education and health care. Migration has enabled millions of families around the world to substantially improve their incomes and living conditions. And expenditure and investment of remittances can have substantial positive effects on economic growth in origin communities and regions, from which also (poorer) non-migrants can benefit to a certain extent. From a perspective of human development that focuses on the well-being and capabilities of people, as proposed by Amartya Sen (1999), this constitutes progress and should be seen in a positive light.

However, the accumulated evidence also demonstrates that migration and remittances cannot overcome more structural development constraints such as misguided macro-economic policies, socio-economic inequalities, authoritarianism, corruption and legal insecurity. Evidence shows that the extent to which migration can play a positive (or negative) role in social, economic and political change in origin countries fundamentally depends on more general development conditions.

In contexts that are unfavourable to human and social development more generally, migration may actually reinforce existing inequalities. High poverty and inequality often mean that international migration (particularly to wealthy countries) remains a prerogative of the better-off groups in origin communities and societies. Such strong 'selection' is reinforced by immigration policies that discriminate in favour of the skilled and against the low-skilled. If it is mainly elites that are migrating, migration might therefore actually reinforce the status quo. For instance, while migration rates from most sub-Saharan African countries to OECD states are rather low it is mainly the higher-skilled who are able to migrate legally, as students, workers, entrepreneurs or tourists. Inasmuch as the lower-skilled are able to migrate at all, they more often do so illegally and tend to end up in structurally disadvantaged positions.

For instance, elite groups in North African countries often send their children to elite universities in France, the United Kingdom and the United States, generally after the children have attended expensive private or international secondary schools in their own countries. At the same time, relatively poor, often irregular migrants working in Europe or the Gulf may struggle to spend their remittances to send their children to private schools in order to avoid the failing public education system, the quality of which has deeply suffered from decades of public disinvestment, partly pursued under the influence of Structural Adjustment Policies. But such expenditure to compensate for the failure of public policies may prevent them from making other investments. While education and labour migration by elite groups are often defended using the argument that they contribute to so-called 'good governance' (e.g., better macro-economic policies[14]), the preferential access of higher- and upper-middle-class groups to legal migration options is likely to reinforce the structural inequalities between rich and poor.

Also on a global level, available remittance data suggest that international remittances may sustain international inequalities, and particularly the gap between the low- and middle- income countries. According to World Bank data, in 2008, 68.7 percent and 26.4 percent of global remittances went to middle- and high-income countries, respectively, while only 4.9 percent went to low-income countries. This largely reflects the fact that the middle-income countries tend to have the highest emigration rates. If we compare remittances with other foreign major currency inflows, such as foreign direct investment (FDI) and official development assistance (ODA), Figure 2 shows that remittances are relatively most important for middle-income countries, and particularly for the lower-middle-income group. For higher-middle-income countries, FDI is comparatively more important. For low-income countries, ODA is still the most important resource flow.

However, if we express remittances as a percentage of total GDP (see Figure 3), a rather different picture emerges. While the bulk of global remittances goes to middle-income countries, the poorest countries have a relatively high dependency on remittances. In fact, their remittance dependency has increased from around 2 percent of total GDP in the mid-1990s to over 6.5 percent in 2008. Although the latter increase may largely reflect improved remittance accounting in poor countries, the figures nevertheless suggest that in relative terms, remittance dependency is comparatively high in poorer countries. Although it is impossible to distil firm causal links from this, the

---

14 It should be mentioned, though, that what is understood by good economic governance also depends on ideological positions; for instance, about the role of states in processes of economic development.

data strongly suggests that high remittance dependency is a feature of structurally weak economies rather than a characteristic of growing, diversifying and strong economies.

Although we cannot assume that these observations with regard to country-level data automatically apply to the analysis of migration on within countries, a considerable number of national and micro-level studies do suggest that migration tends to favour the middle- and high-income groups much more than the low-income groups; and that migration may, under unfavourable conditions of high migration selectivity, thus sustain or even reinforce existing economic inequalities.

Also, low-skilled migration might serve to maintain the political status quo. Many (currently or formerly) authoritarian states, such as Morocco, Tunisia and Egypt in North Africa, Mexico in Latin America and the Philippines in Asia, have used migration of non-elite groups as a political-economic 'safety valve' to decrease unemployment, poverty and political discontent (Castles, 2007; de Haas and Vezzoli, 2010; Gammage, 2006; Kireyev, 2006). The down side is that this may reduce the domestic pressure on governments to implement structural political and economic reforms needed to create more favourable development conditions.

Figure 2: Remittance, foreign direct investment and aid flows to developing countries, 2008

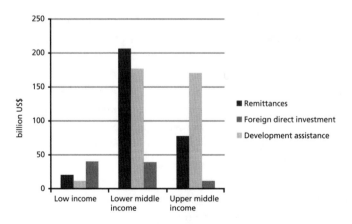

Source: World Development Indicators database, World Bank.

Figure 3: Remittances as a percentage of GDP, 1982–2009

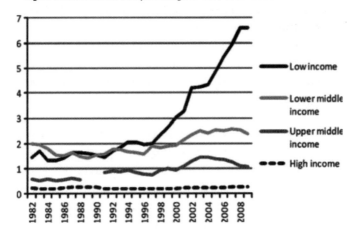

Source: World Development Indicators database, World Bank, with input from the International Monetary Fund, Washington, DC.

Migration, revolution and the political status quo

It seems, therefore, that emigration of the elite and the poor may basically sustain the status quo by even further empowering and enriching elites, and by getting rid of potential troublemakers. In this respect, an interesting question is whether there is a relation between the timing of the popular pro-democratic revolutions in North Africa in 2011 and the reduction of emigration rates in the previous years due to the global financial crisis and the concomitant decrease in demand for migrant labour in major European receiving countries. Although this is unlikely to be among the fundamental causes of these revolutions and political unrest, the diminished emigration opportunities may well have further increased the discontent among disenfranchised middle-class youth, and may therefore have been the proverbial straw that broke the camel's back.

It is important not to conclude from this that migration always sustains and reinforces existing economic inequalities and the political status quo. As recent events in North Africa have shown, Tunisian, Egyptian and Libyan exiles and emigrant communities were extremely swift in organizing themselves to support the revolutions from abroad, through oppositional Internet activism, so-called 'cyber-attacks' on government sites, by demonstrating in foreign capitals, and by influencing public debates abroad and in origin countries. Although further research is needed into this issue, we can hypothesize that while such activism by emigrants has certainly reinforced revolutionary political change, it has not been the main cause of it, and that high out-migration may actually undermine the growth of a critical mass necessary to enforce structural change.

This reinforces a more general point with regard to migration and development: migration seems to reinforce already existing, more general patterns and trends of social, economic and political change – whether these are more negative or positive; and it is unlikely to reverse general development trends unless emigration is truly massive. Under unfavourable development conditions, and in the absence of domestic reform or internal struggles for political change, migration and remittances are unlikely to contribute to nationwide sustainable development.

However, if development in origin countries takes a positive turn, if countries stabilize politically and economic growth starts to take off, then migrants are likely to be among the first to join in and recognize such new opportunities, reinforcing these positive trends through investing, circulating and returning to their origin countries. Such dynamics have occurred in several former emigration countries as diverse as Spain, the Republic of Korea, India and Taiwan – and might be currently happening in a country such as Turkey, where many migrants (and their children) living in Germany and elsewhere in Europe play a significant role as transnational entrepreneurs in Turkey's booming economy (Presseurop, 2010).

The important point here is that migration was not the factor that triggered development but, rather, that development enabled by structural political and economic reform unleashed the development potential of migration. So, it is essential to get the causality right. Notwithstanding its importance as a factor of social change, migration is generally too limited in magnitude to independently set in motion processes of structural reform and social transformation also known as 'development'. As Heinemeijer et al. (1977) have already observed, development is a prerequisite for investment and return by migrants rather than a consequence of migration! As has already been mentioned, migration tends to reinforce (pre-)existing trends, whether this is for the better or for the worse. So, under unfavourable development conditions, migration may undermine development; but under favourable conditions, it is likely to accelerate such positive trends. Skeldon (2008) has argued that although it should be welcomed that migration is no longer viewed as generally negative for development, we should be cautious not to essentialise migration and to place too great a responsibility upon migrant agency at the expense of the institutional change necessary to bring about development.

The neoliberal roots of neo-optimism

Empirical evidence points us to the context-dependency of the development impacts of migration, which should forestall any blanket assertion on the issue. While at the micro- and meso-level, migration can be said to be generally beneficial for sustaining and improving the livelihoods of the families and communities involved, the specific role of migration in macro-level process of social, economic and political development depends on the general development conditions and policy contexts in which migration occurs. It seems most appropriate to talk about migration in terms of having a development potential. If migration enhances the human capabilities of individuals and families, which it often does to a smaller or larger extent, it gives them the freedom and power to invest as much as to disengage from origin countries! This is a key observation. If states fail to implement reform, migration and remittances are unlikely to fuel national development – and can even sustain situations of dependency, underdevelopment and authoritarianism. This questions the 'level playing field' assumptions of neoclassical migration theory, particularly within the context of developing countries, which makes the idea of migration and remittances as an effective, 'bottom up' form of self-help development sound rather naive.

Migration and development neo-optimism largely neglects this point. In order to explain its recent popularity, it is important to observe that the recent migration optimism has strong ideological roots, because it fits into neoliberal development paradigms that have – at least until very recently – downplayed the role of states in bringing about development, and have overemphasized the power of markets and individuals to bring about political-economic change and social transformation. These ideologies have links with neoclassical economic theory and the functionalist paradigm in social theory of which it is part, which in their focus on individual actors and markets largely neglects structural constraints such as ingrained socio-economic and power inequalities (de Haas, 2010a).

On a critical note, Devish Kapur has pointed to the ideological roots of recent remittance euphoria. He argues that remittances strike the right cognitive chords, and fit in with a communitarian, 'third way' approach, exemplifying the principle of self-help, in which "Immigrants, rather than governments, then become the biggest provider of 'foreign aid'." (2003: 10) In a similar vein, Stephen Castles (2007)[15] observes that the 'remittance mantra' has parallels with the 'trickle-down' theory of development propagated by the modernization theories of the 1960s. This is the main danger of the neo-optimism on migration and development: these views are partly ideologically driven, and shift the attention away from structural constraints and the vital role of states in shaping favourable conditions for positive development impacts of migration to occur.

Despite their development potential, migrants and remittances can neither be blamed for a lack of development nor be expected to trigger take-off development in generally unattractive investment environments. So far, most efforts to link migration and development have focused on maximizing remittance transfers through legal channels. However, such policies do not address the larger issue of 'contextuality' and will ultimately have very limited effects. In many ways, governments of sending and receiving countries have become overly obsessed with maximizing remittances, while they have generally ignored the basic necessity to first create a fertile soil where the remittance seeds can be sown and can actually germinate and grow. In the same vein, policies to 'channel remittances into productive uses' are often based on the rather condescending view that

---

15 See http://tinyurl.com/8nmzu2u

migrants behave irrationally. They also miss the fundamental point that in unfavourable investment environments migrants generally have good reasons not to invest in risky enterprises and, rather, prefer to stick to relatively secure investments such as houses or small-scale commerce. In addition, such propositions unrealistically presume that remittances can be 'tapped' by governments whereas remittances are private money; not to mention the deep-seated distrust migrants often have vis-à-vis governments.

An increasing number of receiving country governments have linked the issue of migration and development to return or so-called 'circular' migration. The assumption is that temporary migration is beneficial for both origin and destination countries as well as for the migrants themselves. There is substantial empirical evidence to question the assumption that temporary migration is the most effective 'development tool', while such 'revolving door' policies are very difficult to implement in practice. In fact, their stated development intentions often seem to camouflage a hidden agenda of voluntarily or forcibly returning irregular immigrants or rejected asylum seekers, after providing them some modest financial assistance, or rapid and often ineffective professional training (Weil, 2002).

In fact, policies that try to forcibly link restrictive immigration policies centred around temporary and return migration often seem misguided, not only because of their usual failure to meet their stated objectives (Castles, 2004, 2006), but because they paradoxically seem to reduce the development potential of migration. They do so by infringing on migrants' residency and socio-economic rights and by effectively pushing migrants into permanent settlement. Through raising barriers to immigration, migrants have to assume higher costs and risks to migrate, which also increases the risks of returning. Therefore, the degree of circulation and temporariness tends to be higher under free migration than under restrictive immigration policy regimes. While the latter often officially proclaim that they encourage return, temporary and circular migration, they actually tend encourage permanent settlement. For instance, the post-1973 recruitment freeze on 'guest workers' and the adoption of certain immigration restrictions in North-West European states encouraged many migrants to stay on the safe side of the border (Entzinger, 1985). In the same

82

vein, migrants who either lack legal status and whose socio-economic mobility is frustrated by discrimination and social marginalization tend to have less financial, human (knowledge, education) and social (social networks) resources that can potentially be deployed to the benefit of human and economic development in origin countries.

Therefore, the much sought-after 'issue linkage' between migration and development is generally not desirable, and can actually undermine broader development agendas and justify depriving migrants of their fundamental rights. Rather than crunching the two issues together into a forced and unhappy marriage, it therefore makes much more sense to conduct separate, sensible migration and development policies that improve economic and political conditions in origin countries and that optimize migrant rights and socio-economic mobility. This seems to be the most effective way to optimize the positive role of migration in development processes.

Conclusion

Empirical evidence indicates that although migrants can potentially accelerate development at home, they can neither be blamed for a lack of development nor be expected to generate development in generally unattractive investment environments. Migration alone cannot independently set in motion broader processes of human and economic development. So, the right question is not whether migration leads to certain types of development, but how differences in migration policy and investment environments explain why migration plays a positive development role in some cases and less positive or even negative roles in others.

This shows the need to reframe the debate on migration and development. Because development is a condition for attracting migrants' income-generating investments rather than a consequence of it, policymakers would be wise to reverse their perspective on migration and development. Rather than asking what migrants can do to support development, or to forcibly, unrealistically and harmfully link the issue of return or temporariness to development, governments would be much better off identifying how to make conditions in origin countries attractive for migrant to invest socially, politically and economically. The second question that they should be asking is how they can design immigration policies that empower (instead of exploit) migrants and that maximize their social, human and economic capabilities to contribute to development in origin countries. While migrants' cumulative capabilities determine the development potential of migration, the development conditions in origin countries will ultimately determine the extent to which this development potential will be unleashed.

From this, we can draw clear lessons for policy. First, targeted remittance, 'diaspora' and investment-stimulation policies will have marginal (if any) effects if they are not accompanied by general reform and progress in origin countries. The only way of genuinely releasing the development potential of migration and migrants' resources is to create attractive investment environments and build trust in political and legal institutions of origin countries. Here lies a clear responsibility for origin-country governments, and this also shows the crucial importance of fundamental political change in contexts where governments largely or uniquely serve the interests of the elite and perpetuate structural socio-economic inequalities and the exploitation of the poor.

Public policies that improve the functioning of legal, economic and political institutions, and the access of ordinary people to education, health care and basic rights, are crucial not only for creating a fertile ground for development in general, but also for compelling migrants to invest in origin countries. Discourses celebrating migration, remittances and transnational engagement as self-help development 'from below' are driven by neoliberal agendas and shift attention away from structural constraints and the limited ability of individual migrants to overcome these and the responsibility of states to redistribute resources. This exemplifies the crucial role that states continue to play in shaping favourable conditions for human development.

Also, immigrant-receiving governments can play a significant role in increasing the development potential of migration through lowering thresholds for legal immigration, particularly for the relatively poor and the lower-skilled, and through favouring their socio-economic mobility through giving access to residency rights, education and employment. By deterring the relatively poor from migrating or forcing them into illegal channels, and by discouraging return and impeding circulation, restrictive immigration policies may damage the poverty-alleviating and development potential of migration.

The recent wave of optimism about migration and development was overly naïve and has failed to take on board lessons from decades of research and policies. Because expectations about migration as a development panacea ran unrealistically high, it is therefore no surprise that there is an increasing feeling of disappointment around the issue. For instance, the British government has largely abandoned its Diasporas program while the Dutch government is cutting down the number of officials working on migration and development. As has been argued above, this all is rather reminiscent of the early 1970s, when the high hopes of the past also turned into deep disillusionment and scepticism.

So, we may be at a new turning point, in which case we are heading towards a neo-pessimistic backswing of the migration and development pendulum. This would be unfortunate, as it would also shift the attention away from the real, everyday contributions that millions of migrants around the world make to improving the lives of their families and communities back home; as well as things that governments in sending and receiving countries can do to improve migrants' capabilities to contribute to development in origin countries, and their propensity to do so.

The key issue is to take on board past policy lessons and research insights on the context-dependent nature of migration impacts and, last but not least, to set expectations right. Instead of swinging between exaggerated optimistic and overly pessimistic views, there is a need for much more nuance. Now that the migration and development pendulum has swung from sheer optimism to sheer pessimism and back again, it is time to nudge it steadily towards the middle.

References

Adler, S. (1981) *A Turkish Conundrum: Emigration, Politics and Development, 1961–1980*. International Labour Organization, Geneva.

Agunias, D.R. (2006) 'Remittances and development: trends, impacts, and policy options'. Migration Policy Institute, Washington, DC.

Almeida, C.C. (1973) 'Emigration, espace et sous-de'veloppement', *International Migration*, 11(3): 112–117.

Bauer, Th., and K. Zimmermann (1998) 'Causes of international migration: a survey', in P. Gorter, P. Nijkamp and J. Poot (eds.) *Crossing Borders: Regional and Urban Perspectives on International Migration.* Ashgate, Aldershot: 95–127.

Castles, S. (2004) 'Why migration policies fail', *Ethnic and Racial Studies,* 27(2): 205–227.

Castles, S. (2006) 'Guestworkers in Europe: a resurrection?', *International Migration Review,* 40(4): 741–766.

Castles, S. (2007) 'Comparing the experience of five major emigration countries', Working Paper 7, Oxford: International Migration Institute, University of Oxford, Oxford.

de Haan, A. (2002) 'Migration and livelihoods in historical perspective: a case study of Bihar, India', *Journal of Development Studies,* 38(5): 115–142.

de Haas, H. (2006) *Engaging Diasporas: How Governments and Development Agencies Can Support Diasporas' Involvement in Development of Origin Countries.* A study for Oxfam Novib, International Migration Institute, University of Oxford, Oxford.

de Haas. H. (2007) *Remittances and Social Development: A Conceptual Review of the Literature.* UNRISD, Geneva.

de Haas. H. (2010a) 'Migration and development: a theoretical perspective', *International Migration Review,* 44(1): 227–264.

de Haas, H. (2010b) 'Migration transitions: a theoretical and empirical inquiry into the developmental drivers of international migration'. Working Paper, International Migration Institute, University of Oxford, Oxford.

de Haas, H. & R. Plug (2006) 'Cherishing the goose with the golden eggs: trends in migrant remittances from Europe to Morocco 1970–2004', *International Migration Review,* 40(3): 603–634.

de Haas, H. & S. Vezzoli (2010) *Migration and Development: Lessons from the Mexico–US and Morocco–EU Experiences.* International Migration Institute, University of Oxford, Oxford.

de Mas, P. (1978) *Marges marocaines: limites de la cooperation au de´veloppement dans une re´gion pe´riphe´rique: le cas du Rif.* NUFFIC / IMWOO / Projet Remplod, 's-Gravenhage.

Entzinger, H. (1985) 'Return migration in Western Europe: current policy trends and their implications, in particular for the second generation', *International Migration,* 23(2): 263–290.

Frank, A.G. (1966) 'The development of underdevelopment', *Monthly Review,*

18(4): 17–31.

Frank, A.G. (1969) *Capitalism and Underdevelopment in Latin America.* Monthly Review Press, New York.

Gammage, S. (2006) 'Exporting people and recruiting remittances – a development strategy for El Salvador?', *Latin American Perspectives,* 33(6): 75–100.

Hamdouch, B., A. Berrada, W.F. Heinemeijer, P. de Mas & H. van der Wusten (1979) *Migration de developpement, migration de sous-developpement?.* INSEA, REMPLOD, Rabat.

Hayes, G. (1991) 'Migration, metascience, and development policy in Island Polynesia', *The Contemporary Pacific,* 3(1): 1–58.

Heinemeijer, W.F., J.A. van Amersfoort, W. Ettema, P. de Mas & H. van der Wusten (1977) *Partir pour rester, une enque´te sur les incidences de l'e´migration ouvrie`re a` la campagne marocaine.* NUFFIC, Den Haag.

IOM (International Organization for Migration) (2006) *Mainstreaming Migration into Development Policy Agendas.* IOM, Geneva.

Kapur, D. (2003) 'Remittances: the new development mantra?' Paper prepared for the G-24 Technical Group Meeting, 15–16 September, United Nations, New York.

Katseli, L.T., R.E.B. Lucas & T. Xenogiani (2006) 'Effects of migration on sending countries: what do we know?' Working Paper No. 250, OECD, Paris.

Kindleberger, C.P. (1965) *Europe's Postwar Growth: The Role of Labor Supply.* Oxford University Press, New York.

Kireyev, A. (2006) *The Macroeconomics of Remittances: The Case of Tajikistan.* International Monetary Fund(IMF), Washington, DC.

Lipton, M. (1980) 'Migration from the rural areas of poor countries: the impact on rural productivity and income distribution', *World Development,* 8: 1–24.

Lowell, L.B. & A. Findlay (2002) *Migration of Highly Skilled Persons from Developing Countries: Impact and Policy Responses.* International Labour Organization, Geneva / UK Department for International Development, London.

Özden, C. & M. Schiff (eds) (2005) *International Migration, Remittances, and the Brain Drain.* The International Bank for Reconstruction and Development/The World Bank, Washington, DC.

Penninx, R. (1982) 'A critical review of theory and practice: the case of Turkey', *International Migration Review,* 16(4): 781–818.

Pieke, F., N. Van Hear & A. Lindley (2005) 'Informal remittance systems in Africa, Caribbean and Pacific (ACP) countries'. UK Department of International Development (DFID), European Community's Poverty Reduction Effectiveness Programme (EC-PREP), Deloitte & Touche.

Presseurop (2010) 'Lure of the Bosphorus', 17 November, www.presseurop.eu (accessed 18 May 2011).

Reichert, J.S. (1981) 'The migrant syndrome: seasonal U.S. labor migration and rural development in central Mexico', *Human Organization*, 40: 56–66.

Rhoades, R.E. (1979) 'From caves to main street: return migration and the transformations of a Spanish village', *Papers in Anthropology*, 20(1): 57–74.

Russell, S.S. (1992) 'Migrant remittances and development', *International Migration*, 30(3 / 4): 267–288.

Sen, A. (1999) *Development as Freedom*. Anchor Books, New York.

Skeldon, R. (2008) 'International migration as a tool in development policy: a passing phase?', *Population and Development Review*, 34(1): 1–18.

Stark, O. (1991) *The Migration of Labor*. Blackwell, Oxford.

Stark, O., C. Helmenstein & A. Prskawetz (1997) 'A brain gain with a brain drain', *ECOLET*, 55(2): 227–234.

Stark, O., J.E. Taylor & S. Yitzhaki (1988) 'Migration, remittances in inequality: a sensitivity analysis using the extended Gini Index', *Journal of Development Economics*, 28: 309–322.

Taylor, J.E. (1999) 'The new economics of labour migration and the role of remittances in the migration process', *International Migration*, 37(1): 63–88.

Taylor, J.E., J. Arango, G. Hugo et al. (1996a) 'International migration and community development', *Population Index*, 62(3): 397–418.

Taylor, J.E., J. Arango, G. Hugo et al. (1996b) 'International migration and national development', *Population Index*, 62(2): 181–212.

UNDP (2009) *Human Development Report 2009*. Overcoming Barriers: Human Mobility and Development, UNDP, New York.

Wallerstein, I. (1974) *The Modern World System I, Capitalist Agriculture and the Origins of the European World Economy in the Sixteenth Century*. Academic Press, New York.

Wallerstein, I. (1980) *The Modern World System II, Mercantilism and the Consolidation of the European World- Economy, 1600–1750*. Academic Press, New York.

Weil, P. (2002) 'Towards a coherent policy of co-development', *International Migration*, 40(3): 41–56.

World Bank (2007) *Final Report of the International Working Group on Improving Data on Remittances*. The World Bank, with input from the International Monetary Fund, Washington, DC.

Discussion

Comments by moderator Heidi Dahles (VU University):
Thank you very much Dr De Haas for your comprehensive review of the development potential of migration and remittances and thank you in particular for your thought provoking vision of the consequences of this potential for policy options in sending and receiving countries. To me, your message is loud and clear, migration and remittances alone cannot overcome structural development obstacles. Remittances are no substitute for development aid and donor efforts. Governments cannot relinquish their responsibilities to diaspora and migrant communities or returnees. Without general political and economic reforms in sending countries and reform in development and migration policies in receiving countries, the impact of remittances should not be overemphasised.

I read this as a clear signal to policymakers worldwide and Dutch policymakers in particular – a signal that challenges recent shifts in politicians' thinking about development aid and migration policies. It has currently become fashionable to join in with voices claiming that development aid is ineffective and it is most convenient then to claim that the widely scattered migrant and diaspora communities can take care of their own folks both at home and in host countries. Your analysis, however, shows that there has to be development before remittances can have an impact. Hence, development aid has not become redundant in this neoliberal world.

This conclusion is very much in line with the findings of a small research literature review, which I conducted recently, on entrepreneurial activities among return migrants. The idea exists that migrants are expected to bring back an entrepreneurial spirit when they return to their countries of origin. So I looked into a smaller category of people than your presentation discussed; return migrants, all over the world, in the research literature. What do we find? Surprisingly it seems that return migrants, and I leave out the distinction between high-skilled and low-skilled for a moment, are more inclined to start a business venture upon returning home compared to the people that stayed at home. They seem to bring new skills, and work experience gained from spending time in a more advanced technical and commercial environment. These skills and this knowledge are more important than bringing back accumulated savings. Obviously, having been in a wealthy country helps return migrants enhance their entrepreneurial spirit, and thus their success as entrepreneurs upon returning to their home country. Overall though, returnee entrepreneurship contributes to the establishment of survivalist firms, rather than high potential growth firms. We find return migrants starting necessity driven businesses, which means they end up in the informal sector very quickly, starting firms that aim to secure the livelihoods of their families. So we should not be too optimistic when we speak about returnee entrepreneurship.

It is in some sense similar to the sending of remittances, in the fact that the money is put into consumptive use; these survivalist firms can be seen as a way of consuming the money that migrants earned and saved in the host country. Less educated migrants usually invest their accumulated savings and economic capital in self-employment and micro business start-ups upon their return. Less educated migrants, and those who work in low-skilled jobs in host countries, are unable to learn skills that can be utilised for business start-ups in their home countries. And let's be honest, most migrants in wealthy countries work in such low-skilled jobs, even those migrants who already have the skills when they arrive. High-skilled returnees, on the other hand, have the skills to generate capital through and very often we see, in the literature, that they do not necessarily need a lot of savings to invest in businesses. They start businesses through their networks; networks that spend transnationally in both host and home countries. The point is, however, that high-skilled migrants do not return so easily unless courted by their home country governments.

We know that China, India, Korea and now recently Turkey, have shown to be very successful in creating conducive business conditions to invite high-skilled migrants back home. I heard that associations established especially for this purpose are very important to entice these people to return. So success or failure of returnee entrepreneurship is not only a matter of returnees possessing the appropriate resources, but also of institutional factors, in particular the migration and return policies in the host and home countries. Host countries providing training and education to migrants, in particular training for entrepreneurship in this case, create the basic conditions for returnee enterprises to become successful in their home countries. And on the other hand, home countries providing conditions conducive to business also contribute to the development of their country and the success of their returnee migrants.

So I feel that both our findings argue that in order for remittances and diaspora investments to fully realise their developmental potential, receiving countries need to reform their policies towards migrants and migration. What would then be the recommendations emerging from these findings regarding both the development and migration policy of let's say, the Dutch government, and what might the synergy between reforms in our migration and development policy be? It may sound politically incorrect, but nevertheless tempting to suggest that cooperation between migrant and diaspora organisations and the Dutch government and with the Dutch private sector would be beneficial to return migrants in particular. I am not arguing for what has been called the *oprot premie* (the get-lost policy). I am pleading for finding possibilities to help people return with skills and knowledge that would help them become successful in their home countries as entrepreneurs or professionals. One could think about financial skills training and entrepreneurial education in our country and then leave it to the migrants to either put this knowledge and skills to good use in their host country or to take these skills home and contribute to development in their own country. Wouldn't that be the perfect marriage between development and migration policy, or for that matter, between a neoclassical and a neoliberal policy?

Response by Hein de Haas:
Your research findings are really extremely interesting and seem indeed to fit within the broader picture I sketched. What are policy

recommendations and what is political correctness these days in the Netherlands? What used to be politically correct is now politically incorrect and the other way around, so I don't know. I think very broadly, just forgetting about politics, the more liberal your immigration policies, the more migrants can circulate freely; because obstacles for migration do not necessarily decrease migration, but they certainly do fix migrants and push them into permanent settlement as they no longer take the risk to return anymore. This is the paradox.

I think in this particular time period, there is no political will to free up immigration policies. However, I think you can make a reasonable and well-argued case, without saying that we will open up all borders, that there is a demand for all sorts of migrant labour, not just for the best and brightest, not only the so-called "knowledge workers", but also for those with medium and lower level skills. In that sense, creating mechanisms for labour migration, for people from developing countries, can have a very positive effect. On the other issue, of supporting diaspora organisations, the Dutch, British, French, Mexican and many other governments have all been trying this. In practice it is very difficult because there are all sorts of problems of representation. A lot of home town associations have their own political agendas. The idea that migrants are necessarily superior development workers is another myth. There is a certain danger in thinking that they will do the trick. It also distracts from the fact that 99.5% of all remittances and development contributions go through individuals and families. So we shouldn't only concentrate on these organisations.

I can only agree with the idea of supporting or training people, but why should we link it to return? I think this is another obsession. If you read the last 2 white papers by the Dutch government on migration and development, it is not concealed at all that the real issue is about return migration and actually circular migration is about temporary migration. It is even linked to the asylum debate; forcibly sending back rejected asylum seekers, training them while they are still in prison and then expect them to contribute to the development in their war torn countries of origin. I think it is quite a far stretch, to put it mildly. I actually think it is very difficult to link migration and development agendas and I even think it can be dangerous.

The more I look at it, the more sceptical I am that these two issues should be linked. Let's keep these agendas separate, because linking them might actually undercut the support for development – the development issue may be used as a moral justification for policies of forced return of migrants. So although I support your point, I am just wondering whether it is politically feasible or even desirable.

Question from the audience:
I am bit surprised that the very close association between migration and development has not been opened to a broader agenda. For example, the trade policy agenda may also give some positive, new ways of looking at migration, especially when we consider that trade is not only about goods, but also about people. Something could be done to make temporary migration a positive instrument. To my knowledge, it has not really been investigated in detail and I am wondering why?

Response by Hein de Haas:
Yes, I can only endorse that. I know that these negotiations have been going on, but there is this issue, like with the European Union, that states don't want to give up their sovereignty when it comes to migration issues because it is so politically sensitive. I would agree that migration can also be seen as a service and that trade agreements can be used to facilitate migration, whether permanent or temporary. I can only really hope that politicians have the courage to argue that if we open up more legal possibilities, either through trade agreements or national policies, that we will paradoxically have more control over migration and we decrease the threshold for people in developing countries to migrate, who then don't have to overcome obstacles and circumvent all sorts of rules in order to migrate. The latter has two negative effects. It makes migration very costly because it increases barriers and risks. It also leads to so-called 'brain waste' – the phenomenon of people with graduate degrees driving taxis in European capitals.

Question from the audience:
I have a question with regards to remittances. In the past the Dutch government had a very positive view of remittances, while nowadays, Dutch policy is much more critical towards remittances. Is this also true for England?

Response by Hein de Haas:

I have never heard this argument in Britain. I think it is a particular attribute of the small nation states of Northern Europe – in Denmark these views are also very popular. It is an interesting point because it evokes a broader issue: the link between migration and transnationalism. You can see remittances, or any other involvement of migrants in origin countries – political or otherwise – as a form of transnational engagement. This is increasingly being viewed in a hostile light. Although the global trend has been to create possibilities for dual citizenship, small nation states in Northern Europe have tried to reverse this trend. This is based on the view that integration and transnational migration are substitutes. This view is questioned by increasing evidence that these might well be complements for the following reason. Migrants who are not marginalised in receiving countries and who have the ability to integrate and experience social mobility, especially of their children, have more capabilities in Sen's conception of the term. Their integration enables them to also do things in origin countries. The most deprived migrants, especially irregular migrants, don't have that ability because they can't circulate, they can't travel, they don't have the financial and social means to make these contributions. So those statements are not well-informed by evidence that the relationship might also be the other way around. This relates to the issue of circulation: the most circular migrants tend to be those with two passports.

Question from the audience:

I was a bit surprised that migration was mainly discussed from a South-North perspective. Yet there is a lot of South-South migration taking place as well. I was wondering what the differences are between these two migration flows, both in terms of remittances and in terms of transmittable values.

Response by Hein de Haas:

You are completely right, most migration is between developing countries. But what is a developing country? Again you see that most migrants tend to migrate from the relatively poorer to the wealthier developing countries. The Gulf is a major worldwide attraction of migrants these days. So, the distinction between North and South is very problematic. However, it does matter where people go to in terms of the impacts of migration in origin countries. For instance, a recent study by Philippe Fargues compared the impact of the migration of Moroccans to Europe and the migration of Egyptians to the Gulf on fertility. The outcomes of the study suggest that migration from Morocco to Europe has accelerated a change in family planning norms, which have led to an accelerated decline in fertility rates in Morocco from 7.5 in the 1970s to 2.3 at present. In Egypt, although there has been a decline in fertility, the decrease has been slower and has even been stagnating. The study linked this to the transfer of more conservative norms from the Gulf to Egypt. I am not sure though if you can actually qualify migration to the Gulf as South-South migration because the Gulf is considerably wealthier. One of the problems is a lack of data. We have much more data on migration to rich countries. The evidence that exists shows that if people make it to the OECD countries, the effects on income and poverty reduction are much higher because people tend to earn not just more money, but also have more rights in destination countries. But so-called South-South migration fulfils similar functions. Within Africa, there is a lot of migration to countries such as Libya, to South Africa, to Côte d'Ivoire, which relatively speaking are wealthy countries. Within South America, there is increasing migration to Mexico and Argentina. In terms of impacts, however, we don't have a lot of data to specify them.

Question by moderator Heidi Dahles:
Could this be because South-South migration helps poor people to be more a part of these migration movements, and also helps people to earn more money?

Response by Hein de Haas:
I think that it is a valid point. There is not much new in migration studies. It was already described in the 1960s, that poor people first migrate to cities and once in the cities, they might create the conditions enabling them to migrate further, to Europe for instance. We see this a lot in North Africa; Ghanaians, Senegalese, Somali migrant

groups first go to North Africa, after which some migrate on to Europe.

Question from the audience:
One of the conclusions that we draw from the material that you presented is that it doesn't make sense for policymakers, nor for social scientists, to see remittances as the silver bullet that is going to cure all ills. But the argument was based mainly, if I understood you correctly, on the size of the remittances for middle income countries. You pointed out that it is on average 1.7% of GDP and that we shouldn't expect too much, in terms of economic development, coming from this 1.7%. Simultaneously, you indicated in one of your first slides that the overall size of remittances is much higher than the overall size of development aid. Would you then be willing to draw the same conclusion regarding development aid? That we should stop giving development aid because it doesn't make any difference for economic development.

Response by Hein de Haas:
That is a good question. My main argument, why I said that remittances are not the silver bullet, is based on micro level empirical evidence. But I use that figure to put things in perspective, because, if like me, you discuss remittances on a daily basis, you tend to amplify the phenomenon. I am not an expert on development assistance. It seems to me that the big difference between remittances and development assistance is that remittances are owned by migrants. I always find it intriguing how some governments are talking about channelling remittances towards productive investments. It evokes the image of the migrant as an irrational being who doesn't know what he or she is doing with their own money and that governments should capture this money and invest it on behalf of the migrant. This was an idea that the Turkish government was experimenting with in the early 1970s, and it hasn't worked at all. It is a Western, state-centred vision, in which migrants are expected to trust governments in their origin countries – that is a basic fallacy – and further, that they are willing to put their money in a bank managed by the government. Anyone who has done fieldwork in any developing country will know that

this is an amazing assumption. I think in that sense you are talking about different entities. I understand why development agencies are worried about remittances, it may undermine their agenda and relevance.

Question from the audience:
I was born and raised in Pakistan, but am working and living here in the Netherlands and I feel a connection to both countries. My question is, who is a migrant and who is a global citizen? Are not all migrants global citizens?

Responses by Hein de Haas:
I am not sure all migrants feel as if they are global citizens. On a slightly critical note, I think it is quite an elitist view that we are all world citizens. However, obviously in this world, more people are feeling that they are participating in multiple societies at the same time, which goes against our nation-state system. Particularly in countries like the Netherlands, we see a counterrevolution; we have already become diverse, but policies are trying to somehow reverse this. I come back to my initial point. The paradox is that the increasing restrictiveness of policies has pushed migrants into permanent settlement rather than encourage circulation. This is one of the main reasons why so many migrants are now eager to seek double nationality, as it is the best way to circumvent all regulations. You are then free to circulate. I often use the example of Moroccan migration to Spain; in 1991 Spain introduced visa requirements for Moroccans. Before that time there was no illegal migration, because people could travel with a passport and tended to circulate and migrate seasonally. The moment Spain introduced visa requirements, illegal migration started and permanent settlement accelerated. That is the paradox. A lot of policy documents talk about 'circular migration' when what they actually mean is one-off temporary migration. Migrants don't all aspire to settle, yet when governments block off the possibility for return, they in fact encourage permanent settlement.

Question from the audience:

There have been several questions about remittances and development objectives. I was curious, what percentage of remittances go to different types of activities? Let's say, supporting the education of relatives, purchase of housing, investment etc.?

Response by Hein de Haas:

Most people, all around the world, spend most of their money on consumption and migrants are no exception to that rule. Most micro-studies that I know of in North Africa and elsewhere, show that 70-90% of income is spent on consumption. The problem has been that consumption has always been cast in a negative light – this idea of imported goods and increasing dependency. However, if consumption means you encourage local production of foodstuffs or other products it can have very positive effects. The next category is probably housing, which is generally the fist major investment that most migrants tend to make. This has been heavily criticised by policy makers and researchers as a 'non productive investment'. Even though it might have an inflationary effect in migrant sending areas, there are also many studies that show that it can have very positive multiplier effects on regional economies. Some of Morocco's classic emigration regions have now become moderately wealthy regions, attracting internal in-migration from people seeking work, for instance, in the construction industry. Migrants have often capitalised on existing processes of urbanisation by investing in such enterprises. It is very difficult to generalise about the more risk-taking investments. The general investment environment then becomes very important – whether your assets are safe etc. In my Moroccan research I often asked migrants whether they invested, for example, in agricultural enterprises, and if they didn't, why not? One of the problems was that people couldn't get title deeds on their land, and even if they did, they could not be sure that the deeds would be respected. There are too many stories of people who have built a hotel, or started a farm, only for a local nobleman to come along claiming that the land is his, bribing a judge, and then for the migrant to lose the property. These aren't circumstances conducive to migrant investment.

Question from the audience:

I agree with you that talking about migration and development in conjunction is a problem, but this has been such a constant feature in the externalisation policies and practices of the EU. Talking about the two in conjunction makes migration a very undifferentiated process, yet there are refugees, there are asylum seekers, economic migrants etc. It also creates problems in terms of migrants' access to protection. So I wanted to know your view on the EU policy towards migration and development?

Response by Hein de Haas:

It is definitely an issue. This issue of migration and development is used, or I would say abused, in EU and national policies. It generally consists of a re-admission agreement, often on a bilateral level between, for example, Spain and Morocco or France and Morocco, whereby Morocco accepts to re-admit irregular migrants who come to France in exchange for development aid. The idea then is that this development aid will be invested in migrant sending areas so that migrants won't travel anymore. A good study on this has actually been done in Senegal; it looked at the coalitions that form around these re-admission policies and it emerged that, while nobody actually believed in the policy, it served everybody's interests. Migrant associations get some funding from these projects; the French government can boast it is doing something about the problem and send some migrants back to Senegal; and the Senegalese government can say they are working towards development. The underlying assumptions are, however, naïve. Firstly, it is naïve to think that these policies will stop illegal migration. It is often impossible and also very expensive to expel migrants. Secondly, it is naïve to assume that these programmes are going to encourage development. There is this famous project in Senegal called 'Return to the Farm' or 'Return to the Land' (*Retour vers l'Agriculture*), bringing back illegal migrants and giving them money to set up a farm. Yet, talking about values, these migrants do not aspire to be farmers, even if they had the means; and so they use the money for other things, like, for example, migrating again. So these programmes serve an agenda in which migration and development are linked. It all seems very nice, but again I think the migration-development issue is abused, which is why I am increasingly opposed to linking them – it is a humanitarian justification of return migration and expulsion policies.

Question from the audience:
I would like to pick up on the distinction between a global citizen and a migrant. It has a lot to do I think with the skill level of the individual. You said you would leave this distinction out of the debate, but I was wondering if you could elaborate a little bit nevertheless.

Response by Hein de Haas:
There is reason to hope that there will be more Marxism in social theory again because a global class perspective could help us think more critically about migration, and particularly the differences that governments increasingly make between 'desired' and 'undesired' migrants. Even under Minister Verdonk, who has this image of being very restrictive, the immigration policies for high-skilled migrants became much more liberal. It is very easy now, if you are above a certain threshold of education and income, to migrate to the Netherlands. You can almost get a visa overnight, including for your family. This is happening globally now. Increasing competition for high-skilled migrants will only increase this tendency, especially in light of ageing populations. You can envisage the future of migration in which we are all happy to call ourselves 'global citizens' and 'the transnationals', while on the other hand the term 'migrants' is mainly reserved for lower skilled, non-European individuals. On a global level, we might see these two migrant classes appearing. This increasing stream of privileged people, who have free mobility and who we don't classify as international migrants, but as global citizens, are reinforcing global class inequality.

The role of external interventions redefined

Paul Collier

Over the last ten years the donor community has been inspired by a simple slogan: 'ownership not donorship'. I have much sympathy for the intent behind that slogan, but often it is more rhetoric than reality. For example, last month I visited three different African countries; in one of these countries I met the Finance Minister. He is a member of the new government, the first democratic government the country has ever had. They invited me to advise them on their policy programme, especially concerning the first few months. He admitted they had no money. The main challenge was to get the donors re-engaged, and so his government was particularly keen on discovering which policies the donors would like. He said he had already tried to pick up on what the donors liked at the moment and, as a result, he asked me whether his country should focus on gender and the environment. Realising that this was the reality after a decade of 'ownership not donorship,' I almost wept. Here one finds a Minister of Finance of a newly established democracy, with the responsibility of forging his nation's economic programme, and his main concern is how to design something that will appeal to the current fashions in the donor community. That is inadvertently what we have created. So despite all that admirable rhetoric of 'ownership not donorship', what we have is a kind of 'reflective donorship', whereby governments try to second guess what will appeal to the donor community.

We also need to take another look at the slogan itself, because ownership is not even always the appropriate choice. Recently, United Nations Secretary-General Ban Ki Moon sent me to Haiti to apply the principles of my recent book *The Bottom Billion*, a few months before the earthquake. This disaster changed everything, but even before the earthquake, Haiti had undergone 40 years of governance breakdown. What the earthquake did was massively weaken the government as many government people were killed. It also excessively increased needs, urgent needs. It was in some sense Haiti's international moment; the international community knew it had to step up and help Haiti. Suddenly there was money and along with that the question of how to spend it. Unfortunately, there was no government to come up with a plan, and no government to accept and distribute and manage the billions of dollars being offered. How then could the intention of 'ownership not donorship' be applied? Who was to assume ownership?

The reforming Prime Minister of Haiti, a really feisty, courageous woman who had come out of the civil society movement in Haiti, had just been impeached by the Senate and had been made to resign. Impeachment had taken place because a majority of senators had accepted bribes from Columbian drug barons, who insisted on her departure as she stood in their way. This was the bitter reality of post-earthquake Haiti. The country was in desperate and urgent need of money, but handing it over to the existing government meant giving money to a very suspect and barely competent entity.

I was asked to advise because of my prior involvement with the country. I suggested, and was backed by many others, a dual governance structure, in which a competent representative of local government would work with an international figure beyond reproach, with the prestige and charisma to get things done and to coordinate the great variety of different donors. The plan was put into motion, and President Bill Clinton was invited to come in and work with local Prime Minister Bellerive. They jointly chaired the 'interim commission', which was granted the authority to act. This authority turned out to be most welcome, because no official government was formed – and still has not been formed. Immediately after the earthquake, the government decided to hold an election, distracting the politicians the rest of the year in their attempt to win the race. The elections were deemed corrupt and illegitimate, and the results were rejected by the Haitians. New elections have yet to be held, and the issue is still unresolved. This has left the country without a democratically elected government, and an illegitimate administration.

Effectively attempting to by-pass the original structures of government was the best thing that the interim commission could do under the circumstances. Unfortunately it was very slow in becoming operational: it was slow hiring staff, it was slow taking decisions and it was slow exercising its authority. For example, the most urgent task immediately after the earthquake was to clear the rubble. So an NGO specialised in reconstruction imported a huge rubble crusher to do the job. But the machine was held at customs for five months by certain commercial parties within Haiti, who had planned on earning exorbitant amounts by carrying out the work themselves. The interim commission regretfully failed to act timely and decisively here. It was nevertheless a good idea to establish the interim commission; if local actors had held full power in Haiti and had been given those donor billions, the money would likely have simply disappeared. So let this be a reality check. We can't always assume that outcomes will be good as long as local actors have the power.

Policy conditionality and budget support

Let me turn to some examples of international interventions with typically poor outcomes. Take, for instance, 'policy conditionality'. It was introduced some time ago, but it is still in use. Policy conditionality is where donors give aid to developing countries, and in return the developing countries pledge to adopt certain policies prescribed by the donor. What is fundamentally wrong with this intervention is that it destroys the accountability of government to citizen. Governments have to take responsibility for their policies, and citizens have to know that their government's policies are actually chosen by their government. Policy conditionally was a disaster exactly because it undermined this fundamental characteristic of good governance.

A second example of a poor international intervention is 'budget support'. Once again, this type of intervention is often done with the very best of intentions. To start, there has been recent academic work of the highest quality on what the origins are of effective states. How does one engage in effective state building? To the extent that there is an intellectual consensus, the key step is that the state invests in building a tax system on its citizens. This tax system has two benign effects. Firstly, citizens generally do not appreciate being taxed and thus taxing provokes their scrutiny, which disciplines the government. Such scrutiny does not happen automatically because scrutiny is a public good and as with any other public good, if everybody benefits, nobody in particular feels responsible for doing it. Scrutiny takes time. It also takes effort, and it is costly. And thus it is only the provocative act of the government reaching into the citizen's pocket that actually stimulates citizens into this act of scrutiny of government. And scrutiny of government improves government performance. This is one way in which the act of taxation leads to better governance.

The other way taxation leads to better governance does not depend upon citizens acting. Once the government has built an effective tax system, which captures some of the income of the society, the government has an incentive to try and increase that income. After all, if the society gets better off – if incomes go up – the government captures a slice of the revenue. And the bigger the slice it captures, the bigger is the incentive of the government to try and help the society to increase its income. What can the government do to help the society increase its income? The fundamental step is, having built the tax system, to invest in the rule of law. In other words, the government has to put in place an independent judiciary, settling disputes between private actors and restraining the power of government itself. The rule of law stimulates economic activity, but the incentive for the government to provide the rule of law is fundamentally that it will benefit financially from the growth it triggers. Effective taxation leads to the emergence of an effective government.

The problem with budget support – as a form of aid – is that it is a substitute for tax revenue. It is not the only substitute we see; another example is revenue which drops from heaven, or more probably, bubbles up from the ground in the form of natural resource revenues. To a limited extent, both natural resource revenues and budget support have this common effect of reducing the need for government to raise revenues from taxation. Let me give you an example. A friend of mine was at one stage economic adviser to the President of Nigeria. In that capacity, he visited the thirty-six states of Nigeria and noticed an empirical regularity. All of Nigeria's states were controlled by governors sitting atop a large amount of oil income – half of Nigeria's oil income goes to the states, more specifically it goes directly to the governors of the states. He noticed that the more corrupt the governor, the lower was the local tax rate. Basically governors who were corrupt were opting for a quiet life so as not to provoke any scrutiny. They did not even bother about capturing growth from the state, because they got their money from oil. The best strategy for them was the quiet life which was achieved by zero local taxation. Without any doubt, the most effective state governor in Nigeria at the moment, who is really causing a sensation for his effectiveness, is the governor of Lagos state. Unusually, Lagos state does not get much oil revenue. What the governor has decided to do is to significantly raise taxes. In return for those taxes, the governor began to improve Lagos' infrastructure. And you know what? He is nowadays very popular. In fact, he is a role model amongst Nigerian governors. This is the dilemma: budget support directly helps the society – it provides the finances for government to provide the public goods that poor people need – but it also has this offsetting effect of discouraging the government from imposing its own taxes.

Clean politics and informed societies

Having talked about two rather detrimental forms of international intervention – policy conditionality and budget support – let us turn to some good international interventions. We will start with a variant of budget support. The central question is how to apply budget support effectively. A radical suggestion would be that budget support should only be provided in situations where independent certification has established that the budget process is honest – basically that the budget is watertight. Is that not the same as policy conditionality? No, it is more like governance conditionality. The difference is this: policy conditionality is telling a government which policies it should adopt; governance conditionality is helping a government to enforce its own laws. There is no society in the world where looting the public purse is legal. Looting the public purse is always against the country's own laws; but in some societies it is common practice because governments are not able to enforce their own laws, primarily because there is no satisfactory scrutiny of budgetary spending.

In *The Bottom Billion,* I describe how one of my former students sets up a tracking survey of public spending in Chad. She found that for every dollar released by the Ministry of Finance for rural health clinics only one cent arrived in the rural clinics; 99 cents in the dollar somehow went astray. That sort of system is frankly unfit for budget support. The problem is not that the money leaks and is wasted – if that were the only problem, I would not be advocating what I am suggesting – it is that it is captured by political crooks who use it to finance their political power. Certifying budget support is one way to limit that damage.

A related set of international actions is to try to force Western companies who do business with governments of developing countries to behave with integrity. Every member state of the Organisation for Economic Co-operation and Development (OECD) now has domestic laws that prohibit companies from bribing government officials. The real question is whether or not those laws are enforced. My own country, Britain, has an absolutely shameful record. The laws have been in force for the past ten years and in that period there has been only one prosecution. I know about that prosecution because I was brought in by the Serious Fraud Office as the expert witness. Britain did indeed prosecute this particular company – a small construction company – but only because its new management called in the Serious Fraud Office after finding evidence of blatant bribery in the books; there was an actual paper trail, years of it! The new managers feared they would be held liable, and so they requested that the company be prosecuted. That is the heroic story of the sole prosecution in Britain.

The Serious Fraud Office asked me to testify about the total cost of the corruption. This case was a classic example of corruption – our corruption – undermining their governance. This little company had been building bridges in Jamaica and paying its fifteen percent to a middle ranking official in the Ministry of Public Works who was pocketing the money each year over a long period of time. Now he could have gone off and lived a good life. But instead he decided that his career as a public official in the Ministry of Works was over and he felt a higher calling to politics. So he used his money to buy a seat in parliament, and then he used some more of his money to climb up the greasy pole of politics. By the time this corruption case came to court he was his country's Minister of Transport. My testimony was thus that the ultimate cost of the British company's bribery was to have a crook as Minister of Transport. As soon as this case came to light, the Minister was dismissed.

That is the true nature of our conniving. We foul up the whole political class in these societies. Few honest people will even try to run for political office, because they know they have already lost. They are competing against crooks with vast resources from patronage, and this sours the whole political system; electors are left with the choice of voting between Crook A or Crook B. International interventions aimed at cleaning up the governance of our business relationships can make a big difference. They cannot have honest politics until we have honest business. We can refer to this good international intervention as 'building clean politics'.

Another good international intervention is one referred to as 'building informed societies'. Let us start with a major development that will be affecting mainly poor countries in the next decade: the resource booms. First of all, global prices of resources and commodities are very much higher than what they have been in the past. In addition, African and other low-income countries hold only about a fifth of the amount of discovered sub-soil assets that OECD countries do. But all that figure tells you is that there has, as yet, been a lot fewer searches for assets in those less-developed countries; these are the last frontiers on Earth for resource discovery and during the next decade, by hook or by crook, they'll be discovered.

So huge amounts of money will potentially flow into these countries; hugely valuable resources will certainly flow out of them. This is surely their big opportunity, but unfortunately, the history of resource extraction has been deplorable both with reference to the behaviour of the resource extraction companies and the behaviour of the governments – this is the core subject of my book *The Plundered Planet*. There is an immeasurable chain of events and decisions to be made – what will it take to get it right? What will stop history repeating itself, the history of plunder? Disastrous economic histories don't have to repeat themselves. For example, the most successfully run economy in Europe today is Germany. Why is this the case? Very simply because it used to be the worst. Germans lived through the most searing economic disaster that economic policy is capable of – hyperinflation that destroyed the middle class. Germans learned a lesson and vowed 'never again'.

I hear that sentiment of 'never again' across Africa now. They are well aware that the last time there were big revenues from commodities, those revenues were plundered. Germany managed to successfully harness their lesson learned and created practical institutions that have ensured that 'never again' became a reality. The key institution installed was an independent central bank. The Germans established rules and institutions and embedded them into a society that was very aware of the vital purpose of those rules and institutions, and thus sustained them. That is the recipe that African and other poor, but resource-rich, countries need. There is no substitute for an informed citizenry. There has to be a critical mass of citizens who understand the issues.

Now, the issues that Africans have to understand are not the same as the issues that Germans had to understand. Germany was fighting hyperinflation; in Africa independent central banks are almost an irrelevance. The decision chain for harnessing natural resources for prosperity is quite different, and so too are the institutions they will need. They can't even simply copy developed-country institutional systems, because we never faced the same problem. They will need purpose designed institutions sustained and supported by an informed citizenry. The challenge is to build those informed societies and to build those appropriate institutions. Although their needs differ from ours, we can nevertheless help them, because building the institutions requires a degree of technical knowledge.

In *The Bottom Billion* I floated the idea of a natural resource charter, which would set out the decision chain; and over the course of the last 3 or 4 years, a group of economists, lawyers, political scientists from around the world have built that charter, called *The Natural Resource Charter*, with its own website: www.naturalresourcecharter.org. The charter entails more than an online guide to building a decision chain; it has grown into a large organisation, with its own board. The board is entirely Southern; the chair is Ernesto Zedillo, the former President of Mexico who is now a Professor at Yale. The rest of the board comprises two Africans, an Arab who heads the Arab Development Fund, and a Chinese. So this is not the North telling the South what to do, this is the international South seizing its moment and building an instrument for information, not for coercion. It's a citizen movement rather than Northern finger wagging, and thus its standards have been adopted by the African Union and its economic institution, NEPAD. NEPAD, with African economists, will be presenting the standards to African governments, with which they can conduct a self-assessment, and discover how they stand in relation to the best practices outlined in the charter. The charter is a new way in which the international community can engage with countries in need of help. In this case, the countries do not need our money – they are going to have their own – what they need is the knowledge and organisational principles that will make it easier for the reformers to take charge.

The precursor to *The Natural Resource Charter* was the *Extractive Industries Transparency Initiative,* also a set of voluntary international standards, which was promptly picked up by the Nigerian reformers, who formulated a Nigerian Extractive Industries Transparency Initiative. The EITI was not the same as *The Natural Resource Charter* – it concerned transparency in revenues while the charter covers the whole decision chain, from how you handle the discovery process, how you tax companies, how much you save versus spend, how much you invest etc. The EITI was launched in somewhat inauspicious circumstances. It was, inadvertently, one of Prime Minister Tony Blair's greatest achievements. It was designed as his initiative – for him to announce at the Global Summit in South Africa in 2002. But he got last minute cold feet and never made the announcement. Luckily, due to the deep incompetence of the British civil service, the press office still released the press statement. We figured if EITI could be a blazing success, which it has been, then maybe a civil society movement could also book similar successes.

In conclusion, poor countries of the world no longer necessarily need our money, it's our knowledge they need most. Thankfully, modern technology now allows ordinary people in the rich world to easily communicate with ordinary people in the poor world. Information technology is on our side – more than ever allowing for that well-known adage, 'six degrees of separation', to be true. Information can now flow as never before. Take Cairo in the last couple of weeks. Information flows don't have to be as dramatic as that, but information flowed from Tunisia to Egypt, and Twitter essentially defeated one of the most entrenched autocracies on Earth. So use the information technology to spread the news of The Natural Resource Charter, which can build the critical mass of informed citizens that the poorest countries on Earth so badly need.

Summary

Paul Collier began his lecture by reflecting on the concept of 'ownership'. What does this term actually imply and how is it translated into practice? Collier argues that too often the mantra of 'ownership not donorship' has set into motion a rather superficial and disingenuous reform process in developing countries, by which they simply tap into whatever the tastes and fashions of the donor community happen to be at the time, in order to increase their chances of receiving development assistance. Collier calls this phenomenon 'reflective donorship'. While 'ownership not donorship' therefore makes for a catchy slogan, Collier cautions us to not automatically assume that 'empowering' local actors produces beneficial outcomes. More fundamentally, is it even responsible to advocate ownership when the governments of many developing countries are corrupt and dysfunctional? What does ownership entail in a country like Haiti where, following the 2010 earthquake, there was complete governance collapse. Collier asks the question of how, in a situation like this, donor money can address urgent needs via governments?

A solution Collier and others have proposed is the creation of a dual governance structure. This is in fact what happened in Haiti whereby an international figure, President Bill Clinton, and a domestic leader, Prime Minister Jean Max Bellerive, together formed an interim commission to deal with the pressing issues related to the economic and social reconstruction of the country. Collier moved on to talk about some good and bad examples of international interventions. Collier pointed to 'policy conditionality' and 'budget support' as two problematic forms of development assistance. Policy conditionality – the giving of aid in return for the implementation of certain policies – destroys the accountability of governments to their citizens. Budget support also undermines the link between government and citizenry, but in a more complex fashion. One of the building blocks of an effective state according to Collier is the expansion of the tax system. The reasons for this are two-fold. First of all, levying taxes on citizens' income provokes their scrutiny, which disciplines government. Second of all, the government itself has an incentive to increase its tax revenues through increasing the income of its population by investing in the rule of law. The problem that Collier identifies with budget support is that it functions as a substitute for a tax system, which means that these positive spin-off effects do not occur. However, Collier did not dismiss budget support as a form of development assistance outright. He argued that when the budget process has been certified as being in agreement with certain international standards, giving money can prove effective.

This is especially so when the money is intended to build what Collier called 'clean politics'. International intervention can further clean politics in two concrete ways. The first is through 'governance conditionality', which Collier differentiates from the more nefarious 'policy conditionality', because it is about helping a government to implement its own laws rather than importing a checklist from abroad. The second is by acting to improve the integrity of multinational companies, in particular by putting an end to bribery payments which can poison the whole political class of developing countries.

Another case in which international intervention can be a force for good is in helping to 'build informed societies'. Collier argues that the key to well-functioning institutions and economic growth is to build up a critical mass of informed citizens. In the context of Africa, Collier sees a knowledgeable public as crucial to successfully harnessing the continent's vast resource wealth. Indeed, civil society has already played an important role here in setting up natural resource charters that help ensure that resource revenues go towards the common good and not the enrichment of a corrupt elite. Collier thus concluded that when it comes to international intervention, what poor countries need most is not our money but our knowledge, so that they can build up the skills, expertise and technical capacity to realise their own development goals.

Discussion

Question from the audience:
What could a country like the Netherlands, a country of relatively small size, but with an ambitious development programme and a high level of expertise, do to alleviate the situation in, for example, Haiti or contribute to global development more broadly?

Response by Paul Collier:
Good, this gives us the chance to open up a third front of good international interventions. In Haiti you have an appalling need for healthcare and schooling, which the government has been completely unable to provide – something like 90% of social provision in Haiti is provided by NGOs of various forms. That is going to be common in a lot of the really fragile states. Think of Southern Sudan, which is just becoming independent. Southern Sudan has quite a lot of money of its own – it will also need and receive a lot of aid – but it also has oil so it will easily receive over 1 billion US dollars from oil revenues every year. The problem is that there is no public administration to effectively spend that money to provide the services that ordinary people need. So there is a huge lack of schooling, of healthcare and so forth. What then is the realistic option for providing scaled-up and decent quality services in places like Southern Sudan and Haiti? I think the answer is effective organisations like NGOs, but which should be working to government rather than to us. I would like to see a structure in which NGOs receive money for service provision not through donations, but money that flows through government. It might be Dutch money, it might be that the Dutch government gives the money to a state organisation, which then contracts Dutch NGOs to provide basic services.

That structure would have a number of advantages. Probably the most important one is that it would change the incentives for NGOs. At the moment the incentive for NGOs in these situations is to run a beautiful boutique operation – something that looks good (and is good) – but there are two problems: one is that it is very small and the other is that it is at a very high cost. NGOs shouldn't be providing beautiful boutiques. What they should be providing is cost-effective services that can be scaled-up as money is pushed into the organisation. The tragedy is that we have organisations like McDonalds that can provide hamburgers on huge scales, but we don't have the equivalent to McDonalds in basic services, even though what is most needed in poor countries is to supply basic services on a cost-effective basis and at scale. So NGOs need to turn themselves into the McDonalds of basic service provision. Instead they aim to be like top-end, boutique jewellery shops selling a tiny volume of very fine produce. What I would like to see therefore is a rethinking amongst NGOs. The nearest we get to effective NGOs are churches. Churches provide a mass organisation connected with ordinary people, providing a range of healthcare and schooling, as well as a religious function in places like Haiti and Southern Sudan. Yet donor agencies have very often been reluctant to engage with churches in helping to finance their services. I think that is an ideological resistance to what are actually pretty effective organisations, so I would like to see that overcome.

Question from the audience:
Is there not a hidden agenda behind rich countries' engagement with development issues?

Response by Paul Collier:
The suspicions are real, but they are fantasies – that is to say suspicions are widespread, but I really don't think there is a modern basis for them. There is no appetite in the Western world to return to colonialism; quite the opposite. If anything the sentiment in the Western world is divorce and separation, not engagement on any terms. Isolationism is a much bigger threat than a new wave of colonialism. What is the hidden agenda? Let's face it, the most transparent, potentially dangerous agenda out there internationally, for the poorest countries, is the Asian scramble for natural resources in Africa. If I had to point to one potential danger it would have to be that. It's not neo-colonialism; China has never had an appetite for colonialism whatsoever, but where it is potentially dangerous is in the sentiment of the Chinese President: "we won't ask any questions"; which can sound very positive. However, I just recently returned from Guinea – there was a coup in Guinea in which a young captain came to power.

While he was the self-styled President of Guinea, pro-democracy demonstrations erupted, to which he responded with violence and murdered 157 demonstrators. Three weeks later, in flew the Chinese and signed a 7 billion US dollar natural resource contract with him. He just ran off to Burkina Faso with the first payment. *That* does worry me. As I said, it's not neo-colonialism, it's not a hidden agenda, it's a very transparent agenda. So my advice to you is to get out of this 1960s/70s mentality of an evil West trying to take Africa down; it's kind of nonsense.

Question from the audience:
I think China is being very effective in bringing things such as investment, infrastructure and affordable goods to Africa. So instead of pushing China to the wall, they can better do business with China. Is that what you think?

Response by Paul Collier:
I'm glad you asked that because I agree with that sentiment. China is a two-edged sword; it has a lot of opposing effects, but on balance it is a force for good. China has brought three things that are all positive. One is a greater competition for natural resources, which has raised their prices – surely a plus. Africa is going to earn trillions of dollars in the next decade from natural resources and if it seizes that opportunity, which I very much hope it will, this is Africa's chance to transform itself with its own money. The second thing that China has done is to provide very cost-effective infrastructure. Now that is itself a bit of a two-edged sword because the business model of China is to bring in everything, including their own labourers. That's going too far in terms of a model of cost-efficiency. It's vital that construction actually generates jobs for Africans so it's going to have to modify its business model. The third thing China is doing is that it is bringing in a lot of cheap manufacturers, which has admittedly hit Africa's manufacturing industry, but has really reduced the cost of living for ordinary people. In my mind that is a plus. I think in the next decade there is a chance of a much bigger plus, which is that wages in China are now at last starting to rise quite fast and so some Chinese manufacturing may well be looking to relocate and it would be wonderful

if China started to outsource some of that manufacturing to coastal Africa, which would enable Africa to diversify. So basically I agree with you and I'm glad for the opportunity to counter the negative; the main effect of China is positive.

Question from the audience:
You have spoken a lot about the G8 in the past, especially when you wrote 'The Bottom Billion'; what do you think the appropriate platform is now for conducting a dialogue on development?

Response by Paul Collier:
Thank goodness the G8, which was the only act in town and which was manifestly deficient because it excluded so many countries, has now been replaced by the G20. The move from the G8 to the G20 has been a huge plus and a big beneficial spin-off from the global crisis. The G20 is *potentially* quite an exciting forum for helping the poorest countries. I'm currently engaged with it at the moment, trying to get an item onto the G20 agenda that would be helpful for the poorest countries – but unfortunately I am finding that it is much more difficult to get items that help the poorest countries onto a G20 agenda, than it was with the G8. The emerging market economies that now have seats at the G20 are interested in their own agenda. They still see themselves as "emerging, so we need an agenda that is helpful to us, never mind those that haven't risen to emerging market status yet". In that sense, behind all the rhetoric of 'Solidarity of the South', the emerging market economies actually turn out to not be such trustworthy friends.

Question from the audience:
Say you would have half a billion Euros to serve the needs of women and girls in Afghanistan; would you protect their interests by training police and providing F16 fighter jets, or could you give an alternative to the proposal of our Green Left party?

Response by Paul Collier:
First, I've not discussed security at all, but it is fair to say that without security it is hard to do much else, so we shouldn't be completely

contemptuous of the provision of security. It doesn't have to be the West that provides the security. In Haiti, the big UN peacekeeping mission was predominantly Brazilian, plus some Peruvians. It's been there since 2004 and it's been hugely beneficial. Often the sort of security you need in these situations evolves from military to policing, and building effective policing is really valuable.

Now suppose I a had half a billion to help in Afghanistan and other than security here's what I would suggest. It has actually been tried and sort of worked, but was discontinued. The National Solidarity programme was an attempt to distribute money to local communities, for them to spend subject to a set of checks on governance, so that the money couldn't just be embezzled by the village leader. There had to be some village committee structure in place for taking decisions, some accountability of how the money was spent. The advantage of this programme was that first of all, it enabled localities to take power into their own hands, rather than being dependent upon a corrupt civil service. Secondly, it allowed local leaders to emerge, showing that they could use public money well. Growing an effective politics from the bottom up is, I think, the best we can hope for in situations of very dysfunctional politics. We have tried to do instant fixes of politics from the top: holding a national election in which a divine figure is elected who everyone accepts. This of course never happens. We have exaggerated the benefits of these quick political fixes at the top. The politics at the top is almost always dysfunctional in these societies. It's growing a new politics from below, whilst trying to contain the power of the corrupt patronage systems by scrutinising the flows of the money. That's the best we can do on the politics front, I think. A longer term solution is thus to grow a new politics from below, by empowering local politicians to show how they can do a good job with public money. That's what I would do with half a billion.

Question from the audience:
Do you think, and would you go so far as to say, that sharing knowledge and investing our time in talking to people around the world is even more important than making donations and even more powerful?

Response by Paul Collier:

If we go deep enough into modern economic thinking about the growth process – why some societies become rich and others don't – basically the thinking now is that ideas are decisive. Ideas in various forms, ideas that generate institutions, ideas that generate technical knowledge: ideas shape economic opportunities. The nice thing about ideas is that they are potentially free, they are the ultimate public goods. At some deep level, what modern economics is saying is that ideas are vital. To translate that into practical terms of what ordinary people can do, let me give you an example of something I came across recently in Southern Sudan. A group of people came together and started a website, www.peacediv.com, on which local entrepreneurs in Southern Sudan can post their business ideas. It's particularly pitched to the Sudanese diaspora so that they can fund these local business ideas. Furthermore, where the diaspora is investing, it gives other international actors more confidence and comfort. So you can imagine diaspora money being matched by other international money. So, that's one way of trying to help small businesses in a post-conflict situation. All the post-conflict societies have big diasporas because so many of their able people left; harnessing the diaspora for good is a really important strategy for reviving the post-conflict societies.

Question from audience:

At this moment we are living in the second food crisis of this decennium and you have been talking about sub-soil wealth in Africa, but there is also a lot of soil wealth. According to the statistics, most of the areas that can be used for food production, which are still available, are in Africa – hence the land-grabbing by China, India, Saudi Arabia etc. Most African countries are net importers of food and with higher food prices, a large part of the population is in deep trouble. Is it not of critical importance that Africa becomes more food secure and uses its land better, and what then could the rich countries do to help Africa become more food secure?

Response by Paul Collier:

That's a really good and timely question. I first read about this around the 2008 food crisis because I thought that was potentially a food crisis that was here to stay. The 2008 food crisis was punctured by the global economic crisis. That's a pretty drastic way of bringing food prices down, but for a little while it worked. Now we are back with another food crisis.

Let me run through first, why it is important and second, what we can do about it. So, why is it important? As you say, many African countries are food importers. That such a land-abundant country is importing its food is in itself a tragic situation. What's the most vulnerable group? The group living off imported food is to be found in the coastal cities. The rural population is less exposed because they are growing their own food. The urban population is the one that is buying food at world prices or higher. So, that section of the population is really very exposed to fluctuations in world prices. When there's a shortage on the world market, prices go up and demand falls. What does that mean in practical terms? It means that some people are eating less. Economics has got some nice anodyne phrases for very brutal processes. Who's eating less? Amongst the urban poor in Africa, half of the budget is spent on food. If half of your budget is spent on food and world food prices double, the only way you maintain your food consumption is if you buy nothing else. The group that equilibrates the global food market is the poor, urban households in the poorest countries. Within those households, who's going to go hungry? Here's my fear, at the bottom of the food chain are the children. If children go without adequate food for a period of two years, the condition they develop is called stunting. And in 2008, this was my fear – if the spike in food prices persisted for two years we would have stunting occurring amongst the children. A key fact about stunting is that it is irreversible. In fact, it is so irreversible that is actually intergenerational. There are Swedish studies on height that show that the affect on height can persist for several generations. The other key fact about stunting is that it is not just a physical condition, it also has mental consequences. So here we have irreversible effects, which are so damaging that they also impair mental abilities, which will quite possibly ripple down the generations. So we cannot afford to have a long-running food crisis.

What can be done to increase world food supplies, and in particular food supplies in Africa? I am going to give you solutions that will challenge you and I suggest that your ideology is getting in the way. I'm going to give you two uncomfortable solutions. The first solution is commercial agriculture. By commercial agriculture I do not mean the mega land deals. I do not mean Saudi Arabia trying to buy half of Madagascar. That is not commercial – that is a geopolitical land grab, which has to be avoided at all costs. The whole point of these geopolitical land grabs is to pre-empt the market, so that when food is next scarce, Saudi Arabia gets fed rather than Madagascar. Commercial agriculture is not the same as geopolitical land grabs; it is moving from the peasant mode of production to a larger scale of organisation. It used to be thought that small is beautiful in agriculture, but the latest agricultural economics research suggests that small is not beautiful. As you move from farms of two hectares up to forty hectares, which is the range that has been properly explored, the total efficiency factor increases. Small is actually misorganisation. When you move beyond forty, to two or three thousand, I think the same happens. There are strong scale-economies in things like logistics, finance, and risk-taking, which make commercial agriculture more productive than small farm agriculture. African small farm agriculture has basically had constant productivity for forty years compared to a global trend of rising productivity. Whilst we should do all we can to try to directly raise the productivity of peasant agriculture, I have nothing against doing that, we should also try to open up commercial farming. Commercial farming may be able to produce a lot of food quite fast. The governor of one of the northern Nigerian states was telling me that he is pioneering commercial agriculture and yields are about four times as high as in peasant agriculture. So that's one approach, to which the international development agencies have unfortunately been completely allergic to for decades.

The second approach to which all the European young are adamantly opposed to, again for ideological reasons not science, is genetically modified crops. Here's the bitter reality, Africa is suffering from climatic deterioration and yes, we should try to do our best to reduce climate change and global warming, but even if we stopped emitting carbon tomorrow, the climate would continue to deteriorate for the next fifty years. The challenge for Africa is how to adapt to that likely deterioration, which includes more extreme weather condi-

119

tions, droughts, floods, heat, cold. All these extremes make it harder for the traditional crops to produce decent yields. There's even a danger that, in southern Africa, traditional varieties of maize, the staple in many countries, may become unviable. So Africa, more than any other region on Earth, needs to speed up crop adaptation. Genetically modified crops are part of this process of speeding up. They are not a magic bullet, they are just part of the process. Yet virtually all African countries, except South Africa and Burkina Faso, banned all genetically modified crops. They banned them because we banned them in Europe. It was just a gut reaction. We did it for all the wrong reasons. Our agricultural protectionist lobbies smelt a new excuse for protectionism; the Left thought this was a good chance to be anti-American, Prince Charles thought this was a great way to go back to the 18th century, and so on and so forth. So there was a deeply dysfunctional and very powerful political alliance which messed Europe up.

Question from the audience:
How do you see the whole movement of social investment or triple bottom line investment? Do you see it as a negative or positive intervention from the West?

Response by Paul Collier:
I think it is a hugely positive force. Social enterprise didn't exist in my time; it exists with great passion and ability now. There are a huge number of things young people can do in social enterprises that are beneficial and really exciting. These are the organisations that can innovate, and what we need most is experimentation and innovation, and then the ability for the successful to scale up. That's why social enterprise is so exciting; it allows the successful to expand. I think it is a hugely advantageous thing. It is where young people can bring a whole range of things, business skills, technical skills, social skills – the skills that build effective organisations. It is a great thing for young people to become engaged in.

Social responsibility in a context of change: from corporate and organisational, to networks, markets and territories

Patricia Almeida Ashley

Hopefully, at the end of this lecture and subsequent discussion, we shall have new possibilities of ideas and actions concerning the social responsibility movement towards a sustainable society. I shall start with a question: "Why have certain people, from all different social segments, become interested in, involved in and committed to the social responsibility movement – and what are their motives, expectations, actions and results?"

It could be that social responsibility is a good way of doing business and bringing opportunities for financial earnings, either at the personal or organisational level. It could also be motivated by the need for emotional attachment to social networks of people who hold the romantic belief that incremental social changes can bring a durable and, possibly, irreversible process towards sustainable society. It could be by choice, but also by chance or mistake, or even encouraged by an authority such as a director, in favour of strategic directives, either in private, educational or civil society organisations.

My own story involves the International Institute of Social Studies of Erasmus University Rotterdam finding me hidden away from the world, in a cosy country house, surrounded by chickens, flowers, mountains, and birds, in a simple and friendly neighbourhood of mainly Italian immigrants in rural Brazil. I was contacted by Rector Professor Louk de la Rive Box in June 2009; in an email he informed me that I had been selected by a search committee in Latin America, chaired by Professor Bert Helmsing, to hold the Prince Claus Chair in Development and Equity, from September 2009 to August 2011.

That year was in fact my tenth in which I had been engaged in the research of the social responsibility movement in Brazil. At the end of the 1990s, a Yahoo search for social responsibility resulted in just two hits in Brazil: Instituto Ethos (a business association) and IBASE (a civil society organisation). The literature on the topic was almost all foreign, with only one Brazilian book published in 1981, and a special edition of a management journal published in the mid 1980s. A similar search in 2011 resulted in more than a hundred thousand hits! All of them involving knowledge produced by Brazilians – from civil society, academia, enterprises, business associations, public bodies, consultants, editors, journalists and media.

Now, I come to the heart of the argument I am proposing. Currently, there is still a significant lack of public policies, in all sectors and at all levels of government, that are clearly integrated and aligned with the movement of social responsibility. We, at ISS, started a project in 2010, supported by NWO/Wotro, ISS and Universidade Federal Fluminense (my affiliated institution in Brazil), researching public policies on corporate social responsibility. We have found that there is a lack of systemic applied knowledge among government bodies, in both Brazil and Europe, on the current state of corporate social responsibility. And unfortunately, the mainstream thought held by government is still based on a very cautious and, possibly, fearful political understanding that corporate social responsibility is a matter of the will of enterprises, driven mainly by business leaders and its forums.

Borrowing an analogy from quantum physics, instead of looking at the wave as a whole, the current dominant paradigm in corporate social responsibility considers enterprises as solitary dots and, at the most, networks of dots. Below, I will offer a summary of the current and main global frameworks concerning corporate social responsibility. What I invite you to do is consider the wave, the greater picture; take a step back and regard the institutional context in which enterprises find themselves. This task of comprehending the institutional field of corporate social responsibility requires a more ethnographic and longitudinal approach, in order to fully grasp the relevance of what is within and between the 'dots' of organisational social responsibility.

Then, as an illustration of the complexity and challenges of the institutional field of corporate social responsibility, I will briefly present the case of Sao Joao del Rey. I will outline some of the local challenges for bringing the ideas and practices of corporate social responsibility into a municipal reality of local actors, based on a six year personal experience of living, teaching and researching there. It is not an unusual case in Brazil; it is indeed the typical Brazilian municipality with all its inequalities, expressed in rural and urban environments.

In closing, and with the purpose of reframing perspectives from corporate and organisational social responsibility, to networks, markets and territories, the last part of the paper presents a conceptual framework, which I call the **Master** model of multi-actor and multi-level social responsibility in a territorial scope, connecting layers of stakeholders' social responsibilities towards development and equity goals. The Master model is currently in its infancy, and so I welcome all comments and contributions to guide its further development.

Social responsibility: from organisational to multilevel and multi-actor conceptual frameworks

Too much consideration is generally given to social responsibility frameworks conceived for the organisational sphere, mainly based on hierarchical or 'vertical' power models within the borders of enterprises or organisations. Too little attention, however, has been given to frameworks based on the complexity of the mutually reinforcing alignment of multilevel and multi-actor social responsibilities, which requires cross-organisational and inter-institutional governance and policy models of social responsibilities among different social spheres. The current literature on the concept of corporate social responsibility (CSR) on a global level points to a multitude of perspectives and scopes for the concept of social responsibility within and among countries, and embedded in its specific economic models, institutional fields and culture.[16] Some international perspectives are generating congruence on a multidimensional scope for social responsibility (e.g., ISO 26000 for Organisational Social Responsibility, the Global Reporting Initiative – GRI, the United Nations Global Compact), while others are

---

16 See a more detailed review in previously published papers by the author (Ashley, 2010a and 2010b)

focusing on one dimension for subjects of social responsibility (e.g., the UN 'protect, respect and remedy' framework for human rights).

However, the mainstream of global perspectives on CSR is still very much focused on a corporate or organisational level of social responsibility, rather than in a broader scope of social networks and institutional fields. According to this current mainstream of CSR, we can identify a plethora of tools, principles, protocols, guidelines that have been building a soft law framework through international forums, which still look toward the company as the centre of the social responsibility discussion.

CSR brings its own conceptual weakness when enterprises are faced by the decision criteria of market transactions and relations in competition, financing, supplying, buying, investment, as well as government taxing and other legal and institutional aspects that are beyond the boundaries of the enterprise. At the global level, international capital movement and financial decisions are still embedded in an economic paradigm based on 'short term' timeframes for business performance, based on levels of interest rates and return on capital, decoupled from an increasing promotion of a global movement of corporate social responsibility.

Also, the higher education paradigm is still mainly oriented towards forming professionals in different areas of knowledge for working towards one-dimensional criteria of financial evaluation as a measure of business excellence; in other words, focusing on capital and profit margins growth, which are not necessarily generated by or a result of socially responsible markets and enterprises. Not to mention criteria used in purchasing decisions by organisations, families and individuals, which are mainly based on accessibility, price level and product quality related to its function and social appeal, regardless of the quality of social, economic and environmental history of products.

Thus, it can be argued that CSR is facing a global dilemma for its future. Business managers leading the way in socially responsible behaviour are confronted with an ethical dilemma when having to face investors, regulations, lenders, buyers, suppliers, professionals, and competitors, who are not embedded in a culture of social responsibility. Some questions can be raised connecting CSR, development and equity in this global dilemma; such as, what is the future of corporate social responsibility within the global context of non-ecological models of development that contribute to climate change, urbanisation, violence and inequalities? What are the possible limits to and contributions by corporate social responsibility for development and equity, especially considering the UN millennium development goals, reinforced by the UN's latest report on human development, showing how high the levels of inequality still are in human societies, among and within countries? What are the social responsibilities of different social actors towards development and equity goals? How could public policy in government contribute to social responsibility among market players? How could policy align development and equity goals and multi-actor social responsibilities? How could global partnerships for development contribute to building a culture of practice of multi-actor social responsibility, aligned with goals of development and equity? How do we balance soft and hard regulation concerning multi-actor and multilevel social responsibility in different territorial scopes?

The contribution of negotiated global frameworks on social responsibility

Here I offer a selection of global voluntary frameworks on corporate social responsibility in the form of principles, guidelines and standards for best practices. The selection includes those frameworks led by the United Nations, the OECD and the International Organisation for Standardisation.

The United Nation Human Rights Commission and John Ruggie's framework[17]

The UN Commission on Human Rights adopted a resolution on 20 April 2005 requesting the Secretary-General to appoint a special representative on the issue of human rights and transnational corporations and other business enterprises. In July 2005, Kofi Annan

---

17   Source: Business & Human Rights Resource Centre at http://www.business-humanrights.org

appointed Professor John G. Ruggie to be Special Representative of the UN Secretary-General on business & human rights. The Business & Human Rights Resource Centre created a portal at John Ruggie's request, to facilitate communications and sharing of materials related to the mandate, which read as follows:

- To identify and clarify standards of corporate responsibility and accountability for transnational corporations and other business enterprises with regard to human rights;
- To elaborate on the role of States in effectively regulating and adjudicating the role of transnational corporations and other business enterprises with regard to human rights, including through international cooperation;
- To research and clarify the implications for transnational corporations and other business enterprises of concepts such as 'complicity' and 'sphere of influence';
- To develop materials and methodologies for undertaking human rights impact assessments of the activities of transnational corporations and other business enterprises;
- To compile a compendium of best practices of States and transnational corporations and other business enterprises.

In June 2008, the United Nations Human Rights Council unanimously accepted the policy framework proposed by the SRSG, and extended the SRSG's mandate for another three years, asking him to operationalise the framework in order to provide concrete guidance to States and businesses. The framework was also endorsed by the major international business associations and by leading international human rights organisations. A new consensus advancing the business and human rights agenda was formed in a policy framework comprising three core principles: the State's duty to *protect* against human rights abuses by third parties, including business; the corporate responsibility to *respect* human rights; and the need for greater access by victims to effective *remedies*.

In March 2011[18], the SRSG will present to the UN Human Rights Council his final recommendations, which will include a set of Guiding Principles for the operationalisation of the UN 'protect, respect and remedy' framework, which will elaborate and clarify for companies, states, and other stakeholders how they can take practical steps to address business impacts on the human rights of individuals. The Guiding Principles consider the complementary roles of the States, the business enterprises and judiciary or non-judiciary bodies in relation to the effective implementation of human rights.

The ISO 26000

ISO 26000 was published in November 2010 and is the result of a five-year global discussion involving multi-stakeholder committees from more than 90 countries. Brazilian and Swedish national standards bodies were appointed president and vice-president of the ISO working group on social responsibility. ISO 26000 boasted an incredibly transparent process in reaching a global consensus on the scope and depth of organisational social responsibility. Since the beginning of the activities of the working group, all documents and participants were publicly available on the ISO website. The multi-stakeholder global discussion generated an experience of multi-actor governance with appropriate level of systematisation and transparency for all participants and observers.

A remarkable innovation of ISO 26000 is that social responsibility is proposed not only for business organisations, but for any organisation; business, government, educational and other non-state organisations. Another note to be made is that ISO 26000 has defined guidance on the necessary core subjects or themes of organisational social responsibility: governance, human rights, labour practices, environment, fair operating practices, consumer issues and community involvement and development. These core subjects are embedded in the principles of social responsibility: accountability, transparency, ethical behaviour, respect for stakeholders' interests, respect for the

---

18 This paper was written prior to this date. As an author's additional note, I inform that John Ruggie's final report was publicly distributed at the seventeenth session of the Human Rights Council (21 March 2011).

rule of law, respect for international norms of behaviour, and respect for human rights. The core subjects are to be observed in policies, strategies and evaluations of social responsibility, within any organisation (business, government and non-state actors), and to be supported by the use of tools for managing social responsibility.

In summary, ISO 26000 as a non-certifiable guidance standard is indeed an emergent conceptual framework to be considered as a major reference for research and other international and national standards and tools concerning corporate social responsibility.

The Global Compact

2010 celebrated the 10th anniversary of the Global Compact 10 principles[19] for business social responsibilities. Currently, the UN Global Compact is the world's largest voluntary corporate sustainability initiative with over 8,000 business participants and non-business stakeholders from 135 countries. Global Compact Local Networks can be found in over 90 countries.

The Global Compact has generated several tools and documents to reinforce complementary initiatives and a learning environment on business social responsibility. Examples are the Principles for Responsible Investment (PRI) and the Principles for Responsible Management Education (PRME), which are spreading rapidly among different actors in the global arena, encouraging institutional change within the business environment, specifically in investment bodies and higher education institutions.

---

19 *Human rights:* Principle 1 - Businesses should support and respect the protection of internationally proclaimed human rights; Principle 2 - and make sure that they are not complicit in human rights abuses. *Labour:* Principle 3 - Businesses should uphold the freedom of association and the effective recognition of the right to collective bargaining; Principle 4 - the elimination of all forms of forced and compulsory labour; Principle 5 – and the effective abolition of child labour; Principle 6 - and the elimination of discrimination in respect of employment and occupation. *Environment:* Principle 7 - Businesses should support a precautionary approach to environmental challenges; Principle 8 - and undertake initiatives to promote greater environmental responsibility; Principle 9 - and encourage the development and diffusion of environmentally friendly technologies. *Anti-corruption:* Principle 10 - Businesses should work against corruption in all its forms, including extortion and bribery.

The OECD guidelines in a revision process

The OECD Multinational Guidelines are recommendations by governments covering all major areas of business ethics, including corporate steps to obey the law, observe internationally-recognised standards and respond to other societal expectations. The 42 governments adhering to the OECD Guidelines for Multinational Enterprises are working on an update of the Guidelines, which aims to ensure their continued role as a leading international instrument for the promotion of responsible business conduct.

Following an agreement on the terms of reference, work on the update started on the occasion of the June 2010 Roundtable on Corporate Responsibility, where discussions centred on supply chains, human rights and environment/climate change. A special consultation with stakeholders took place in Paris on 13 December 2010. Discussions focused on human rights, employment and labour, due diligence, supply chains and procedural provisions, including those relating to the functioning of National Contact Points.

There is a close collaboration between the two parallel processes of revision of the OECD guidelines and John Ruggie's mandate on the UN 'protect, respect and remedy' framework on business and human rights. John Ruggie submitted two discussion papers for the 2010 Roundtable, one with his contributions to the revision process and another including the application of the UN 'protect, respect and remedy' framework for business conduct concerning human rights in supply chains (Ruggie, 2010). In a specific decision making diagram for dealing with issues of human rights in supply chains, it is shown how it is the duty of enterprises to respect human rights, and thus they are expected to terminate contracts with any party found to be ineffective in using strategies for upgrading standards concerning human rights.

In the next section, I illustrate the complexities of discussing and turning the ideas and tools of corporate social responsibility into a reality within a specific territory, in this case a municipality of 85.000 inhabitants, in Minas Gerais, Brazil.

Sanitation in São João del Rey

"The social responsibility of business is to make business survive. Sanitation is none of my business." This statement sums up the feelings of the majority of micro, small and medium size companies in Sao Joao del-Rei (which are incidentally not suppliers of multinational companies). Survival of the enterprise is to stay in business, which means that labour, environmental, consumer, or other laws cannot always be obeyed. Prices can be kept low if the additional costs of legal compliance are avoided. Trust is key to social networks in Sao Joao del Rei; once customers are known by name or face, a notebook suffices to keep track of goods sold and amounts due. The conservation and reproduction of collective traditional habits and beliefs in trade and business are most valued by business forums and associations. In addition, gender empowerment is not part of the business game; and career plans, respect for health and safety at work, schooling, training and development, are not budgeted for by local businesses.

The improvement and expansion of higher education by the Universidade Federal de São João del Rey has brought lots of public budget into the local economy, new events, bachelor courses, research and extension projects. However, the university has always been seen by common people as an ivory tower of elite professors, mostly concerned with their own isolated national and international research networks and publications. A few exceptions were found in the small number of professors engaged in transformational research that actually brought about social innovation. They comprised no more than 5% of the academic staff there.

One such projects was the Ecocidades project, which I was responsible for and that was funded by the Ministry of Cities and the Ministry of Education. It commenced in 2007 and, in 2009, entered a partnership with the Environmental Justice Project run by Professor Eder Jurandir Carneiro. The Ecocidades project organised a series of activities, such as qualification events for public agents, business representatives, educators and civil society organisations, in the form of short courses[20], field research, events[21] and a communication tool[22]. The Ecocidades Project focused on a number of topics for its capacity building aspect, including sanitation, environmental policy, urban environment, urban development and local governance. The project was later expanded to include research on retail business policies on human resources; a participative evaluation on the implementation of the Municipal Director Plan; meetings with trade unions, city committees, the city council, the city hall and local secretaries; radio interviews; opinion articles in local newspapers; meetings with political party leaders during the 2008 election campaigns; and so on. The use of an ethnographic and longitudinal research methodology illuminated the limits and possibilities for spreading social responsibil-

---

20 An eighteen-hour short course on Planning and Urban Management, with an emphasis on Sanitation and Environment Protection – September and October 2007 – with 71 participants, among them public agents from civil society organisations and community-based movements, the city government and commissions' members. Lectures and workgroups included topics such as City Planning and Financing, City Environment Management, Environment Education, Management of Urban Solid Remains, Water Resources and Sanitary Sewer Systems and Urban Water Drainage. What resulted, as the end-of-course task, was a contribution of all the regular participants in the diagnosis and participative planning of the topics dealt with during the course. It also offered two three-hour short courses on Environment Ethics and on Sustainable Cities – November 2007 – with 50 participants in each course, including university students, teachers, civil servants, community-based movements and civil society entities.

21 Seminar for Ecocities in the Vertentes Region – May 2007 – with 120 regular registered participants from the civil society, the government, city commissions' members, popular movements and educators; Seminar for Ecocities in the Vertentes Region and Exhibition of Initiatives in Environment Education in the Elementary Education Schools in Sao Joao del-Rei – November 2007 – with 100 participants from the civil society, the government, city commissions' members, community-based movements and educators; Exhibition of Academic Production in Sanitation, Environment Protection and Sustainability by UFSJ Students – November 2007 – with the participation of 50 university students and teachers.

22 www.ecocidades.org enjoyed over 1000 visitors between August and November 2007, plus the expectation of 3000 annual visitors between 2007 and 2010, during which time the website maintained didactic materials and results of the extension project research. In October 2009, visits to the website surpassed expectations, with over 16,000 visitors since the creation of the website.

ity into the business community, within a non-aligned institutional context and influenced by the cultural aspects of the municipality concerning social responsibility.

The situation in Sao Joao del-Rei is a good example of an extremely low level of collective social responsibility shown by the various social actors (politicians, residents, business, and workers) towards the city and its environment, society, collective health and local economy, which mainly involves tourism, mining, agriculture, trade and services in health and education sectors. No one has ever taken responsibility, and never has a multi-actor approach to the sanitation conditions of the city been developed or implemented. In general, the government has always been blamed for the sanitation problems. During political meetings, all social segments are present, representing the different economic activities, but the focus is typically on discussing the survival of businesses and ways to boost the economy, and rarely do people seem interested in discussing the sanitation issues.

The city experiences severely poor sanitation conditions; domestic waste is still thrown straight into the local streams and rivers, greatly jeopardising the water supply. The Lenheiro river, which runs through the city, has been severely polluted by raw sewage; a fact confirmed by Oliveira et al. (2001) in a study that collected water from the river at seven different spots – from its source, to where it flows into the Rio das Mortes. At one point in its course, the river receives, in addition to domestic waste, industrial waste rich in organic matter, thus decreasing oxygen levels in the water considerably. The results of the study showed that the Lenheiro river is clean with 'class 1 water' near its source, but it quickly becomes an open sewage after just the first four kilometres. Lenheiro Hill, which lies on the left bank of the river, is occupied by informal settlements of poor households, without any public policy for housing and sanitation. The soil on Lenheiro Hill presents high permeability combined with excavations (veins) produced after three centuries of gold mining. Domestic sewage drains into the veins or directly into the many little streams, infiltrating the permeable soil and contaminating the ground water.

Such facts are either unknown or disregarded by the inhabitants and by the great number of tourists who come to visit Sao Joao del

Rei – they come on account of its cultural and historical heritage, the architectural riches of the buildings in the historical center, as well as the culture preserved in its art and tradition in sacred music, cooking, craftsmanship and works of art.

The institutional structure and mechanisms of the local City Hall seem to have been demobilised along the years, with mayors in office devoid of any engagement with public transparency and the quality of public services, damaging municipal management and the necessary investments in urban infrastructure, especially with regards to sanitation and the use of urban soil. The mayors and city aldermen of the last 20 years have had a basic education at best; they have been supported by local business associations and leaders, and elected through practices of privilege distribution and assistance programmes, even though most are/were undergoing law suits claiming administrative improbity.[23] There is a significant lack of qualified staff among the technical personnel at City Hall for planning and government budgeting.[24] Public budgets are not presented to or discussed with the Urban Planning and Development Commission and no public hearings are prepared.[25] During the research undergone by the Ecocidades project in 2009, we found that all municipal commission Presidents complained about institutional weaknesses, mainly as

---

23 Based on data for Mayors elected in Brazil for the mandate period of 2005-2008, according to the Brazilian Institute of Geography and Statistics (IBGE), 50% of the elected Mayors in the class group of Municipalities with up to 50.000 inhabitants - 4.996 municipalities - have never graduated.

24 A fact that reflects on the quality of the Pluri-annual Plan (PPA), taken from the Act of Budget Directives (LDO) and from the Act of Annual Budget (LOA). The PPA for the 2010-2013 office was forwarded to the Aldermen Chamber in incomplete format, lacking the annexes demanded by law, which would define the government programmes and acts, together with the respective budgets for the following four years.

25 Which are necessary for the budget presentation by the City Hall for the fulfilment of the PPA, the LDO and the LOA, as demanded by the City Statutes.

the result of a lack of technical and political support from City Hall.[26]

On the other hand, the Ecocidades project was able to compile and offer freely available information, through its website, about the majority of activities conducted during the period 2007-2009; the information had been supplied by web visitors from Sao Joao del Rey, from Brazil and abroad. It is amazing how powerful online social networking of communities can be. Also remarkable is the potential strength of partnerships between higher-education institutions and civil society in order to contribute to social, environmental and economic innovation, by means of transformational empowerment and collective awareness of all actors in a municipality, using information technology, the organisation of events and courses, socially relevant research, and the publication of experiences and results in different languages and media, for different audiences.

However, such partnerships require funding. Restricted budgets for education, research and civic driven change, of all actors (public, private and civil society), could limit its result to a multitude of papers published in international journals read only by highly skilled and intellectual workers. Fortunately, Lula's government has reinforced budgets for Science and Technology, as well as for federal universities, after a long history of privatisation of education. With a country the size of Brazil, continuity of investment and education, research and civil society organisations, as well as policies for micro, small and medium enterprises, give Brazilians hope that social innovation is a priority for Brazil.

Next, I wish to present the Master model for reframing corporate social responsibility as part of a broader concept of multi-actor and multilevel social responsibility in a territorial scope, aiming to turn CSR into an institutionally viable concept, supported by collective social responsibility from different actors towards specific territories.

---

26 The more dynamic members use their private resources to pay for communication devices among themselves, because City Hall does not provide the necessary support. It is very common for City Hall to demand political support from the commissions only at those moments when City Hall needs their approval for federal and state budget resources when the applications have to go through the commissions, as is usual in areas of health, education, housing and social assistance.

From corporate and organisational, to multi-actor and multilevel social responsibility in a territorial scope – the Master model

In previously published papers (Ashley, 2010a and 2010b)[27] I presented the multidimensional, relational and multidirectional model for business social responsibility – the MRMRSN model – as an analytical framework for analysing and classifying current different perspectives, standards, tools and business strategies on CSR. In summary, it proposes a typology of three levels of ethical challenges – legal compliance; social expectations; and ethical ideals – to all business-society relations oriented to relational governance in specific institutional, legal and cultural contexts of business operations. It also proposes mutual social responsibility among stakeholders by means of policies, strategies and actions – stakeholders' social responsibility[28], as to create a coherent institutional field that could facilitate and promote a culture of social responsibility in society:

I will briefly describe some ideas that are to be conceived in a coherent system of stakeholders connected to business-society relations, rather than as a sole fragmented action by one group of stakeholder social responsibility. Thus, we need to think as collective social actors learning from each others experience and progress towards stakeholder social responsibility. I should emphasise that business associations, educational institutions, the financial sector, the State, civil society and trade unions have a primary and direct role in the concept of stakeholder social responsibility. As result of their combined social action, we can think of the media and publishers on the one hand, and the consumers and families on the other hand, as responding to a new institutional and cultural context which will create social demand by them. (Ashley, 2010a:26)

As a further conceptual development, the concept of stakeholders' social responsibility is proposed, here, to better clarify when defined as multi-actor and multi-level social responsibility in a territorial

---

27 Earlier versions of the MRMRSN model have been presented in Brazil since 2002.

28 Stakeholders' social responsibility by: the enterprises; the business associations; the financial system; the State; the civil society organisations and trade unions; the educational system; the consumers and families; and the publishers and media.

scope, of and among different layers of stakeholders: the Master model.[29] The Master model is proposed as a mapping tool for building research questions linking policies on social responsibility, governance, development and equity. The building blocks of the Master model can be unfolded by means of a related set of research questions. These are presented below.

Multidimensionality of social responsibility themes

What theme(s) of social responsibilities are to be researched as a focus for policies? Human rights only, as currently thoroughly proposed by Ruggie (2010); community involvement and development, as is the case for development assistance government policies; or the strategic philanthropy of enterprises? Aren't we losing synergy when we detach human rights from the environment or from fair operating practices? Or should we continue to focus on one-dimensional perspectives for themes of social responsibility policies?

ISO 26000 proposes the themes of social responsibility as: governance, human rights, labour practices, the environment, fair operating practices, consumer issues and community involvement and development. These are also the themes considered in the Master model, based on the current literature on social responsibility.[30]

The territorial dimension

What is the territorial scope of actors´ social responsibilities? Are we looking at the organisational, sectoral, municipal, provincial, national or international territorial scope of social responsibility? The multilevel governance discussion previously presented points at jurisdictions and territories as variables that contribute to frameworks

---

29 The Master model is an original idea resulting from a proposal by the author of this paper, which is not only based on the references quoted here and current research activities, but it also is a result of a long personal deconstruction of CSR, which generated a proposal for a new synthesis for dealing with perceived CSR conceptual gaps.

30 See documents of the ISO 26000 for a more detailed description of the eight themes of social responsibility.

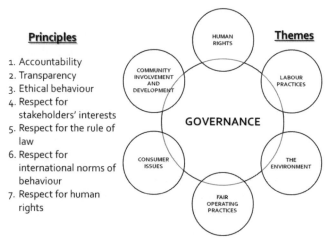

Principles

1. Accountability
2. Transparency
3. Ethical behaviour
4. Respect for stakeholders' interests
5. Respect for the rule of law
6. Respect for international norms of behaviour
7. Respect for human rights

Themes

HUMAN RIGHTS

LABOUR PRACTICES

THE ENVIRONMENT

FAIR OPERATING PRACTICES

CONSUMER ISSUES

COMMUNITY INVOLVEMENT AND DEVELOPMENT

GOVERNANCE

Figure 1: Principles and themes of social responsibility – according to ISO 26000: 2010

of governance systems. As such, conceiving of the social responsibilities of stakeholders requires us thinking within a territorial frame of social, economic and environmental relations affecting policies of social responsibilities. The territorial dimension of the Master model also points to the need for impact measurement of social responsibility policies towards goals for development and equity indicators.

Multi-actor social responsibility

Whose actors' social responsibilities are the focus of research or policies? State and government organisations; science and knowledge institutions; public and private media; public and private capital investment agents; public and private financial institutions; trade unions; business associations; enterprises involved in different economic sectors and of different sizes; non-profit and community-based organisations; and so forth?

Social responsibility literature is mainly focused on the voluntary policies of enterprises. As previously presented, stakeholders are part of the discussion of my inaugural address at ISS (Ashley, 2010a), proposing to reframe from a corporate to a stakeholders' social responsibility in a multidirectional perspective. In each social sphere of categories of stakeholders, we find organisations embedded in institutional fields, and thus, it is a cross-organisational and inter-institutional perspective that brings the need to answer whose social responsibilities we are talking about and towards whom these social responsibilities are directed.

The UN protect, respect and remedy framework

What is the scope of complementary roles on social responsibilities based on the UN protect, respect and remedy for Human Rights? What other social responsibility themes can be appropriately framed in the UN framework? The Master model proposes an extension of the contribution made by Ruggie (2010) and the UN framework to include all themes of social responsibilities as defined in the ISO 26000.

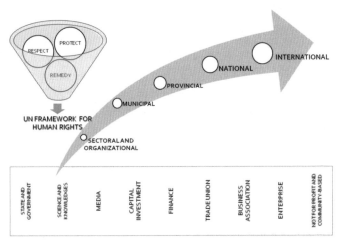

Figure 2: Territorial scopes, multi-actor social responsibility and complementary roles according to the UN protect, respect and remedy framework

The levels and territorial scope for ethical challenges

What is the level and territorial scope of ethical challenges? First level related to legal compliance? Second level related to current social expectations beyond the law? Third level related to ethical ideals expressed in codes of principles and ethics? Are we looking at ethical challenges framed at organisational, sectoral, municipal, provincial, national or international territorial scopes?

Based on the previous MRMRSN model for social responsibility strategies (Ashley, 2010a and 2010b), the three levels of ethical challenges can be applied for regulations and expectations on social responsibilities. Legal compliance, social expectations and ethical ideals are culturally dependent and institutionally embedded, and thus, bring a dynamic concept to different territories and societies.

Figure 3: Multilevel ethical challenges and territorial scopes for multi-actor social responsibility

Selection of economic sector

What economic sectors or industries should research and policies on social responsibility focus on? How can comparability be possible, if desirable for social responsibility policies, within economic sectors and among different economic sectors? When considering inter-organisational and inter-institutional relations, it is easier to research and build policies in specific contexts of a determined sector, because environmental, social and economic variables and impacts can vary substantially. Building research scopes and modelling policies of social responsibilities for specific economic sectors, agents and institutional fields could raise empirical results to alter the quality of competition within industries, upgrading ethical levels in the whole sector. Suppliers to specific industries could be most affected; but so too could buyers, if indeed the whole sector is subject to social responsibility policies.

Governance phases for policy process

What are the multilevel governance phases in the policy process for multi-actor social responsibility? Networks among actors which are not only one-time transactions could be improved in governance systems that are multilevel and that bring a learning environment based on ethical values, coherent with trust in socially responsible behaviour. Political commitment to values and policies of social responsibility is conceived here as necessary for a framework of multilevel governance systems of multi-actor social responsibility.

An assessment of current alignment of values and policies would be a second phase of governance, followed by a further phase of renovation of values and policies, in which the old, the present and the future is subject to renewal in terms of legal requirements according to social expectations and ethical ideals. Innovation of values and policies would be a more mature phase of governance, completing the four phases for multilevel governance for multi-actor social responsibility.

Link with development and equity outcomes

What development and equity outcomes are expected from social responsibility based on MDG and UN Human Development indicators? If we combined the previous described parts of the Master model and think of its purpose in contributing to development and equity social, economic and environmental impacts, we are considering not only the efficacy, but also the effectiveness of social responsibility policies. The Master model includes the UN Millennium Development Goals and the UN Report on Human Development as some of the development and equity frameworks to be considered as purposes for social responsibility policies. Other UN frameworks could also be considered, as well as other institutions' frameworks.

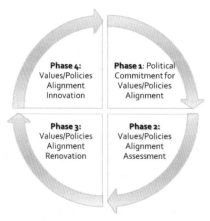

Figure 4: Governance development phases of policies on multi-actor and multilevel social responsibility in a territorial scope

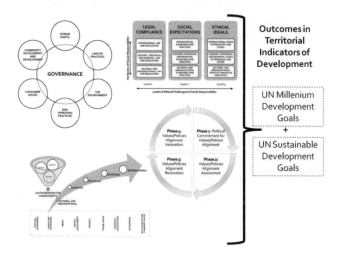

Figure 5: The whole combination of parts of the Master model linking social responsibility, development and equity

Final remarks

This paper is an introductory discussion, which expects contributions and critique from readers. It aims to open a discussion about reframing the concept of corporate social responsibility into a broader conceptual framework of stakeholders' social responsibility. It also points to a similar conception for policies and research on social responsibility into a multilevel governance of multi-actor social responsibilities in a territorial scope, as described in the Master model presented here[31].

It is proposed that social responsibility is still based on the conception of organisations as 'dots' instead of waves that are part of a larger institutional context. Multi-actor and multilevel social responsibility in a territorial scope, illustrated here by the case study in Brazil, could be a better conceptual framework for the purpose of governance and social responsibility policies towards development and equity goals in specific territories.

The path brought by global frameworks as proposed by GRI, the UN Global Compact, the OECD guidelines, the UN protect, respect and remedy framework and the recently published ISO 26000, may bring awareness to policy makers to realign public policies with the paradigm of social responsibility, development and equity into a multilevel and multi-actor coherence.

References

Ashley, Patricia Almeida (2010a), 'Corporate social responsibility: A role only for business leaders?', Prince Claus Chair Inaugural Address Series. The Hague: International Institute of Social Studies.

Ashley, Patricia Almeida (2010b), 'Interactions between states and markets in a global context of change: contribution for building a research agenda on stakeholders´ social responsibility', Working Papers Series at ISS/EUR, n. 506, The Hague: International Institute of Social Studies.

Bache, Ian and Flinders, Matthew (eds). (2005). Multi-level governance: Interdisciplinary Perspectives, Oxford: Oxford University Press.

Committee of the Regions of the European Union (2009). The Committee of the Regions' White Paper on Multilevel Governance. Available at www.cor.europa.eu .

Kohler-Koch, Beate and Eising, Rainer (2006). The Transformation of Governance in the European Union: Routledge/ECPR Studies in European Political Science Series. Taylor and Francis. ISBN: 9780415430371, 336 p.

---

31 Contributions can be sent to Patricia Almeida Ashley at redeeconsciencia@gmail.com or ecocidades@gmail.com

Marks, Gary and Hooghe, Liesbet. (2005) 'Contrasting Visions of Multi-Level Governance', in: Ian Bache and Matthew Flinders (eds). Multi-Level Governance: Interdisciplinary Perspectives. Oxford: Oxford University Press, pp 15-30.

OECD (2010). Cities and climate change, OECD Publishing. http://dx.doi. org/10.1787/9789264091375-en

Oliveira, E. P. ; Linhares, L. A. ; Araujo, D. A. ; Gorgulho, H. F. (2001) . Avaliaçao da Influência do Esgoto Doméstico na Contaminaçao das Nascentes do Córrego do Lenheiro, Sao Joao del Rei, MG. In: XV Encontro Regional da SBQ-MG, 2001, Belo Horizonte. XV Encontro Regional da SBQ-MG. p. 1-1.

Ruggie, John. (2010) The Corporate Responsibility to Respect Human Rights in Supply Chains. 10th OECD Roundtable on Corporate Responsibility. Discussion Paper. 30 June.

United Nations (2010a). Keeping the promise: United to achieve the Millennium Development Goals. Draft resolution referred to the High-level Plenary Meeting of the Assembly by the General Assembly at its sixty-fourth session. Washington: United Nations.

United Nations (2010b). UN Global Compact and International Standard ISO 26000 Guidance on Social Responsibility. Available at www.unglobal-compact.org

Winter, Gert (ed.) (2006). Multilevel governance of global environmental change: perspectives from science, sociology and the law, Cambridge: Cambridge University Press.

Summary

The focus of Ashley's lecture was how we can expand the concept of corporate social responsibility (CSR) so it may function as a more inclusive and all-encompassing framework for social responsibility. This requires a fundamental reworking of the concept of CSR, moving it away from simply a business model towards a multi-actor and mul-tilevel theoretical construct, which can be applied to different social spheres, cultural contexts and territorial settings. By re-imagining the underpinnings of the CSR concept, there is a greater chance that the inherent potential of CSR initiatives to contribute to the creation of sustainable societies may be realised.

Ashley began her lecture by critiquing the lack of up-to-date knowledge governments have about the current state of corporate social responsibility. She noted that public policies are still largely informed by an understanding of CSR as a business-driven enterprise. Ashley argued that this understanding of CSR has severe limitations. Leaving CSR efforts in the hands of business leaders does not take into account the fact that businesses operate in an environment in which competitive pressures often militate against socially responsible outcomes. These conflicting priorities do not make business leaders the best placed to spearhead the CSR movement.

Ashley illustrated some of the problems of the current approach to CSR by looking at the example of sanitation in Sao Joao del Rey, a city in the state of Minas Gerais, Brazil. Here the dumping of domestic sewage and industrial waste into the Lenheiro river and its surrounding banks is causing considerable water pollution and environmental damage. Ashley commented on the difficulties of implementing a solution to the problem under the rubric of the CSR model. She noted that companies did not see sanitation as an issue they should be concerned with, encapsulated by the quotation, "The social responsibility of business is to make business survive. Sanitation is none of my business", which Ashley believed to be a widely shared sentiment amongst the companies in Sao Joao del Rey. For Ashley, this demonstrated the limits of relying solely on business leaders to act as agents of change.

She therefore invited the audience to think of a model of social responsibility that does not take the company as its central unit of analysis, which recognises the need for a multidirectional strategy to be devised and which understands that in order for social responsibility to take hold in society, collective action needs to be undertaken by many different actors working together. To this end, Ashley proposed a multidimensional, multilevel and multi-actor conception of social responsibility. It is *multidimensional* because, drawing on the ISO 26000 guidelines, social responsibility themes include: governance, human rights, labour practices, the environment, fair operating practices, consumer issues, and community involvement and development. It is *multilevel* because it looks at three different types of challenges confronting the social responsibility agenda including legal compliance, social expectations and ethical ideals and how these are expressed at different territorial scales. Finally, it is *multi-actor* because it looks at all the stakeholders that are involved in social responsibility from enterprises, to governments, to civil society organisations, to consumers, to the media and so on.

By putting forward this new model of social responsibility, which stressed the importance of social networks, institutions and the cultural embeddedness of organisations, Ashley hopes that a new ethic of 'before profit' responsibility can be realised. She argued that this will require a deeper drive by public bodies to fully get behind the social responsibility movement and apply this new model of CSR to all social spheres.

In the discussion following Ashley's lecture, a number of interesting points were raised. A couple of questions probed further into Ashley's new model of social responsibility, in particular into the ways in which it is possible to differentiate between the three levels of responsibility. Ashley answered by saying that one should not conceive of these levels as fixed, but rather context dependent, exhibiting considerable variation in time and space. So, for example, what are ethical ideals in one country might already be legal compliance in another. In a similar vein, when asked how the 3 different social spheres in the model relate to specific stakeholders, Ashley stressed the interconnectedness and unity between the spheres. This means that we should not think of markets as only the domain of the private sector or territories as simply the jurisdiction of governments – these separations are an illusion. This related in part to a question on the role of the state in the social responsibility movement. Ashley commented that given the discrepancies in the legal frameworks pertaining to CSR, governments should work towards updating and aligning their CSR legislation to ensure that a coherent discourse around CSR emerges. A question was also asked about the relationship between trade agreements and CSR. Ashley replied that trade agreements can play a major role in creating sustainable global supply and value chains and are therefore of critical importance. On a more personal note, an audience member wished to know what Ashley's personal experiences and lessons were from her involvement in her CSR project in Brazil. She stated that the key success factor in her project was the generation and distribution of information regarding CSR practices and that the media was a great support in this capacity.

Discussion

Questions from the audience, with responses by Patricia Almeida Ashley:

1. I would like to know, looking back, what were your lessons learned? Also how did you generate support for your project in Sao Joao del Rey?

That project only had one year of funding. This was a complaint from all the universities involved because we wanted at least three years. But the Ministry of Cities and the Ministry of Education, instead of giving us a longer time to allow for the maturation of the project, ended our funding after one year. We published a book, but I don't think it was enough because we did successfully manage to generate high expectations at the local level, and so people were disappointed.

Regarding the lessons learned, the success factor in my project was information. We could generate and organise information, we could evaluate the implementation of the city plans, and we were opening doors. I was feeling a bit threatened because some government people were starting to complain about us but we did not care because we found support from the media: radio, TV and the newspapers. So the information is there, freely available for downloading and people are still accessing it.

2. I would like to ask you to elaborate a bit more on the role of the state in the social responsibility movement. How can we upgrade our legal framework here in Europe and in the West more generally to make it more compatible with CSR goals?

For the issue of legal compliance, I agree totally that we take it for granted in Europe. In Brazil, we need to reform our law. The legal frameworks we have are outdated; they are unaligned with social responsibility. So that's why I say that public sector has a role because there are legal frameworks that don't even consider social responsibility as a value which should be upheld.

3. What is the relationship between trade agreements and CSR? Shouldn't we focus our attention more on reforming the WTO and coming up with equitable trade agreements rather than pushing for CSR?

Moving on to the European/Western legal system and the trade agreements. I understand that a major policy move that Europe could make is pushing forward sustainable global supply chains, also for overseas development assistance. Because if we invest in building capacity in countries so that they can realign their production systems in accordance with the goals of environmental protection, social development and economic inclusion as well as reforming the tax systems so as to give a premium to those that are compliant with social responsibility schemes, then we are adding a different value to the market place. So trade agreements should consider creating sustainable global supply and value chains instead of just doing philanthropy. This is not the role of business. The role of business is to do business and to do business it must be sustainable, both in economic, social and environmental terms. That's the game. In order for a business to be sustainable, it has to have an institutional field, a legal framework, a market, a financial sector, and investors which are coherent and aligned with the goals of social responsibility.

One of the measures that would have an impact would be a market that gives incentives for consumers to buy products that have been produced in a socially responsible way, but I think that consumers, individually, are less powerful than for example consumers in cooperatives or consumer groups that have the support of sustainable retailers that are applying a social responsibility policy as part of a business association policy. So the movement for change has to come from civil society engagement, business association involvement, education and research policies, public sector actions which help to reframe the legal frameworks which are not coherent with the future of sustainability and social responsibility.

4. What does it mean for companies to be responsible and to be moral actors?

When looking at the different spheres and matching markets to the private sector and territories to governments, it is not a coherent discourse. For instance, when we speak of markets everyone wants freedom but when there is a financial crisis, everyone wants protection from the market by the government. This discourse on freedom and free will of the market is not coherent. We are teaching freedom but we are not considering the ethics of care. We need to build markets for socially responsible business. In Brazil, the government is a big buyer of goods and services in the market. We are developing sustainable procurement policies. We need to develop this at the international level, to incorporate sustainable buying practices into international trade agreements.

5. How do you distinguish between the different spheres you have identified of the political, the economic and the social, and how they relate to the government, business and civil society respectively, given the increasing networks between them?
6. You talked about three levels: legal compliance, social expectations and ethical ideals. I was wondering in which level we should invest our scarce time and resources? My opinion is that we can make the most impact at the level of social expectations.

Maybe the diagrams are not clear enough. They are not meant to be static. What are ethical ideals, might be social expectations in another country. What are ethical ideals in Brazil might already be legal compliance in Europe. Because of these different cultures and different contexts it is difficult to have a catalogue of indicators that are applicable to every country. So to frame your thoughts in static terms like this is very difficult.

How do we change social expectations? It's by education, by information, by experience, by exchanging, by partnering and sometimes by force. Companies in Brazil that started the movement of social responsibility were forced to do so by external pressure, especially from Europe to prove that they didn't use child labour, they weren't polluting the environment, etc. Only if they complied with CSR guidelines would they be kept on as suppliers. This is all down to external pressure.

So these categories are not fixed. What are social expectations can, in the future, turn into legal compliance. Because what does the law express? It expresses a consensus of society's social expectations.

Yet we cannot import these legal frameworks from Europe, which are so much more advanced than other regions, to countries where the culture doesn't allow for its understanding and application. In Brazil, it is only since 2004 that legal frameworks have started to incentivise policies on social responsibility and higher education institutions have begun to monitor, evaluate and analyse these legal frameworks. So legal frameworks can be a good way of creating new social expectations.

Final comment by Patricia Almeida Ashley:

I feel that these questions are still looking too much at the dots. I'm not talking about *corporate* social responsibility anymore; I'm talking about multi-actor social responsibility based on the ISO 26000 framework which shows that we cannot only think of public policies for businesses but also for organisational social responsibility.

When I mention territories, I'm not saying that territories are only a matter for governments or that markets are only a matter for businesses. There in Sao Joa del Rey, I could see that everyone was engaged in everything. These separations are an illusion. Territories are a matter for everyone and we are also part of a market. What I present is a theoretical scheme.

Concluding comments by Teresa Fogelberg
(Global Reporting Initiative):

I think that there is a bit of a paradox because on the one hand, you criticise the CSR concept for being too limited but on the other hand, the reason why it was created was specifically because the corporate entity escapes national borders and national legal compliance and therefore we needed something to regulate the multinational companies. Now CSR has become very broad and encompasses a lot a things but I think it is good to remember where it comes from.

I also think it is fascinating that in Brazil and other emerging market countries, and comparing them with the Netherlands and other European countries, business associations are so innovative; meanwhile in the Netherlands, sorry to say, they are often the most conservative organisations that lobby against any change and any regulation. I think it would be fascinating to look deeper into this, how businesses can be drivers of change.

You also made a point about the lack of public policies on CSR. An exception, however, is India where there is a lot happening. They are considering, for example, making it mandatory for state-owned companies to report on their environmental and human rights performance. The same is happening in China. Today in Europe there is also a growing consensus that it should become mandatory for all companies to disclose and report on their CSR policies. That happened in Denmark last year and is going right now, as we speak, through the parliament in Norway.

What I also loved was the concept of 'protect, respect and remedy'. Protecting is a role of the state, respect is the responsibility of companies and remedy is the right of citizens to be repaired when injustice has been done against them. I think it is a wonderful idea to take that model that has been developed for human rights and apply it to the issue of CSR.

Meeting global challenges: regaining sovereignty

Inge Kaul

I would like to talk about 'Responsible Sovereignty', a key to structuring and organising a next World Order. With this I invite you to 'think big', as I thought it best not to come here with a small issue, something found on the side-lines, a topic merely referring to changes in the margins.

I am more and more struck by how we are continuously told, on the one hand, about the prosperous life that we could lead: we could live longer and healthier, we can travel more, and are now globally better connected than ever. But at the same time, and increasingly so, in the papers, but also in actual fact, we live in a time of war. There are attacks by people who we call terrorists, and the resulting war on terror; recently we have experienced the currency wars, in which we manipulate our currencies for reasons of competition, so that our industries and our jobs may survive. Our public language has such a military sound to it these days. My most recent reminder that we are truly living in 'war' times, was in India a few days ago, where I was attending the Energy Security Meeting. I was surprised, not only by the fact that as usual there were only a few females present, but also because most countries had sent their military guys – to a meeting about energy. And they were rattling their sables in the fierce competition and real race for the last drop of oil and land in the world.

These times of war have made me think of related problems; we live in a globalising world, in which we have opened our borders and now face an increasing interdependence between nations. But policy-making still lags behind, both in terms of institutions and in perspectives. Our ways of political thinking have not yet caught up to the global reality we face; we still think too much in terms of zero-sum, rather than recognising the fact that global cooperation is really the best strategy for realising all our national interests.

Now, before I elaborate on this point and try to show a possible way out, I would like to ask you to not immediately think of Africa – or the 'developing world'. Think about yourself and your daily life and I will show you how that will also be good for Africa. My request is motivated by the fact that at an international level we all tend to turn towards Africa, looking for ways in which to 'fix' it. As a result, we exclude ourselves from the international debate and continue to meddle around in others' affairs. When I say we, I mean us here in Europe, and the West.

The first point I would like to make concerns the growing compulsion to cooperate globally, whereby the cooperation makes sense for all parties concerned. Why is this so? Well, after a long period of establishing borders and building nation-states that claim non-interference and national policy-making sovereignty, we started opening up national borders, with the intent to increase economic trade and wealth. We, as in the richer industrial countries primarily – the impetus has often come from us – have promoted trade liberalisation, the removal of capital controls, and the harmonisation of global infrastructure. As a result, economic globalisation has occurred with an increase in cross-border economic activities. We have frequently insisted, mainly through Structural Adjustment Programmes, on regulating national policy regimes, tax regimes, investment regimes and the business climates in other countries. However, as a result of our actions, we have witnessed the uninvited cross-border spillover: food security problems, health contagion effects, communicable diseases. Furthermore, since 2008 we have experienced the consequences of toxic financial products and the ripple effects throughout the world. One of the results of the uninvited cross-border spillover and (un) intended globalisation, is that former national public goods have been globalised. We now find that most of our policymakers agree when Mr. Obama, in virtually every speech he gives, explains how the major global challenges of today are of such a nature that no country can tackle them alone and that international cooperation is required.

This is of course true; take tuberculosis for example. With international travel as it is these days, a TB programme in one solitary country would be of no sense whatsoever; all countries must participate. The same goes for greenhouse gas emissions; we have to take corrective action everywhere. Most global public goods that affect us result, in order to be adequately provided, from a summation process; corrective action taken everywhere, but in a concerted way. Notably, the levels of input by international agreements on how to tackle a global public good are usually minor compared to what needs to happen at the national level. So, when you hear about a global challenge, do not think that we should rush towards the international level of agreement – that could in fact be the last thing on the list. What we should be considering, as our very first reaction to a global issue, is what can we do on a national level? Are we concerned about the issue enough to act nationally? What will the costs and benefits be to us? What, for example, will have to be done in terms of new banking regulations and supervision at the national level? So even though the G20 can come to certain agreements, they really are just a 'dot on the i' compared to all the corrective actions that have to be taken on a national level. Global public goods are basically our globalised national public goods – we still have to take national action.

At one point in our histories, our societies fell into a situation in which the state had to be called in to regulate and control a number of issues: public goods, such as street lighting, sewage systems, drinking water, disease control, safety, etc. Now, because of our open world in terms of finances, borders, travel, communications, and so forth, our public goods have become globalised. Where the state once set up the tax system, so that we would all be adequately provided for, we now lack the equivalent of that state at an international level. States meet internationally as sovereign and as quasi-private actors; they pursue particular interests, namely their national interests. So what ends up happening, at for example the UN, is that all states agree on the goal, they can even come to agreements for particular issues – but none of the resolutions ever specify in advance who will be doing what, and who will be paying for it. There is a strict separation between stating policy priorities and making financial arrangements. Statements such as "let's half poverty" or "let's stabilise the climate" are wonderful; but an agreement on the goal, without an agreement on an action plan or budget, is meaningless.

I find it astounding that companies producing even the most insignificant products, pencils for example, will have a concrete production plan: where to produce, how many workers, how to package, where to sell, how to transport....and what the price will be! Yet entire states are seemingly incapable of setting a concrete plan to establish public goods for the planet as a whole. More common is that policy-makers sent to international meetings make sure to come home with the message that they negotiated a good financial deal, that they will not have to pay too much – that they 'won'. Yet the global public goods continue to affect us all – soon there will be no more hiding.

So, what we need is better cooperation between states. All sides should stop trying to out-do the others; stop trying to win the deal. The point is, that if the efforts and costs are shared fairly, we will all have a chance to win. Yet for some reason we are rarely able to behave in this manner. More often than not we make insensible deci-sions, based on the need to protect our *own* needs, failing to under-stand that global issues affect us all.

First of all, we have learned from institutional economics that it is very difficult to change institutions; so what you see is that, although we have all these global challenges, we still have a ministry of *Foreign* Affairs, as if the problems are out there and not in here. If you then consider the budgets of the Health and Environment ministries, they only have small sums allocated for global matters. More frequently, they will look towards the country's aid development budget if they need to step out into the global arena. As a result, you find that on average, among donor countries, thirty percent of aid today flows into concerns that in fact reflect our priorities, regardless of whether it is also a priority for the donor country. So you have the foreign domestic divide as an institutional lock-in; we are now actually con-sidering international cooperation as a form of aid, which is why we have this tendency to stare at Africa when global issues arise.

Zero-sum thinking is still very prominent and even though power relations are changing, they are changing slowly. You still see power politics being exercised, where economics should play a much larger role. International cooperation should make good business sense – which includes considering the potential negative returns (in terms of global goods). We have done many studies, trying to figure out how big the gain would be on a global scale if we were to cooperate fairly and how we could compensate everybody, so that you have a win-win rather than zero-sum situation. The results of our studies show that the global gains would be so large, that the 'winners' could easily compensate those who perhaps fell behind.

Mutual advantage is a possibility, but at that point we are confronted with the 'real' enemy of cooperation: the scarcity of natural recourses. In our frantic race for the last drop of oil we are often neglectful of human rights in order to foster our own energy security. Instead, we should be thinking in cooperative terms, which would be to consider what we can do together in order to speed up the energy transition and to avoid this fierce competition, not only for oil, but also for agricultural land. By now you are all familiar with the phenomenon of land grabbing, which is a really nasty new trend, in which some countries may one day wake up and realise that they are perhaps still political owners of their territories, if that, but no longer economic owners.

So what to do? Finding the magic bullet is no easy feat. But consider this: why is it that despite our European history and the many struggles we have experienced, we have managed to live relatively peacefully in recent times? It was in fact 'a big idea' that allowed us to come together and live side by side. It was the understanding between European countries to no longer solve our issues with war. Military should be the last recourse. So, is it not possible to come to a similar agreement on a global scale? An agreement that would end this desperate competitive race for natural resources, which is at the base of inequalities in the world. Can we not, like in Europe, agree to act within a global cooperation?

Certainly we are approaching a general agreement that the current style of politics and ways of achieving political aims is very costly, uncertain, instable and unsustainable. So maybe we could start the process by expecting our governments to no longer be this selfish, and to remind ourselves what the concept of sovereignty was designed to entail; we should recall the UN charter in which the rights and duties of sovereignty are emphasised. States have rights for determining their own policy priorities, but they also have duties. In the past, rights and duties were somewhat limited to within a country. But no longer. In our globalised world we now also have rights and duties towards outsiders – we must recognise Human Rights on a global level, not just national. Because, I would argue, you cannot have an open world, globalisation, and not feel a certain amount of respect for your neighbouring countries and for their sovereignty. So my proposal is that we look at sovereignty as we look at freedom. We can learn from Nobel Prize winner Amartya Sen and his writings on freedom, in which he posits that by respecting others' freedom, your own chances of freedom increase as well, i.e., if we all accept the norm of respectful freedom, whereby my freedom is not enjoyed at your expense, then we will all enjoy greater freedom. So, if we choose to employ respectful or responsible sovereignty, we would decide to no longer spew pollution into the world, or toxic financial products, because in the long run it will only hurt ourselves as well as cause the immediate negative effects on others. We should therefore try to minimise negative cross-border spillover effects that can undermine the welfare and wellbeing of other states.

But how do we get states to be willing participants in responsible sovereignty? My experience of all my years at the UN is that one way, but not the only way, of successful cooperation is a lengthy one, but it works. It will take an ongoing and lengthy debate on the 'big idea'. Just consider the fact that Human Rights were contested when they were initially pronounced, but bit by bit they were picked up by civil society organisations and state actors the world over, and very slowly such ideas took root nationally; finally reaching the international level. These days, a world without the belief in Human Rights is unthinkable - they are being reconfirmed, reasserted in other resolutions, and there is a thickening normative global framework that is actually beginning to reign in state-behaviour. I think it would be wonderful if SID were one of the non-state actors, stirring up debate on responsible sovereignty, and I wouldn't be surprised to even find support among some business actors.

Another step in the process, as the global debate on the 'big idea' continues, is that we as voters hold our states responsible and demand that they behave in a responsible way. But there is also an opportunity for states themselves to tame each other; and the opportunity for keeping others in check is in fact increasing. One could argue that we are seeing a small shift towards multi-polarity; China and India complain about the US and vice versa. States are watching each other and certain acts are not tolerated. But of course, this is a lengthy process; you are talking about thirty, forty or fifty years for an idea to become a norm, between the time it enters public domain and when it takes root. Only then do you see a bottom-up globalisation process that lasts. Most top-down quick globalisation processes don't last, but some do stir up lively global policy debates.

And therefore my last recommendation is, and I hope the Dutch government will take it up, is to install a new international commission on responsible sovereignty. Because you can discuss and discuss, but a summing-up process is necessary. Norms are global public goods, because they want to be consumed by everybody. However, simply being public in consumption, does not mean that we all like these goods that we are supposed to consume. Sometimes they really do not taste good to us. So therefore it is very important to have a good debate, a good shaping of norms and of policy regimes, like the trade regime. It was the UN that granted sovereignty and recognised the sovereignty of all states, so it should probably be from within the UN context that we move from the more narrow concept of national sovereignty - "stay out of my borders" - to this new and more globally embedded concept of national sovereignty. It should be through UN-commission action and a general assembly that we come to accept such a norm for state-behaviour in the future.

Now, I am quite optimistic that this is possible. I have conducted multiple empirical studies and have spent thirty years at the UN, during which time I, with great pride, 'invented' two notions: 'human development' and 'global public goods'. Perhaps I can add 'responsible sovereignty'.

In conclusion, let me return to Africa. Although you have some serious and real issues here in the Netherlands to consider, such as the safety your dikes provide you and the fear of flooding, or the next outbreak of swine-flu, you should start seeing these issues as global goods. We need provisions for *global* health and *global* climate control to provide solutions to *national* issues. In addition, besides the ethical or moral aspect of providing aid to developing countries, there is a good national reason to be concerned about inequality in the world. Global public goods effect us all, but so too does the spill-over from states in less well-off situations. Aid has an element of self-interest, which is why we are concerned with failing states. It makes more economic sense to prevent a storm than to spend money on clean-up programmes each time a storm hits. Somehow we tend to always find the money for a crisis, but we rarely find the money for more constructive thinking. I hope that responsible sovereignty, looking at the state as an intermediary between the outside and the inside, and thinking globally, could really be cheaper than what we are doing now.

Summary

In her lecture, Kaul spoke of the concept 'responsible sovereignty' as the key principle of a new world order. In the divided world we live in today, filled with challenges that cross national borders, policy-makers need to find strategies to secure the value of our currencies in the competition for energy security and other problems related to globalisation, such as climate change and the spread of communicable diseases. To find solutions for this ever-denser web of crises, international cooperation based on global coherence is required instead of the zero-sum game based on the national interest that states are playing today. Kaul elaborated further upon the benefits to be found in international cooperation. Together with increasing market integration and a growing volume of cross-border economic activity, many unintended and negative spillover effects of globalisation seem to challenge nation-states all at once. In order to mitigate the effect of these negative consequences, corrective action based on strong global coherence is needed. However, negotiations in the field of international cooperation are still shaped by individual countries that are solely interested in achieving their own relative gains.

To come to a solution, Kaul asked the public to review the actions of our governments in a broader sense, and to remind them of their duties, not only within their own country, but also on a global scale. Kaul outlined her concept of 'responsible sovereignty': to create a norm of living in the world, in which we have a certain amount of respect for each other's freedoms. This global freedom is a key public good that fosters social cohesiveness and peace at local and national levels. We can fulfil this ambition by enabling a worldwide debate on this issue, as was done in the process of formulating the Universal

Declaration of Human Rights. The concept of human rights slowly took root locally and then spread internationally. Furthermore, states should hold each other responsible for their actions. Kaul argued that it is time to create an international commission on responsible sovereignty in order for the idea to move beyond pure academic discussion and into the realm of policy.

Discussion

Comments by the moderator, Anton Hemerijck (VU University):
The argument is that new long-run and very serious collective action dilemmas are hurting the global compound and that states are in fact very ill-prepared to solve these problems, especially with respect for dilemmas that have salient global distributive implications. Even worse, I would add, there is an incipient retreat from supranational integration, which has everything to do with the new populist isolationism in mature democracies of the OECD-world. Responsible sovereignty is central to any effective solution. I believe you, but I also think we need to be wary of functionalism. In your talk, and also in the paper, there are statements like "global public goods are no longer an option, it is a compulsion". I do understand the functional imperative, but we know that the problem of functionalism is its neglect of power relations. So when we search for solutions, even if we understand the direction of available options, we need to rely on sober political analysis, whether these options are really viable.

With respect to the concept of "responsible sovereignty", I am not sure we mean the same thing with "sovereignty". National sovereignty in terms of policy autonomy has become something of a myth. It is cherished by domestic political leaders for obvious reasons – because that is where electorates are – but in fact, nation states are becoming increasingly institutionally incomplete, in terms of regulatory coverage, as they are increasingly embedded in a complex multilateral system of governance. This is true par excellence for the EU and its Member States.

But first, I wish to go back into history somewhat to see whether there ever was a time when we had a social contract based on "responsive sovereignties" in the plural. I think there was. The period of 1945 to the mid-1970s, there was, what John Ruggie coined an era of "embedded liberalism". We all know Keynes'advocacy for demand management and for his economic defence of the welfare state, but in fact Keynes was perhaps even more important as an international economist. Paradocially, he argued that for international economic integration there was a need for capital controls, for the political imperative to guarantee full employment (only for men) on the domestic level. The core functional imperative of the post-war era was social and political stability after a decade of political, social and economic chaos. Stability required full employment and capital controls. Embedded liberalism at the global level relied strongly on domestic social contracts. It seems to me that what you are searching for is something akin to that experience. Keynes and Beverage and other thinkers of the post-war era had a very positive theory of the state; based on the memory of the 1920s and 1930, when markets failed. Stability taken too far results in institutional inertia. The rigidities of the post-war Bretton Woods system were exposed in the 1970s oil crises. This experience triggered the shift to neo-liberalism. The new imperative was the opposite of stability, namely flexibility. The easiest way to gain flexibility was through deregulation, based on a negative neoclassical theory of inefficient welfare states. There has been a thirty year period of neo-liberalism, which some people believe ended with the 2007 crisis (not true in my opinion), in which our understanding of the state in its functions debilitated significantly. Therefore, if you want a shift towards "responsible sovereignty" in the wake of the failire of neoliberalism, to move towards a kinds of "embedded globalisation", there is a lot of state rethinking needs to be done.

Where problems of cooperation or solidarity involve distributive consequences, politically this requires elements of closure and proximity. After the era of "embedded liberalism" we moved to a new period where supranational economic integration, especially in the EU, was driven largely by market making, that is 'negative integration', trumping domestic social contracts somewhat. And to my mind with significant success. The EMU is quite a courageous step in that respect. But it made things very difficult for non-market actors, such as the trade unions. So now, when we move to a domestic politics, and we really have to think through the post-crisis precarious politics of the nation-state, because on the one hand we have state capacity, that is massively constrained in practice, but also intellectually; and in the realm of the political there is this isolationist populism that is particularly jealous of external political space or international cooperation. So in terms of international cooperation, we moved from a division of labour, whereby the 'low politics' of international cooperation is left to the diplomats, and the 'high politics' of the welfare state is left to domestic politics. Now that most citizens are quite fearful, they are fully aware that the status quo is unsustainable; but that is also exactly the reason why they do not like to cooperate into the unknown which does not bode well.

On the positive side of the story may be that these are simply the 'growing pains' of a more political European Union or a more political supranational government. But if you look at political leaders today, they are afraid of isolationist populism in their backyard, so there is a really big political problem if you want to move to on the one hand 'responsible sovereignty', and on the other hand 'embedded globalisation' in terms of legitimacy. Because, you have to do so much more to expose the drawbacks of the status-quo, to confront institutional resistance as highly problematic, to legitimate new substantive principles – because they are not procedural principles, like the ones of Keynes and Beverage full employment – and then you have to organise consensus and governance capacity, again at the national and supranational level, and this in a climate, after the crisis, of distrust, not only in markets, but also in states, with very little budget resources to solve these problems.

So my bigger question to you is: where is the ray of hope? Is it the G20? I think in the last couple of years, at some moments you thought yes, the G20 is living up to its expectations. The IMF? I think it is improving its records indeed. The World Bank? Maybe not. The EU? That is difficult. The ECB? Certainly, but with political leaders such as Merkel and Sarkozy, I do not think quantitative easing is sustainable. Is a rebalancing between the Chinese and the US economy taking shape? I do not think so. This comes back to something I said earlier, that given the fact that we have had this experience of neoliberalism, with all its goodies as well as its baddies that went along

161

with this experience, a fundamental rethinking of state functions is really at stake. State functions cannot be governed by sovereign polities, because basically, they are not sovereigns anymore, they are only semi-sovereign nation states.

Response by Inge Kaul:

With many of the comments I can agree. Especially with the point of rethinking the state function. I may not have highlighted enough my thoughts on what the role of states is. We see, especially when experiencing state delegations internationally, that they are particularistic private actors, pursuing their national concerns. Therefore we lack today a theory, and there academia have let us down. We only have a market-failure theory. Any textbook of public economics will assume a single closed economy. I looked at 176 textbooks, in all sorts of languages, and not only did we find a lot of plagiarism, but they all state to assume a single closed economy. That includes the textbook by Joseph Stiglitz, who writes about the wins of globalisation. Most of the textbooks tell us that public goods are still similar to what they were in the Middle Ages, or in the 1950s: state provided goods. But that is no longer true. There is barely a public good today, and there never was, which is really fully state provided. The state played a larger role before, but now we have strong financial markets, we have non-state actors and most of these global public goods are multi-actor goods.

But what worries me most about states is that they perform as private actors, and that we have to learn to look at international cooperation as a market, where goods and services are being traded; i.e., if you promise to reduce greenhouse gases, I will pay or reward you for that. What happens more often today is that we are still thinking through power politics and national interest maximization terms and we cheat, for example, Costa Rica for the precious services they provide. We give them five dollars for a ton of carbon, whilst Costa Rica could probably get thirty dollars at a certain moment of time. When you look at bodies like the annual meeting of the Bretton Woods institutions, the WTO or the UN General Assembly, these are political markets that are plagued by all factors and conditions that make markets fail. We know that. We have the hegemony, like the monopolist; we have the EU-American relation, which is an oligopoly in certain situations, information asymmetries abound. So we indeed have to fundamentally rethink the role of the state. Whether the state is a state when it appears internationally or whether we rather have to use the market lands.

Then we have to think of the role of the state nationally. What can states do individually? Today, states take us for a ride before elections mainly, promising full employment and health care and what not. When elections are over they blame the financial markets for their inabilities to act. So I think the populist movement and the isolationist movement is a reaction out of fear. Because the state is not waking up to the fact that we are truly living in a globalised world, where you have to have a whole new approach to making social policy and reaching a stage where we can continue living well; all of us, also the Chinese and Brazilians, as well as the Africans. So we are kidding ourselves today. We do not really know how to do social policy domestically and we do not know how the state should behave internationally. The problem is that the academic disciplines, since we are here at the university I have to emphasise this, have remained in silos. There is public economics looking down, international relations looking up, not to even mention other disciplines. We are not coming together. What is surely lacking is an "issue organisation". For example, if you want to control a disease like swine flu, you have to think of intellectual property rights, of the trade regime, you may have to think about certain biogas considerations that may emerge. So it is a multi-issue, multi-actor situation and at present, we are empty-handed when it comes to thinking through the role of the state and often we may be even giving the wrong advice to states.

Question from the audience:
Where are we on the global side? How does the regionalisation in Brazil or India fit in your story? These are processes in which nobody is truly in control. Is the concept of responsible sovereignty triggering enough and don't we need more mind catching and broader concepts? Is there also a chance for change from above; do the people who are really in power realise that they have to take into account the impact of their actions on others? How about concepts of environmental and social debt and offsetting pollution?

To start with the last question. I have not mentioned environmental debt, but it does exist. A responsible sovereign, who takes the outside into account and respects the freedom of others, would probably think to reduce the ecological footprint at home and abroad. One should not overextend oneself in using common resources, but that does not mean that we have to do everything at home. One can still carry out emissions trading and things like that as long as we pay a proper price for it and as long as it becomes a sort of a fair deal. So I agree with you on both points that you mentioned. But through this notion of responsible sovereignty, I think one could get a better hold of these concerns than we do now, accepting that we have an environmental debt.

Coming to the first question, I think there are some people in charge in India, Thailand, China and elsewhere. Actually, what is most amazing is that the state is so much in charge of the run for resources, because nowadays you can forget to go to the UN Security Council; that was the field of high diplomacy before. Now you better qualify as an energy diplomat, because the state is either supporting state-run companies in accessing resources of all kinds or facilitating access of private companies to resources of bilateral diplomacy primarily. So the states are very much facilitating the current run on resources that we see all over the world. They probably know very well, and even close their eyes when some companies behave inappropriately, but let it go for the access of resources.

Coming to the question of the big idea. My main concern these days, and I know that responsible sovereignty sounds a little statist, but since I am so concerned about the failure of states, I am addressing myself to states a lot nowadays, that is one reason. The other thing is that I will probably be never be able to fully clean this term responsible sovereignty, because others are launching this concept too, but it is a different concept. I am engaging here in intellectual competition and I would like to invite you to join. So it is not that I think it is the greatest heart-warming concept, but because states have to change and see that they should not facilitate such resource-runs and that it can be done differently. And, because there is this hegemonic way of pledging this concept into the global public domain, we should also give our version and have it debated. And maybe through global dialogue it will change in the end, that is fine. But something along these lines would be required as an organising principle for the world in the future.

Now, US-China relations could achieve a lot, but at the same time you can see that the US is also trying to divide and conquer in Asia. One goes to India and builds up India vis-à-vis China, and China vis-à-vis India, and probably South Korea. So I think some of the policies of the US at present are more concerned with strengthening their world position and slowing down the rise of China and India, but at the same time, I am convinced that someone is in charge in China; I am part of a globalisation project in Singapore on how Asia sees globalisation – the Asian world and their nations and cultures have a lot of time and their position is to not rock the boat. They just go slowly and they speak softly, so that there is not too much opposition. So I think we will see a rise and a more multi-polar world. Indeed, Obama would probably already subscribe to responsible sovereignty.

That brings us to your question of hope. Now, things are bad and if you say that one should be a political realist, then you will not be ready when the right political moment comes. Therefore, those things are not going to happen the day after tomorrow. We have to have our concepts and we have to have, in civil society and among different states, a ready agreement on such a concept, whether it is precise or not, so that when the right moment comes we can use that window of opportunity. Therefore I am hopeful that it will come with the next crisis.

Comments by Anton Hemerijck:

I am hopeful too, but I am really struck by certain facts. People like Trichet and Bernanke are doing effective and courageous things – but they are not national political leaders. That is my big worry. We have had to create an independent national bank, to do the right thing, because if we would allow a Trichet to run for government, he would not be voted into power and he would probably not make intelligent policy choices. There is the real problem. It has something to do with the elite and the way they talk to the larger public. I do not have an answer to this, but it is a combination between responsible sovereignty, both at home and abroad, together with a concept of embedded globalisation, in which you seek international polyarchy, a re-definition of a policy space. Let us put it this way, in the context of the global crisis, you see China and Brazil developing healthcare and pension policies, giving money to mothers if they invest in their children. You can have a substantive discussion that is not a procedural discussion about markets and trade. It is really about human values and capabilities, how you deliver them and how you organise necessary institutional capacities. But if you look at the political momentum in mature democracies, in which you expect citizens to be interested in these things, they do not want to hear it. They understand what is going on and they are fearful of the consequences, which is why Geert Wilders is popular in the Netherlands. I think it is here where the political elites, not the independent elites at Central Banks, have to stand tall.

Question from the audience:
Where is the concept of accountability in this story of global common goods? Should we not also discuss global values before talking about responsible sovereignty?

Response by Inge Kaul:
We live in a very divided world with widely varying preferences and tastes. The 1999 book on global public goods maintains the more traditional definition of public goods, in which they are goods that benefit us all. But when I visited Manmohan Singh in India with this book, he responded with the sentiment that the multilateral trade regime is a global public good, it hits us all, we are supposed to consume it, but it does not taste good. And from this remark I learned that we have to clearly distinguish between public-ness in consumption and public-ness in utility. Just look at climate change and global warming. Norway probably is not so concerned with it, as it would make life easier for them, and they could start producing wine! But other countries are extremely concerned because for them it will mean flooding or drought. So we have quite varying preferences for things that concern and hit us all and that we all have to consume. When you travel around the world, you get fierce resistance to a notion like common good. As long as there is no democracy really effective in many coun-

tries nationally and participatory policy dialogue internationally, stop talking about what is common good in a value-sense. The concept of public good is like it has always been in *public goods theory*, it has no value connotation. You always have to ask yourself whether a good that provides utility for you, is in the same way appreciated by other people around the world. Another example, if you have a life expectancy of just 45 years then you are less likely to worry about maternal.

So I am a little worried about this global common good. I would suggest that we first cautiously discuss things that are in the public domain, issues that affect us all, and to then through participatory international dialogue figure out where our preferences overlap, and if they do not overlap spontaneously and automatically, figure out how to persuade others. This may involve paying a handsome price. We should not ignore that – international cooperation should make sense. In Germany, this global public good discussion has been totally perverted, because the Green Party in Germany defines global common goods as things that belong to all of us.

But is there accountability? Yes, that is a good question and therefore I am so concerned about the state. We knew that Greece was fudging their books and even our Central Bank knew it. And they knew it was getting worse and worse. So therefore I am convinced that most market failure is preceded by state failure. I am a social-democrat, I would love to see the state come in and correct market failure. But the state does not do that these days. And therefore there is this need to think through a multi-actor failure scenario. And what is very intriguing is that there are so many civil society organisations in the field of climate change, but very few dealing with financial matters. And that has to change.

What follows from all of this is that you have to be prepared for all kinds of actors, dealing, pushing and pressing each other; there is a term for that: messy multilateralism for the next time to come.

Question from the audience:
What are you recommendations to work with other actors in civil society? What do you think about valuation on public goods? How is your theory taken up in other countries?

Response by Anton Hemerijck:

With respect to the latter question, the thing I like about Dr Kauls approach to global public goods is that they allow for contextualisation. I think that common good is too abstract a term, so you need to make it concrete. This reflects a major difference between the OECD, until quite recently, and the EU which is much more into contextualised bench-marking when they compare employment and other kinds of policies. So I think that is important, because contextualisation allows for differences between countries and also triggers for politicisation. Whether pricing is a good or a bad thing, I do not know, because that depends on the context at hand.

The follow-up to the question of accountability is always: to what and to whom? I think transparency is a much better term than accountability, because accountability always leads to the blame-game. I think that transparency could lead to social learning, because the Greeks messed up and Ireland is in huge trouble and why is that? Because we were targeting public policy according to the wrong benchmarks. We were only looking at inflation, deficit and debts. We assumed that markets would work perfectly. So if you only control the public sector, because it is unproductive and inflexible, and you do that through inflation-targeting, then everything is well. Things should have been well in Spain, Ireland and Portugal – maybe not Greece though. But we have the wrong policy theory and that is what should be brought to the fore. The good news now, given what is happening in Greece, I think for the first time in a hundred years, is that they are in a process of creating an effective state. That element of social learning, to really learn from this disaster, to look at the policy theory we had and then to step beyond that and try to think of a better one, will take another ten years. But that is the way to go ahead and I am fearful of the blame game.

Response by Inge Kaul:

Briefly on the question of what civil society can do. Mr Sarkozy and Kouchner created a new commission on international financial taxes and I was invited to join. We came up with a very modest idea, but very doable. It is the collection of a currency transaction tax at a central market place in London – it would generate 30 billion dollars.

And so we thought about creating a joint body, with representative participation, and to channel the money to purposes agreed upon. We projected this not as a tax, but as a user fee, for more stable globalisation from which we would all benefit. We are all involved in currency transactions, so we would all pay a little bit; but states rejected this idea absolutely, because they just want money for their national budgets.

Now, where does the debate stand? In recent times, you see the term global public goods popping up everywhere. The risk is though that people are using it intuitively, because the theory still needs to be fully developed. We have to be very careful for it not to end up in the same situation as the term "common good". But it is in any case being used more and more. For example, the report on the Swedish-French commission has been mentioned; that report misused the term and defined global public goods as things that we all enjoy. But no, we do not. It is very contested and very contentious. To which good to give priority, how to shape the good, whether an intellectual property rights regime should benefit more the inventor and less the sick people in Africa, etc.

But you see a tremendous amount of views of the concept in the regional context. Regional public goods as stepping stones towards global public goods. So in Asia and Latin-America, but also in Africa, they are thinking about how they can first agree regionally, because of similar tastes, on what to do about global stability, health and peace and security, etc. Then with more regional consolidated ideas about global public goods we enter the debate. So a Google search for the term "regional public goods" will keep you busy for weeks. So I think as academics we have a lot of homework to do, so that policy makers can feel more comfortable with picking up the concept. But before that can happen, there needs to be an incentive for academics to start working on it.

China's complexity in addressing 'global' security challenges[32]

Shi Yinhong

Everyone knows that, compared with 10-15 years ago, China is now involved in a much deeper international cooperation. This is in part a result of its own unilateral efforts to deal with adjusting global security challenges and other challenges, such as climate change. I would like to say more about China's complexity in general, and to name some fundamental elements that played their roles and have resulted in a remarkable complexity and sophistication embedded in China's attitude about, position toward, and policies concerning global challenges, and the corresponding multilateral cooperation that consistently requires analyses and assessments that are based on China's various particular situations.

These elements have generally made China's response to global challenges slower and less than the expectations of the West, which so often perceives the world in universal or absolute terms. These elements mainly include: firstly, various huge and often grave economic and social bottlenecks within China, demanding or even forcing the Chinese government to give priority to them in terms of policy concern and resource distribution; secondly, China's rapidly increasing capability is at large almost always remarkably insufficient for the large-scale and quick expansion and escalation of China's international responsibilities – China has an overwhelming concern that the West's demands will surpass their capabilities and as a result hurt their economic and other interests; thirdly, the multiplicity of China's foreign policy interests often means that a policy intended to meet a

---

32 An extended version of this lecture was previously published as "China, 'Global Challenges' and the Complexities of International Cooperation", in *Global Policy* (2011) 2:1; London: London School of Economics and Political Science and John Wiley & Sons Ltd.

particular global challenge will conflict with another that is compatible with other foreign policy interests (especially a long-established policy), resulting in hesitant, small revisions in an attempt to balance needs, instead of the creation of a new policy. Moreover, several factors in 'ways of thinking' also have a major impact. A large part of China's attributes and situations make its opinion often significantly and profoundly different from that held by most Western countries, leading to China's limited rather than complete cooperation, or actions, concerning global affairs. China's more particularistic or relativistic way of thinking has restrained its international commitments. So these are China's limitations in general, now we will go into more detail about security challenges.

Global security challenges

There are different perceptions on global security challenges – not every state and not all their citizens agree on what constitutes a true global challenge. In the area of global security challenges there has been much disagreement and divergence, underpinned by universalistic versus particularistic views held, respectively, by many Westerners and most Chinese, which has hindered global responses. However, the ongoing global challenges in the security category mainly include nuclear proliferation, transnational terrorism, and severe man-made humanitarian disasters including genocide and ethnic cleansing.

Nuclear proliferation

Regarding the extremely difficult nuclear problems in North Korea and Iran, China has made important contributions to the cause of international nonproliferation. I personally have no doubt about that. China's protracted, arduous, and partially effective efforts in the past six or seven years aimed at the peaceful denuclearisation of North Korea are quite distinct, constituting a major part in the considerable increase of China's security role and political influence among the international society. China's relationship with the United States, and its reputation for taking responsibility in international security, have benefited most from its efforts regarding North Korea.

However, since US–DPRK bilateral talks based mainly on American concessions began in January 2007, generally the 'particularistic' dispositions on the part of those concerned have been strengthened in comparison with the 'universalistic' cause of denuclearisation of North Korea. Beijing seems increasingly determined to avoid serious alienation from Pyongyang for the sake of denuclearisation, enduring patiently the latter's arrogance and unfriendly attitude, while conducting bilateral trade and direct investment in increasing volume. The first recent major development is China Premier Wen Jiabao's visit to Pyongyang in early October 2009. This is a turning point, the beginning of a change in the China-North Korea relations. Premier Wen's visit resulted in a much-increased Chinese economic aid to North Korea, without Pyongyang even paying lip service to the principle of denuclearisation.

This shows a very remarkable divergence between China and the United States in the North Korea problem. It has come from a sharp separation China determinedly made sometime in 2009, probably not long before Premier Wen's visit to Pyongyang: the separation of the nuclear problem from the maintenance and development of China–DPRK relations, making the latter for the first time since 2003, the clear and undisputed priority in its North Korea policy. An even broader gap now exists between China and the hawkish US with its northeast Asian allies. China has experienced an extraordinary weakness in its influence on both sides in the Peninsular confrontation, and has displayed a remarkable diplomatic awkwardness – not including its efforts in persuading North Korea to withhold further retaliating action against ROK's artillery drill on *Yeongpang* Island and thereby preventing the very dangerous situation to deteriorate further. After the quite important concession President Hu made to Obama over the North Korea problem in Washington, and further improvement of the Peninsular situation, North Korea is now, much more than before, dependent on China's support.

As for Iran's nuclear problem, China has on the one hand always promoted denuclearisation of that country in the UN Security Council, Six-Nation Meetings on Iran and the International Atomic Energy Agency, as well as in bilateral diplomacy with all parties concerned. On the other hand, China has preserved and even developed its relations with Iran, which are important to its interests in terms of energy and diplomatic influence, while firmly maintaining the principled 'Chinese understanding' of the whole issue. China's attitude is and will continue to strike a balance. China wants to see a diplomatic solution rather than hurrying to sanctions; it is willing to give selective cooperation to Europe and the US, but it is conservative. China might eventually back very limited sanctions, but would be reluctant to do so and might well oppose them outright. Iran is an important country for China, which has dramatically increased its energy links as well as substantial diplomatic interests.

Transnational terrorism

As to transnational terrorism, China has consistently demonstrated its firm opposition, and joined in any international anti-terrorist cooperation as long as the act in question is perceived by China as reasonable, relevant, and within her capability. However, at the same time China has insisted on several principles that have both universalistic and particularistic elements, but are more characterised by differentiation and careful treatment of specific situations, an approach that differs from the American 'antiterror universalism'. These principles, as declared by the Chinese government, are as follows:

- all sorts of terrorism must be opposed, and the international community should take legislative, administrative, judicial and other necessary measures to resolutely combat them;
- any form of terrorism is hazardous to the international community and no country, party, or individual group should take double standards based on political or other selfish intentions while dealing with terrorism;
- the measures, means, and methods adopted in combating terrorism should not aggravate national rivalry, religious hatred, conflict between civilisations, and estrangement between people;
- anti-terrorist actions should conform to the aim and principles of the UN Charter and international law, have firm evidences, define distinct targets, avoid hurting innocents, and be limited to reasonable extent;

- China opposes the linking of anti-terrorism policies with specific religions and nationalities;
- in the process of fighting terrorism, the settlement of existing problems should be taken into account and a solution in the long run borne in mind as well;
- countries should fully employ various means combined rather than merely rely on military force.

In opposing terrorist forces and their actions, China's primary concern has mainly focused upon those that directly target China and its citizens. So also in this area, China takes a more particularistic approach.

Severe man-made humanitarian disasters

With regard to genocide and ethnic cleansing, because of the complexity of the situations and perceived impropriety of interventions, China did not join the multinational action (except in the case of the Rwandan genocide), and condemned NATO's Kosovo war and opposed the proposed UN sanctions against Sudan about Darfur. In future, the most challenging question China may face could be whether the decades-long tradition of self-imposed restriction on its military involvement in the world, reinforced by the inflexible doctrine of non-interference, should be revised according to the requirements of particular cases.

These cases are all based within the security field. The attitudes and policies of China in adjusting global security challenges are dependent upon the type of field. If we look at the financial field or the field of adjusting climate change, we will get a different picture. China still has particularistic policies, but also accepts international cooperation and is more and more open for cooperation with Western countries and the idea of general universal norms. But still, China is China. And China overwhelmingly has its own way of thinking and its particularistic interest concern. This is not only an issue of interest, but also that of a 'way of thinking', or one of philosophy. China will continue to have its complexities. We are in progress; there are more and more cooperative fields and issues between China and the

West. But China also feels differences and disagreements; some are very fundamental, some are dependent upon the situation, and some are declared by both sides. These differences will continue to exist for a long time as the Chinese and Europeans will have to adjust to particular situations in order to achieve fruitful cooperation.

Summary

Professor Shi began his lecture by giving some remarks on China's complexity in general. In comparison with the recent past, China is now engaged in a much broader and deeper international cooperation. China deals with global security challenges with increasing responsiveness and even takes the initiative to assume greater international responsibility. However, there is a remarkable complexity and sophistication embedded in China's attitude, positions and policies in the area of global challenges and corresponding multilateral cooperation.

Shi then turned from a general description of China's complexity in the area of global challenges to a more detailed explanation of China's way of addressing global security challenges, in particular nuclear proliferation, transnational terrorism, and severe man-made humanitarian disasters including genocide and ethnic cleansing.

Professor Shi concluded his lecture by reflecting on China's complexity in addressing these global security challenges. China does accept international cooperation and is more and more open for cooperation with Western countries. In this sense, there has been some progress. However, China remains tied to her particularistic interests driven by its own unique philosophy and way of thinking. China's complexity therefore looks set to continue for some time.

Discussion

Question from the audience:
As a professor at a Chinese university, you sit on top of a very important group in China: the students. Thousands of Chinese students are spreading out over the world in order to study at universities abroad.

I wonder if you could explain what view the Chinese government has of those students who have studied abroad and then come back to China with different western views and ideas? Don't you think that there will be an explosion sooner or later about what they want, such as freedom of internet, e-mail, etc.?

Response by Shi Yinhong:
Of course this is one of the biggest issues China faces. I think the government's official policy is to attract students and professors back to China, where they do enjoy a considerable degree of freedom. China is substantially different from Western countries, but for students and professors there is generally no information restriction. This is because the Chinese government mainly controls Chinese language internet and media – and generally speaking, they never block foreign language internet or other media. Personally, in the past 20 to 30 years, I have been able to access the newspapers and websites of the New York Times, Washington Post, among others, every day without restrictions. If you can read English, then there are few obstacles to information. Why is this? Maybe it is because of China's trust of intellectuals; those intellectuals might have different views, but they also have satisfactory incomes, and they don't want to go too straight.

I am in Western countries very often, and I am well known for speaking frankly. But I do not have any responsibilities towards the government. In the past 20 years, I have issued a lot of independent opinions, and my university and government have never intervened or have given me any trouble. Maybe the Chinese government think: "you are weak and cannot launch big waves". But they also know that many people like me are independent. In terms of China's interest, they tolerate us and learn from us, sometimes. For students it is the same. They can say a lot of things. If they speak publicly and have a public impact, this may be tolerated once, but if it happens ten times, then maybe not.

China has its laws and constitutions, there are some things to be improved. But before improvement, this is Chinese law, and that is different from the constitutions of US or EU countries. China's constitution has some stipulation against the subversive elements. The Chinese government will react (overreact at times) and we still need to build up rule-by-law. So I don't think that every case is justly treated in China, but generally, I believe that the majority of scholars, professors and experts don't have any troubles. Of course at times China is traditional and not tolerant, and hopefully things will be improved, because China is far from perfect.

Comment by moderator Tom Zwart (Utrecht University):
Thank you for your very illuminating answer. Just a quick follow-up concerning the question of what will happen to Chinese students when they come back to China from having studied abroad. The School of Human Rights Research is conducting a human rights project together with the Chinese University of Shandong. It is the first common Western human rights project in the history of the People's Republic so we are quite proud of it. As a part of this project we interviewed people on their thoughts about human rights, and we found some interesting notions, including the surprising fact that, generally, Chinese people who have travelled or studied abroad tend to cherish Chinese values more than those who have never been to the West; the latter group are in fact more susceptible to Western values than people who have witnessed them firsthand. You can only hypothesise that, probably, students who go abroad are challenged, and as a result become strong supporters of their own values. That is at least the outcome.

Question from the audience:
I would like to bring together the concepts of universal norms on the one hand and Chinese complexities on the other hand. Considering the international complexity of contradictions, how do you see a harmonisation of different values in the world, e.g., Asian values on the one hand, and the European or international values on the other hand? How would you conceive of the universal norms transcending the values of different parts of the world, in order to attack or to solve the problems in today's world?

Response by Shi Yinhong:
Some people feel that there are already too many 'universal norms'. If you want universal norms to be truly universal, you should decide to

listen to different nations. Of course, there are developments of some important principles in this area, but still some norms are not really actually 'universal'. Importantly, in order to become universal, norms must be sufficiently generalised. Otherwise, if you want to make very concrete laws, then different nations will have considerable hesitations and will be reluctant. Norms have to leave space for accommodating different understandings and laws. So of course, you can continue to point out some other fundamental conditions for norms to become really universal, but in the international society, 'practice' is so important in the making of norms and laws. Practice can make some norms more universal. On the one hand, the world leaders in 1946 did a great job. From lessons learned, mainly after the experiences of fascism, they emphasised the need for universal norms. But, you shouldn't have so many universal norms – it diminishes the value and possible impact of them all.

Question from the audience:
In the United States, a lot of times when we study China, a lot of professors talk about 'China's peaceful rise' in the world. What do you think of this statement, and do you believe that it will continue to be the same in the 21st century or will we see a more offensive China in terms of its military, economics and diplomacy?

Response by Shi Yinhong:
This is quite a difficult, but also easy question to answer. The Chinese government repeats its 'peaceful rise' again and again, and firstly, I have to say, I don't doubt this. Because this peaceful rise is hugely beneficial to China, peaceful rise is a prime act policy. Peaceful rise means: 'do not use force', which generally means less cost. Anyway, China benefits a lot from a peaceful rise. For this generation and the next. Peaceful rise is so beneficial for China so why would they abandon this strategy? China is very pragmatic, and the peaceful rise is beneficial. Secondly, if you understand the traditional China and Confucianism, then you know we are extremely patient. Compared with Western people, we are not so great in combat. Our armed forces have not fought a single battle in the past (more than) thirty years; therefore China *has* to rise peacefully. Of course, one cannot know

if China will indeed be peaceful forever. Everything can change, the generation of now says 'peaceful rise, peaceful rise', because they know that it is beneficial. But maybe in the future, some leaders will attack Japan just to win the votes. Who knows? One thing is certain: we are Chinese, and from 2500 years ago, even much earlier than Confucianism, we are a particular people, and among us there are many more great poets than great commanding generals.

Question from the audience:
According to some, the West consistently tries to 'teach' China its Western norms and values. Looking at it from the other, Chinese perspective, in terms of universal values, what would you like to teach the world from a Chinese perspective? What would be the norms or values that you would like to give to the world?

Response by Shi Yinhong:
China, in the 1930s before Mao Zedong, was a nation that very much liked to teach others. In fact, Confucianism *is* universalism – this means that what is best for the Chinese is best for everyone. This was the Chinese mainstream ideology before Mao Zedong. Mao Zedong changed this, and despite his many mistakes, and despite him causing so much suffering for millions of Chinese, he made a wonderful contribution to China, and the world. He battled against Western universalism in the 1930s, and whether issued against Lenin or Stalin, Mao felt that every people should decide by their own practice, according to their own situations, in their own countries. What is best for Washington or The Hague is definitely not necessarily best for China, or other people. Many people now like or dislike Mao Zedong, and everyone should decide for themselves, *by their own practice.* There is no certain answer; there's no ready answer from west or east, but you should learn lessons and answer vital questions. This is the particularistic perspective at its best. Whether China is great or not, peaceful rise or no peaceful rise, China has contributed to world history, fundamentally. Of course maybe China will forget it, or China will become too proud and will launch its own universalism. But there is no ready universal answer that can be applied to every situation. There is something like independent practice and it is more effective

in solving its own problems and learning from other people's experience. These are universal norms, from local experience.

Final comments by moderator Tom Zwart:
Thank you. You have rightly emphasised the particularistic approach of China at the international level, which in other publications you have called *Chinaness* which I have always thought to be a very good way of phrasing it. Perhaps we should make the effort to move towards a situation in which we accept that Western norms are Western norms and that China has its own views on issues, and still we are able to reconcile the two. That is actually what we are doing at the Dutch School of Human Rights Research; as I said we are working with the Shandong University School of Law – Human Rights Centre, which is the oldest human rights centre in China. And we are trying to combine the Western view on human rights, which focuses on individual and forcible rights, with the Chinese view, in which individual and forcible rights are less popular.

We believe that it is possible to combine and reconcile the two, therefore we have developed the so-called *receptor approach*. We are looking for receptors of human rights in Chinese society, which is quite easy, because many social institutions in China can be seen as the Chinese implementation of human rights obligations at the international level. For example, we all know how important the family is: the network that will provide for you and take care of you. In addition, Marxism brought gender equality to China, at least on paper, but also to a large extent in practice, because under Confucianism the position of women was subordinate to that of man. So there are several receptors in China, which I find most interesting. I don't know if we will succeed in enough receptors to meet the international human rights standards, but I am quite optimistic. And if there is a gap, we will fill it with Chinese home grown solutions.

The interesting thing is that all those who are participating in the project have agreed to two commitments: first of all, every country that signs up to a treaty, a human rights treaty, has to honour its commitment faithfully, so you can never not implement a treaty by relying on your own culture. Secondly, and this is a principle of international law, states under public international law and human rights treaties can themselves choose the means by which they want to implement these human rights institutions. So, they don't necessarily have to do this through individual forcible rights, which is the western way of doing things. You could also rely on other social institutions such as the family and the network, as I mentioned. So we are hopeful that that will happen, and what I like most, is that the Chinese in this project are the most enthusiastic; they are very proud of their culture so they keep coming up with elements that can serve as a receptor, which of course is contrary to what we now see, but happens in the EU-China dialogue, which is not a dialogue at all. EU Commissioners go to Beijing and release a statement to their counterparts from China and then they have dinner and leave the room. In order to make this a little bit more fruitful, they decided to add an academic seminar to the political meeting. But I have friends on both sides, and its as dead as a dodo. People exchange statements, but it is not a real dialogue. And what I find interesting about the *receptor approach* is that everybody is fully engaged in the debate, whether they agree or not; if we don't agree there's always the dinner and the drinks.

We are citizens of the world?

Kate Nash

'World citizenship' is still a utopian idea, but it is no longer banished
to the realm of science fiction or of idealist political theory. Today
it seems instead to be directly related to quite practical questions of
development. The idea of world citizenship moves the whole debate
about development from thinking in terms of *charity* to thinking in
terms of *justice*. As a 'world citizen' issues such as life-sapping poverty, appalling working and living conditions, and lack of hope for
the future that is the experience of many people around the world,
become a matter of rights and responsibilities. The responsibility is
ours: how do 'we' in over-developed states contribute in practice
to securing human rights that really make a difference to people in
other countries? Put like this, it may sound as if 'rights' is just a com-
plication; it comes between 'us' – the comfortably well-off in rich
countries, and 'them' – the really poor in other countries. And it may
even seem paternalist and disempowering: 'we' secure 'their' rights.
Certainly, realising human rights in practice is far from a simple matter. But what I think is implied in world citizenship at the very least
is that we have *obligations* to others as well as rights. Rights and
responsibilities are two sides of the same coin in structures of global
interdependence. It is in this sense that 'world citizenship' is close
today – perhaps emerging already.

What I want to talk about first of all are the realities that condition our idea of world citizenship in practice. What is it about the
changes we've seen in recent years that now make us think quite
seriously that being a global citizen is somehow plausible, even possible in the relatively near future? Indeed, for human rights activists,
it's just around the corner. 'The world' for them is already a relatively
unified political space, and the idea of world citizenship – involving
human rights and obligations that are realisable, practical ideals –

has a resonance for many that it didn't have until quite recently. In this respect I will talk about two main types of practices that seem to encourage imagining ourselves as world citizens. Firstly, our experience of global digital media, which is making changes to our daily experience of being part of humanity. Secondly, structures of human rights, which perhaps make less of a direct impression on most of us, but which nevertheless embed us in obligations to people in other countries through our *national* citizenship.

In an era of global digital media in which it is very difficult to avoid knowing about details of 'distant suffering', combined with the structures of rights and obligations that are remaking national states, the very idea of human rights carries with it implications about how the world works, and what justice means, that make the responsibilities of citizens in over-developed countries more pressing than ever before.

Who are our fellows?

In terms of world citizenship the most important question is 'who are our fellows'? With whom do we belong, and how? This question has two main dimensions, both of which have a long history. As a political ideal (rather than a moral imperative, which is much older), human rights go back to the great revolutions of the 18th century: the American, the French, and the less well-known Haitian Revolution that was fought to free the slaves of that island. Consider for a moment, that slaves were not regarded as *humans* by the American and French Revolutionaries. Slaves had to win their humanity – the Haitian Revolution was only briefly and locally successful in doing so. Winning rights to basic freedom took a lot longer and involved art, literature, music and images, as well as changes in politics and law.

So 'humanity' has to be fought for – who counts as a fellow human being. But so too does 'fellowship' itself. Fellowship implies solidarity; it involves more than just tolerance, living alongside each other as fellow human beings. It's a question of solidarity rather than tolerance in the sense that we share a sense of common conditions, common hopes, fears, opportunities, threats. Fellows are those with whom we share what is sometimes thought of as a 'community of fate'.

Ever since human rights became a political ideal, fellowship became a *national* construction. National citizenship is the direct legacy of universal human rights. Who enjoys human rights according to the French Declaration of the Rights of Man? It is French citizens. The Declaration goes from 'men' (who are 'born and remain free and equal in rights') to 'citizen' in just the first three Articles. Article 1: Men are born and remain free and equal in rights. Article 3: The principle of all sovereignty resides essentially in the nation. No body nor individual may exercise any authority which does not proceed directly from the nation.

National citizenship is how the modern 'community of fate' is organised. Again, of course, in many cases this has had to be fought for – as the long struggles against imperialism in the 19th and 20th centuries demonstrated. Nevertheless, the ideal of sharing a community of fate with our fellow nationals has to some extent been realised in the 20th century – certainly in Europe, North America and Australasia; less clearly elsewhere. Most importantly, of course, it is the *nation* that is supposed to govern itself through its own sovereign state – but this has also entailed the construction of a 'national economy' (through statistics on trade and manufacturing, national debt etc), policies oriented towards the well-being of the population understood as territorially bounded, the expectation of a common language amongst citizens, and so on. And this community of fate is also an 'imagined nation'; commonality is created through symbols and practices that represent 'us' as belonging together (Anderson 1991). This imagined nation is not only a product of extreme patriotism, with hatred of foreigners, war and violence. On the contrary, as Michael Billig has argued very carefully and convincingly, most nationalism is 'banal' (1995). Banal nationalism involves everyday flagging of the nation – it's completely naturalised, and we're barely aware of it. My favourite example is the weather map.

Banal nationalism is very much with us. We have only to consider an example that is a somewhat 'hotter' form than the weather map, such as the interest in names and faces of fellow nationals over all others in media coverage of accidents or disasters. For example, coverage of the tsunami on the BBC and in British newspapers was to a large extent organised around the names and faces of British people who'd been affected by it. This is taken to extremes during times of war; when British soldiers are killed in Iraq and Afghanistan, their names and faces appear as news – the killing of civilians in these wars is more often marked by the names of places: Kandahar, Helmund Province, Basra.

But banal 'nationalism' is now accompanied to some extent by banal 'cosmopolitanism' (Hannerz 1990; Beck 2002; Szerszynski and Urry 2002). Cultural referents to the global and the non-national are as frequent now as flags and weather maps – in everything from food to pop videos and advertising, through literature, and not forgetting the frequency with which we're shown the very form of the globe itself to stand in for everyone in the world as well as for planet Earth (something which, as a photographic image has only become possible in the last 50 years).

Most important from our point of view, however, and the remarkable interest we take in the names and faces of our fellow nationals notwithstanding, is the range and frequency of images and stories, we now receive directly transmitted into our homes, of what Luc Boltanski calls 'distant suffering' (Boltanski 1999). Distant suffering is not necessarily the suffering of foreigners. What is distant about it is that it is mediated – the person who is suffering is not physically present; we have knowledge of them only through the images and stories of the media. Nevertheless, according to Boltanski, such images do require action from us – just as they would if the person were actually present. He suggests that feeling that we can do something is part of 'the spectatorship of suffering'. In fact, as long as we look we are acting – and if we turn away, or turn off, that is acting too. We are bound to act then when confronted with images of distant suffering. Boltanski shows that there are a number of different kinds of responses, and not all of them directed towards alleviating the suffering. He deconstructs what is involved in different models of response to distant suffering. One of the models stands out as most relevant to world citizenship.

What kind of response to media images and stories of distant suffering is appropriate to world citizenship? What kind of response is appropriate to a world in which we share a community of fate with fellow *human beings*? Rather than exclusively with our fellow nationals. How might suffering be made a matter of justice rather than of charity?

Boltanski suggests that pity is not such a bad start in such instances – but that it is not enough. Unlike Hannah Arendt, who sees pity as a wholly inadequate response to suffering except where people who are close to us are concerned, Boltanski sees pity as a starting point for various different forms of response – the political, the sentimental, and the aesthetic. He argues that there are many different ways in which feeling pity for those who are suffering can develop. If pity is to develop in a way that motivates claims for *justice*, he suggests, the appropriate emotional response to such images and stories is indignation, and the appropriate form of action is the denunciation of those responsible for the situation. It is through feelings of indignation and the attribution of responsibility that feelings of pity can feed a politics of *justice*.

This seems intuitively right. Consider the response when fellow nationals suffer – it is the government that is responsible. In cases of humanitarian crises, our government must ensure that our fellow citizens are airlifted to safety, that they are given medical supplies, and whatever is needed to help them cope, if they are caught up in revolutions or wars, or natural disasters. It's not guilt and shame that we feel – we don't turn away overwhelmed by our inability to do anything. On the contrary, we're energised with indignation if nothing is done. Consider, for example, the outrage at the lack of the US government's response to the disaster of Hurricane Katrina in New Orleans. Justice and our fellow feeling requires that something should be done.

But what if our fellow feeling leads us to indignation over the plight of people whose suffering we see and pity, but who are not fellow nationals? Where then can we direct our indignation? Who can we denounce as responsible?

According to Boltanski, indignation and denunciation invariably imply a 'theory of power'. That puts causality in the picture. That is to say, indignation and denunciation imply not just an identifiable agent who is responsible for the suffering, but also connections between their actions, or lack of actions, and the suffering that is caused. Such a theory need not be enormously elaborate – we're not necessarily talking about fully worked out theories of the kind that fill books. They can be more schematic, and they're often quite taken for granted. Indeed, to be really effective, theories of power need to become common sense rather than academic. What kind of theory of power is implied in world citizenship as it is developing through human rights?

What are our rights?

According to human rights activists, we are world citizens already. As individual human beings we have rights and we also have legal and political obligations. Preventing and dealing with distant suffering is not just a matter of a charitable response to people who are in difficulties at a particular moment. Not that we participate in one common public sphere, or world government, but there do exist common structures of rights in international law.

Civil and political rights, as defined by the UN system, are often considered to be basic or fundamental, especially by over-developed countries. These are the first 12 Articles of the Universal Declaration of Human Rights, and the basis of the International Convention on Civil and Political Rights. They include rights to life and liberty, fair trial, freedom of movement, to association and expression, to property, and to participation in choosing the government.

Social, economic and cultural rights are also well established in international law – in the Universal Declaration of Human Rights, and the International Convention on Social, Cultural and Economic Rights. They are as detailed and extensive as civil and political rights, though much more highly contested, and resisted, especially by Northern states. They include the right to fair wages and working conditions, social security and social assistance, adequate food, clothing and housing, education and healthcare.

But what are human rights beyond declarations and fine sounding words? How are human rights secured? Who is responsible for making sure that human rights really exist? Most people would say 'the United Nations' or perhaps 'the European Court of Human Rights' or 'the European Union'. To some extent this is right; Inter-Governmental Organisations are crucial to ensuring human rights in practice. Yet the answer to the question is actually much more simple and closer to home; international human rights law holds national states themselves responsible for human rights.

Far from becoming redundant, abolished or sidelined by international human rights law, it is only through states that human rights make sense. It's in the name of states that international agreements are signed. It's states that are bound by these agreements; they create obligations for their own future actions. On the other hand, of course, states are the chief violators of human rights. In legal terms, and in reality. It is regimes that have access to state resources of money and force, as well as legitimacy, that abuse human rights. In terms of civil rights, they imprison without charge, torture, kidnap and kill; in terms of political rights, they rig elections and physically attack opponents; they persecute people on the basis of skin colour and ethnicity, refusing to recognise alternative ways of life; and in terms of socio-economic rights they misuse state resources for political ends or simply to enrich themselves and their supporters. Human rights were *designed* with just such violations in mind: the violations committed through and by states.

So here is the responsibility for suffering that is implied in discourses of human rights: it is states that are responsible for guaranteeing human rights. But which states? And which responsibilities?

Let's consider socio-economic rights, which are arguably the most important for the majority of people in the world who lack security of food and shelter, healthcare, the possibility of seeing their children educated and growing up with what they need. And social and economic development is inextricably linked to civil and political rights, which create accountability for government budgets, distribution of public goods (like healthcare and education), investment and the regulation of business.

The point here is that globalisation means that states, responsible for socio-economic rights, are no longer quite the *national* states they once were. Saskia Sassen argues that states are 'denationalising' (Sassen 2006). What she means by this is relatively simple. She's arguing that much of what we associate with globalisation has been created by states. It's not, as politicians would have us believe, that globalisation is happening in spite of states, or by eroding their power. It's happening through states, because of what government officials and bureaucrats are putting in place in terms of regulation (which we often think of as de-regulation) of financial markets, trade and labour conditions. It is as a result of states' orientations towards global agendas and systems, and a turning away from constructions of 'national economy' that globalisation is possible.

Sassen is most concerned with the construction of global capitalism and with its effect on democracy and the workers' movement. She sees the denationalising of states as benefiting global neo-liberalism. But what then of human rights in denationalising states? Do states, in orienting themselves towards global agendas and systems, then become more subject to constraint in terms of human rights? Do human rights begin to supplement or even to replace citizens' rights as what makes it possible to tame capitalism for the benefit of ordinary people?

The short answer here is 'no'. For the most part governments around the world negotiate the global harmonisation of terms of business and the regulation of markets at the international level undisturbed by considerations of their impact on human rights and the kinds of conditions they produce for poor people in other countries. And yet, social and economic rights, which most states have accepted (with the glaring exception of the US) by signing and ratifying the ICESCR, committed themselves to, in the words of Articles 2 and 3: 'take steps, individually and through international assistance and co-operation... to the maximum of its available resources, with a view to achieving progressively the full realisation of [all economic, social and cultural rights]'. In other words they have committed governments to doing their utmost to ensure the socio-economic rights of people both in their own countries, but also in others.

Of course, this is not what we see in reality. Even where states have signed up to human rights agreements, there is actually no universal framework of rights as such. Human rights are at best *universalising*, and it's better to understand them in this way, rather than as already existing as universals. But what such agreements do enable, potentially, is mobilisation to bring states to account for the international human rights agreements that are apparently a global consensus.

So to recap, then, the argument so far: images of distant suffering require a certain emotional response and a certain action. Where they invoke pity, to become part of a politics of justice appropriate to world citizens they must involve indignation and denunciation of those responsible. And it seems that human rights agreements have built in a rudimentary theory of who is responsible: the state. And not just the state of which the people who are suffering are citizens. But all states. Including our own. It is in this sense that we are already world citizens: it is states, our own and others, that must be denounced as the causes of distant suffering.

From national into world citizens?

But if states are denationalising, i.e., government agents are increasingly oriented towards global agendas and systems, it is also the case that they remain banally national. It is politicians, who may be household names nationally and completely unknown elsewhere, who are responsible for government at home and abroad. Even where media is owned and managed by global conglomerates, it continues to orient its readers to a large extent through banal nationalism.

Human rights and nationalism aren't necessarily opposed. Nationalism is of course mobilised in conservative or reactionary forms against the realisation of human rights – whether it's a matter of national security, or bailouts to heavily indebted countries that apply conditions that impoverish the most vulnerable. But it may also be mobilised to support them. Let's consider a case I've studied in detail, that of Make Poverty History in the UK (known as *Maak Het Waar* in the Netherlands) (Nash 2009). It was part of a campaign in 2005 that united hundreds of NGOs through the Global Call for Action Against Poverty, organised around the slogan 'Think globally, act nationally'. It continues today; campaigning, for example on the so-called 'Robin Hood' or 'Tobin Tax'.

In the Make Poverty History campaign in the UK 2005, nationalism worked quite differently, for the realisation of socio-economic rights to alleviate distant suffering. Make Poverty History was an unprecedented media event, over several months, involving everyone from pop stars and celebrities to students and school children. It became a national obsession – in a way that may be peculiarly British, with our populist media. Whole days of BBC coverage were dedicated to it, and every single newspaper took up the theme. Of course, there are many criticisms that can be made of the campaign itself. It called for fair not free trade, demanding that 'odious' debt should be dropped for all those countries that had incurred it, and increasing aid. I don't want to get into what would be necessary in terms of radical restructuring of global governance for poverty to be really become history. What I do want to talk about is the cultural, emotional and political terms of the campaign.

On the one hand MPH was a very important phenomenon from which I think we have to learn. I think it was unprecedented, possibly unique, but perhaps it may be indicative of a new sensibility. Or at least new possibilities. It involved citizens in Northern states (not just in Britain, but nowhere else was it so widespread) coming together to denounce authorities that were not prepared to do what they could to alleviate the suffering of non-citizens in far off countries. To express indignation, not pity, for distant suffering; to denounce governments, their own and others (especially the US); and to demand justice, not charity, for people with whom they do not share a national bond or a common government.

On the other hand, the denunciation was largely framed in terms of what I have called 'cosmopolitan nationalism'. The framework was 'cosmopolitan' because it was oriented towards politics through the state, but for people outside the nation. It was 'nationalist' in that it enabled the celebration of the nation as superior, as benevolent, caring, the saviour of the poor and mistreated. This is a construction that is highly problematic not least because it is rather prone to be self-satisfying – the gesture towards caring becomes a celebration of oneself, one's own sensitivity, enjoyment of one's own indignation. It became sentimental and narcissistic, and tended then to silence those who were 'to be helped', except insofar as they joined in the celebration of the nation's benevolence. This is hardly a basis for dialogue or a way of building democratic exchanges amongst 'world citizens'.

In conclusion then, in what way are we world citizens and what are the limits of that citizenship? We are world citizens in that we are responding on a daily basis now to images and stories of suffering elsewhere in the world. We may, we often do, turn away. We are world citizens in that we have political obligations to those people, albeit indirectly, through the states of which we are nationals, insofar as they have signed the international human rights agreements. A more direct obligation, we might say, is to denounce the authorities when they do not live up to those agreements. In this respect, world citizenship is exercised as national citizenship. Of course, for the most part, most people are unaware of such obligations, and they might well disagree that they are implicated in any way. It is for this reason that there is still much to be done to frame issues of global poverty as matters of *justice* not *charity*; to elicit responses of indignation (rather than guilt, shame or indifference); and to encourage denunciation of authorities that do not keep their promises. And if this seems impossibly utopian, we should consider that it is also necessary.

References

Anderson, B. (1991) *Imagined Communities*. London: Verso Books.

Beck, U. (2002) 'The Cosmopolitan Society and its Enemies'. *Theory, Culture and Society*, 19: 17-44.

Billig, M. (1995) *Banal Nationalism*. London: Sage

Boltanski, L. (1999) *Distant Suffering: morality, media and politics*. Cambridge: Polity.

Hannerz, U. (1990) 'Cosmopolitans and Locals in World Culture' in M. Featherstone (ed.) *Global Culture*. London: Sage.

Nash, K. (2009) *The Cultural Politics of Human Rights: Comparing the US and UK*. Cambridge: Cambridge University Press.

Sassen, S. (2006) *Territory, Authority, Rights: From Medieval to Global Assemblages*. Princeton: Princeton University Press

Szerszynski, B. and Urry, J. (2002) 'Cultures of Cosmopolitanism' *Sociological Review*, 50: 461-481.

Summary

The idea of world citizenship moves the development debate from thinking in terms of *charity* to thinking in terms of *justice*. According to Nash the idea of world citizenship implies obligations as well as rights in the structures of global interdependence. Two relatively recent developments have encouraged our sense of being 'world citizens': global digital media has changed our daily experience of being part of humanity, and the structures of human rights legally embed us in obligations to people in other countries through our national citizenship.

People have not always been, and still are not, treated equally; they have even had to fight to have their humanity recognised (think of, e.g., slaves), they have had to struggle to find common ground and shared values to create a fellowship that goes beyond mere tolerance, and then in a national construction of common fate we have developed national citizenship. Now we look further, toward world citizenship – all are based on the concept of, and political legacy of, 'universal' human rights.

Nash continues with the topic of 'distant suffering': the suffering of people that we only know of through images and stories of the media. Images of distant suffering require action from us and create a feeling that we should do something. What kind of response would be appropriate in relation to world citizenship, in a world where we share a community of fate with our fellow human beings? Emotion needs to develop from pity to indignation, followed by denunciation of those responsible. From this point of view, preventing and dealing with distant suffering becomes a matter of *justice* and not one of *charity*. And whilst there is no world government, there are common structures of rights in international law that states have agreed to, and signed up to. States are thus responsible for securing human rights – yet they are also the chief violators.

We are 'world citizens', in that we daily respond to images and stories of suffering elsewhere in the world. We are also world citizens in that we have indirect political obligations to those people, through our states of which we are nationals. It is in this respect that it is possible to frame issues of global poverty as matters of justice not charity, to elicit responses of indignation (rather than guilt, shame or indifference) and to encourage denunciation of immoral authorities.

Discussion

Opening words and questions by the moderator, René Cuperus (Wiardi Beckman Foundation):

On behalf of the SID I want to thank you, Kate Nash, for the very inspiring, rich and crystal-clear lecture on global citizenship and its limits. I think it's great food for thought and for discussion. I shall kick-off the discussion with some brief comments and observations myself. As author of the book 'The World Citizen Does Not Exist' I will of course do that in a very neutral and objective way.

I think the lecture and arguments made are of great importance for the Dutch debate. What I like about Kate Nash is that she is not a dogmatic cosmopolitan, but interested in the limits, contradictions and hypocrisies that are sometimes associated with one dimensional cosmopolitan thinking. She is not interested in the utopia of global citizenship, but she is interested in the sociology of global citizenship. And I think that we have to thank Kate Nash for a fine and important contribution to the Dutch debate. Holland needs to hear arguments like these today, especially now in these days. Because as many people in this room will confirm, Holland has lost much of its international appeal in terms of its image of tolerance and passionate engagement. It has instead become an inward-looking, populist, protectionist country and at the same time, a selfish neoliberal country, only interested in money. But it may be more complex than that.

I would say that Holland, these days, is suffering from the battle of globalisation and populism. Holland is one of the areas where the clash between the so-called 'globals' and 'locals' is taking place. The clash between people who feel internationally connected, the frequent flying academic professionals, versus those who feel threatened by globalisation, by migration and the international knowledge-based economy. And what makes things worse is that some observers, like Peter Spiegel from the Financial Times, consider the Netherlands to be a trendsetter for what is happening in Europe at large. He called Holland the California of Europe, setting trends and public moods. I think this clash between globals and locals is part of a bigger picture, and you refer to that in your lecture. I believe that it has to do with the dialectics of globalisation; globalisation implies two contradicting things at the same time. On the one hand, the world grows closer together, becomes more familiar, interdependent, interconnected. But domestically, in the nation-states, because of globalisation and migration, national society becomes more global, more diverse, more strange, more fragmented. So we witness a dialectics of more familiarity and more strangeness at the same time. In one sentence you could say: 'the world is becoming flat, but national societies are becoming less flat', just to paraphrase Thomas Friedman.

So my first question to you, Kate, is, what does the concept and idea of global citizenship mean against this new decor, this new background of a clash between globals and locals within our western European societies? Between academic cosmopolitans and more or less lower educated locals. In addition, how are feelings of international solidarity affected if people sense a declining national solidarity as a result of globalisation? Do you need national solidarity to get to international solidarity? Is there a link?

My second question is, what is your exact definition of citizenship? What are the elements of politics in this citizenship? A lot of analysts think that citizenship has to do with political community. I do believe in global engagement and concern, but, to make it very concrete, does the outpour of emotion for the victims of the Fukushima nuclear disaster equate the type of citizenship ties that are expressed in the Euro Crisis with the Greeks? Or, does the Euro Crisis deal more with a shared fellow citizenship because we share a currency, which is more or less a political link. Does citizenship, in other words, presuppose a shared political community, a social contract or reciprocity?

Response by Kate Nash:
They're very big and difficult questions. Of course I think all European countries are going through a situation in which some people are feeling more threatened by strangers, people who are visibly strangers. I don't think that this is really new though. For example, France has been a country of immigration throughout its history, but it only started to think of itself in those terms when people of a certain colour started to arrive. So it now has a problem with people from North Africa. But before that, Spanish, Italians, and so forth came,

and France didn't even bother to make them into French citizens. They live, they do what they like. So I don't think it can be separated from questions about race, ethnicity, culture, etc. I think people are feeling very threatened, but then the white working class in Britain felt threatened by people coming from elsewhere in the 1960s. And they more of less adapted to greater or lesser extent, there are always new challenges. Now there are many people who are third generation immigrants in Britain, for example, who would like to close the door on other people.

So it is an ongoing issue, but it seems to me to be part of our pluralist society. It's not something that you can solve, in a way. And there are those who do talk about how pluralism will undermine national solidarity. Some on the left in Britain hold the argument that a welfare state is only possible if all the people share a very strong sense of national history and national customs and communities which are local, and so on. But I believe there is a possibility of solidarity that allows other people to be part of that national picture. We see it in sports (sport teams are made up of many nationalities, yet still act as a cohesive entity). I don't think there is a finite answer to the question whether or not a pluralistic society can function and experience solidarity.

It is interesting that you think that it is easier to identify with the Greeks as part of the same community of fate in this way. I agree that it is easier to experience a common fate when there is reciprocity, when there is the idea of 'they sink, we sink'. But this is something that is part of any community, the idea that you're sharing dangers and sharing a common fate. This is one of the problems with the cosmopolitan nationalism, because e.g., in the Make Poverty History-campaign it became all about us, and you didn't hear any of these other voices. Some politicians did try to introduce the idea that you have to have development, you have to build up other places because they will otherwise all start emigrating, or we won't be able to sell them our goods. So they try to do it more on the basis of reciprocity, rather than a sort of justice. So they try to do both in a way. It is interesting, there is common currency, but it's also a construction. Some people have reacted, in response to the Greeks, with: 'let them go. We don't have to be in it together.'

– I have the same, semantic question that you, René Cuperus, had, and that Kate Nash hasn't answered yet, namely: what do you actually mean by citizenship? It seems citizenship presupposes that you can say citizen of... what? That is usually a state I think, citizen of a state, you can't use it in any other way. Maybe instead of global citizenship you should use something like: 'responsible global fellowship'. Constitutions of any country just talk about their own citizens and nothing else, that's why you're a citizen of that state. So that brings me to one aspect of your talk which I liked very much, but one aspect you ignored, it seems to be. You should have said, if you really want to stick to the notion of citizenship, that it is a problem mainly because there is no global state. I think that this is the most important aspect if you want to use this term.

– My question is very much in line with the previous question in the audience. You started out by saying 'world citizenship is utopian', and towards the end of your presentation, what struck me, is when you showed the pictures of the British politicians, you seemed to contrast British politicians with European politicians. And the question that popped up in my mind, is, do you think that there is a role for European citizenship as an intermediate step towards global citizenship, or even instead of?

– I wonder, it seems that global citizenship in your definition is demanding governments to take responsibility. But what is the responsibility of citizens? Because now it seems that you can just ask a government to take responsibility and then sit back and relax. Is that true, can you explain a bit?

Response by Kate Nash:
I agree completely that you can only be a citizen of a state. But what I was trying to get at, is that there is indeed no world state, but there are global networks and institutions tying states together. So the way I see it, is that it's as citizens of states, which we still think of as national states, but which are themselves internationalising. That's the direction, the way that some notion of citizenship develops,

through a kind of legal and political structure at that global level. But which only comes to us through states, but we are citizens of internationalising states. In terms of economic globalisation, we are quite aware that governments, in the name of the national economy, now make all sorts of arrangements to attract investments and so on. So we are already used to thinking about the state as globally oriented around questions of economic development, but we're not yet used to thinking of states going global in terms of political, with legal institutions and rules.

Europe as intermediary between world citizenship and national citizenship. The thing about this I suppose is that it's not entirely clear what role Europe plays in the world. Europe, when it comes to Europe and the rest of the world, breaks up into national states as far as I can see it. There's not much of a common foreign policy, there is not much in the way of speaking for Europe at a global level. Nation states make Europe. We are European citizens, that is true, we literally have that status through our national citizenship – but it goes through our national citizenship. Cosmopolitans are very keen to say 'look it's working in Europe', but I think it's a big leap from Europe to the World. So let's see what's happening in Europe first, as it is very interesting. But it won't necessarily lead you further.

Then the idea that this is a kind of passive citizenship. I have focused very much on the kind of rights and obligations, and it's true that that is quite a liberal citizenship model. The republican citizenship is much more about the involvement of citizens directly. And in fact, this notion of world citizenship can only develop if citizens themselves take a very active role. Make Poverty History didn't work, they didn't keep any of their promises. And I don't get the sense that many people took much of an interest in it after the huge populist media campaign. So it would require citizens to a lot more active. I don't think that that is really happening.

Comment by René Cuperus:
For me the European experience is rather negative and problematic. Europe is still expanding, there isn't even one unity – it's very hard to become part of an ever-moving target. For me the European experience is actually fuelling my scepticism towards cosmopolitan citizen-

ship at large. For instance this Greek case, we know how the financial markets react, but we don't know how the electoral market will react now or within 10 years time. It can give an enormous populist backlash. We are experimenting, and Europe is a very interesting experiment for global citizenship and its (psychological) limits. There are limits in terms of the enormous inequalities between people – some who would like to be a part of the European story, and others who feel threatened by it. It is related to education, and other developments in our societies. I also see that the international and NGO world is very elitist, and very threatening to the non-elites. I have a very strong democratic problem with all these developments. So my sceptical position until now remains: as long as we fail to see, in the world, a successful post-national democracy, or a post-national welfare state experiencing solidarity, I choose to stick with the national case.

Response by Kate Nash:

But the response to that, would be to turn it around and ask: "what exactly are you sticking to?" Because the state is also a moving target. So if we think that national states are becoming more globally oriented, well they are responding in part to their citizens and to electoral pressure. We still have political parties, we still vote for them, we still lobby and all these other things. But no one in Greece voted for the government that is now putting in place the austerity measures, they didn't vote for that. That is because they're part of Europe. So they have to put up with it. So the question of citizenship is not what it once was.

Questions from the audience:

Can I push that argument a little bit further? Because I think it's a very relevant point. What we are seeing is that on a global level, the private sector is basically defining the speed of globalisation, with nation states facilitating them. And the private sector is not democratic. All these quasi umbrella organisations that we have (G8, G20, etc) are not democratic either. If that's where the world is going, what happens to the concept of citizens? Because then the national state becomes an illusion. Then the concept of citizenship becomes an illusion. But what is left? Subjects, beings? Because that relationship between state and citizen is gone. Is it just the formal legal kind of citizenship, or also a moral citizenship, that is not necessarily state bound?

Response by Kate Nash:
Well, I was kind of arguing in that direction. I can't stress enough how unusual the Make Poverty History campaign was. It created a kind of solidarity that we very rarely see; so it was absolutely exceptional. It would be wrong to say that democracy makes no difference now; it would be going too far to say that we have no control over how governments address citizens or non-citizens. But I think it's clearly a very difficult issue. Equally you might say, precisely then, if we are in this position now where our national citizenship gives us relatively little hold over fate, if you like. Then what happens to that notion of citizenship? This seems to be one of the things that is actually happening. This is not me recommending it, this is one of the things that is going on. People are looking at other forms for their political life. You could say that something is emerging precisely on that basis. The politicians very much manage it as well – politicians have to play to something. They have to have some stage to play on. So this global thinking also partly comes from the political arena.

Question from the audience:
I have a question about your critical remarks about the role of the private sector. You have said that they're focusing on reciprocity and trade, and not so much on human rights. But I would argue that, even you were saying that one of the necessities of global citizenship is considering others as your equals. I think when you act in a more trade-like context, they actually treat them as equals because they expect reciprocity. Considering this, don't you think that creating a middle class isn't always the way to improve human rights everywhere in the world?

Response by Kate Nash:
I am not an expert on trade and economics. But as a sociologist I am quite sure that the state is absolutely essential nevertheless, to distribute. The state is necessary to regulate and distribute. Equality

between people cannot only come from trade, I am sure about that. But I really don't know – 'trade or aid'.

Question from the audience:
I see two dimensions that also might be important in this discussion and I didn't hear them yet. One is the factor 'time'; so we are discussing mostly short-term problems and I think long-term problems are also quite important (e.g., sustainability of the world and our own nation). The other dimension is the connection between citizens, also within our nation – including on the spiritual level. Perhaps that is also a dimension on which we can connect easier with people outside of our nation. Maybe first we should work on these dimensions, within our nation.

Response by Kate Nash:
I am not sure whether you can work on sustainability within one nation, surely that is absolutely impossible. My understanding of economic and environmental sustainability is that you can't do it in one place. There are many things to be said about it. It seems to me that dialogue the other way around is very important. I think that populist politics is extremely difficult in questions of sustainability. It's a whole other set of questions I think. And in terms of the religious dimension, one of the things that comes out very much, also from this campaign itself, is that it was very much sustained by churches.

Closing comments by René Cuperus:
We would like to thank you for your very inspiring and rich lecture. I like your beautiful words 'indignation' and 'denunciation' – very important emotions for all kinds of emotional attachments to world problems. People's indignation about distant suffering can also be overplayed. These feelings can be very media-driven and temporary. We have to stretch a balance between real indignation and more media-driven indignation, which can be very hypocritical at times.

So how to enlarge our community of fate from nation states to a global level? That is the hundred-billion dollar question. And I tend to be rather sceptical: are we, as national democracies already communities of fate? To what extent are we that really? And is it not decreasing?

There is a final point I would like to make; there is a famous book by a German philosopher Rudi Safranski: 'How much globalisation can we bear?'. As you pointed out, we are confronted with distant suffering more than ever before because of the media capabilities. But, how many images can we bear? Do we have to respond to every incident of suffering – send in the troops? Libya, Iraq, Afghanistan... How much globalisation can we really bear?

PART II

Challenging Universality

The universalisation of human rights: reflections on obstacles and the way forward

Willem van Genugten[33]

State of the art: four warnings against simplistic answers

Reminder: what is the notion of human rights all about?

The history of human rights has many starting points, both in documents and in the writings of philosophical authors. In history, reference is often made to the *Magna Carta Libertatum* of 1215, the document with which the British King at that time responded to complaints about the abuse of power on his part. It states that "no freemen shall be taken or imprisoned or disseised or exiled or in any way destroyed, nor will we go upon him nor send upon him, except by the

---

33 Professor of International Law at Tilburg University and the North-West University, South-Africa (extra-ordinary chair). Chair of the standing Committee on Human Rights of the Dutch Advisory Council on International Affairs. Vice-chair of the Council. Former Professor of Human Rights at Nijmegen University (1991-2006). Some descriptive parts of this lecture are partly based on previous writings, updated where needed: Willem van Genugten, Kees Homan, Nico Schrijver and Paul de Waart. 2006. *The United Nations of the Future; Globalization with a Human Face*, Amsterdam: KIT Publishers (Chapter 3); Magdalena Sepulveda, Theo van Banning, Gudrún D. Gudmundsdóttir, Christine Chamoun and Willem van Genugten. 2010. *Human Rights Reference Handbook*, fifth edition, Costa Rica: University for Peace and Reykjavik: Islandic Human Rights Centre, passim; Willem van Genugten. 2010. 'Protection of Indigenous Peoples on the African Continent: Concepts, Position Seeking, and the Interaction of Legal Systems', *American Journal of International Law*, p. 29-65. Further to this, use is made of the 2008 advisory report on *Universality of Human Rights; Principles, Practice and Prospects* by the Advisory Council on International Affairs, prepared under the chairmanship of Prof. Kees Flinterman and this author, and the background study to that made by Dr. Cedric Ryngaert, Leuven and Utrecht University.

lawful judgment of his peers or by the law of the land" (Article 39). In short, this was a first indication of *the rule of law*. Philosophers such as John Locke (1632-1704), Jean-Jacques Rousseau (1712-1778) and Immanuel Kant (1724-1804), left an important mark on the ideas about human rights in the 18th and 19th centuries. Their writings, together with documents such as the French *Déclaration des Droits de l'Homme et du Citoyen* (1789) and the American *Declaration of Independence* (1776), served as a departure from the thinking up to that time, in which, to put it crudely, the people were there for those in power, rather than the other way round.

The first signs of the *international* protection of human rights date from a much later time, namely the late 19th century and the beginning of the 20th century. Reference can be made to the Brussels Conference of 1890, where a multilateral anti-slavery treaty was accepted and the Hague Peace Conferences of 1899 and 1907, where about fifteen conventions were drawn up in the field of the humanitarian aspects of waging war as well as international dispute settlement. At that time, the first treaties also appeared for the protection of national minorities, such as the 1878 Treaty of Berlin, in which the Balkan states such as Bulgaria, Montenegro, Serbia and Romania were required to observe freedom of religion for the Muslim minorities in Bulgaria and Montenegro and the Jewish minority in Serbia and Romania, if they were also to participate in the 'European Concert'. The Covenant on the League of Nations also contained a number of provisions relating to matters such as the achievement of human labour conditions (Article 23) and the protection of national minorities (in particular, Article 24, paragraph 1), although it did not actually amount to very much. The real breakthrough in the field of the international protection of human rights is linked to the establishment of the UN, founded on the rubble of WW-II.

It was partly because of the persistency of NGOs, such as the American Jewish Committee and the Carnegie Endowment for International Peace, that the UN Charter ultimately contained seven provisions that in one way or another related to human rights. One of these is Article 68, according to which the Economic and Social Council of the UN (ECOSOC) shall set up commissions for, amongst others, the protection of human rights. The Article serves as the legal basis for the Commission on Human Rights, later on replaced by the UN Human Rights Council. It was this Commission, established in 1946, that was responsible for the drafting of the Universal Declaration of Human Rights (UDHR, 1948). Despite the fact that some later developments, such as the threat to human rights as a result of large-scale environmental pollution, exhausting natural resources and combating terrorism, are not provided for in the UDHR, and that the notion of collective rights, such as the right to self-determination of peoples and (parts of) the right to development, are also of a later date, the UDHR can still be seen as the worldwide core document in the field of human rights, the 'mother' of all human rights instruments.

In the UDHR, the different human rights – civil and political, as well as economic, social and cultural – appear comfortably together, from the right not be tortured to the freedom of expression, from the right to seek asylum in other countries to the right to adequate food. The latter is, together with other basic needs, expressed in Article 25 of the UDHR:

> Everyone has the right to a standard of living adequate for the health
> and well-being of himself and his family, including food, clothing,
> housing and medical care and necessary social services, and the right to
> security in the event of unemployment, sickness, disability, widowhood,
> old age or other lack of livelihood in circumstances beyond his control.

According to Article 28 of the UDHR, everyone has a right to the existence of a social and international order in which the rights and freedoms set forth in the Declaration can be fully realised. This article clearly shows that human rights are not only concerned with the obligation of states to refrain from violations, but also with an obligation to provide support if people are not able to achieve human rights for themselves on their own strength. The Preamble to the Universal Declaration also refers to this when it speaks of the "inherent dignity and worth of the human person" and the task to fully realise this all over the world, as "a common standard of achievement for all peoples and all nations".

The UN protection of human rights is primarily covered by a series of international conventions in which these human rights are worked out in more detail, and a huge number of politically and quasi-legal oriented instruments, particularly the instruments that are these days available to the UN Human Rights Council. One can look at all these instruments in terms of a continuum, moving from soft law instruments, like views on specific human rights or elements thereof adopted by resolution by, for instance, the UN General Assembly, to binding international human rights law, and, within the latter grouping, the special category of peremptory standards of international human rights law *(ius cogens)*. As of now, the UN works with a catalogue of 17 Core International Human Rights Instruments – such as the international conventions on civil and political rights; economic, social and cultural rights; the rights of the child; the rights of migrant workers etc., and a range of protocols thereto, and more than 90 other Universal Human Rights Instruments, varying from a Declaration on the Rights of Mentally Retarded Persons and a Declaration on Social Progress and Development to the Statute of the International Criminal Court.

Note the broad scope of all this, and the high numbers of instruments; it is clear that one must be cautious when assuming universality of *the* human rights. It would be impossible to claim that all these documents/instruments do indeed reflect universally accepted norms as the UN labels suggest. Each of the instruments would deserve close scrutiny, before that statement could be made. *Consider this warning number one.*

Universality of human rights from a quasi-legal and a legal perspective

Dealing with the universality of human rights from a quasi-legal and a legal perspective is the easiest part of the story. The UDHR infers the notion of the universality of human rights in its name. And despite wanting to take their word for it, it remains important to be cautious with the word – even in relation to the Universal Declaration, because, amongst other good reasons, in 1948 the UN comprised only 58 states, eight of them abstaining from voting for various reasons, compared with 193 now. It was particularly during the 1950s and 1960s that many sovereign states were added, mainly as a result of the process of de-colonisation, and subsequently through more incidental events such as the disintegration of states like Yugoslavia and the Soviet Union.

The question of what the 134 new states would have contributed to the discussions on the UDHR in 1946-1948 and what they would have done in a vote on this is obviously hard to answer with absolute certainty. However, for many of them it is well known that they subsequently supported the UDHR, be it in various ways, especially while meeting at the two World Conferences on Human Rights, in Tehran (1968) and in Vienna (1993). In the document of the latter conference, the UN member states endorse sentences in which the UDHR is characterised as a "common standard of achievement" and a "source of inspiration", even though it was also determined that the "significance of national and regional particularities and various historical, cultural and religious backgrounds must be borne in mind". In a September 2005 core document, adopted by the UN General Assembly at the occasion of the 60th anniversary of the UN, the words of 1993 were repeated:

> We reaffirm that all human rights are universal, indivisible, interrelated, interdependent and mutually reinforcing and that all human rights must be treated in a fair and equal manner, on the same footing and with the same emphasis. While the significance of national and regional particularities and various historical, cultural and religious backgrounds must be borne in mind, all States, regardless of their political, economic and cultural systems, have the duty to promote and protect all human rights and fundamental freedoms.

Commenting upon similar words, used in successive UN documents, the Dutch Advisory Council on International Affairs stated twelve years ago that "universality is not uniformity".[34] This refers to the "margin of appreciation", which states do have with regard to the achievement of human rights. There is an inherent tension in the wording of the 2005 document, but on a positive note, it repeats, in line with numerous other documents, the indivisibility and inter-relatedness of all human rights; it underlines the notion that they are mutually reinforcing each other; it restates the significance of national and regional particularities and various historical, cultural and religious backgrounds; and it emphasises that all states have to

---

34 Advisory Council on International Affairs, *Universality of Human Rights and Cultural Diversity*, The Hague, June 1998, p. 14-16.

live up to all human rights, "regardless of their political, economic and cultural systems".

But, what about the interaction between these four notions? What does it mean for daily international practice that states have to "bear in mind" the significance of national and regional particularities and various historical, cultural and religious backgrounds when discussing human rights practices? Most would be willing to believe that the 1993 and the 2005 documents can be seen as progress, because, as former US President Jimmy Carter once noted, "in the life of the human spirit words are action"; but one cannot easily hold that such a typical UN consensus formula solves the problem of universality, not in the field of the norms, let alone in the field of practice. *Let this be warning number two.*

Standards and outside interference

Besides the warning against easy answers, it is of course imperative to keep in mind that, in approximately 65 years of legal development of modern human rights law, a lot has been accomplished as well. One can easily think of the UN human rights treaty system, the Universal Periodic Review as conducted by the UN Human Rights Council, etc., but also of the human rights conventions adopted by the International Labour Organisation, on issues such as forced and child labour. Some of these conventions are even older than 65 years, and, while updated in some cases, are still very much alive and kicking.

Linking all that to the discussion on universality and/or non-uniformity, the starting point (terminal station or borderline) should time and again be that there is a series of human rights that have to be observed in any case, whether states want to or not (thus bypassing the "consent to be bound", the traditional fundament of international law). These are the rights that John Locke would have described as (pre-state) "natural rights", and of which Jean-Jacques Rousseau would have said that people would have included them without hesitation in their "social contract". Examples are the prohibition on torture, the freedom of expression and religion, but also, for example and most likely, seen in the light of later developments, the right to food or maybe the right to (clean) water, being a right indispensable to the realisation of many other rights, such as the right to life. In human rights doctrine and conventions, some of these rights are referred to nowadays, in line with Locke's notion of 'natural rights', as 'non-derogable'; *i.e.*, rights which may not be deviated from, even in times of emergency.

Apart from thus identifying some rights as being more important than other rights, my starting point (terminal station or borderline), would also be that in principle all internationally recognised human rights are universal rights, *unless* states can argue on good grounds that an exception to the rule is desirable or acceptable in their situation. A traditional case concerns the prohibition on torture and the case of the ticking bomb: is it permissible to exercise serious physical pressure on persons deemed to know about a threat of an attack? States have regularly appealed and still do appeal to these types of cases to make exceptions to rules, sometimes even leading to the internal legal recognition that such physical pressure is permissible. We all know the position of the previous legal advisor to the US government on such issues as water boarding. The core approach in human rights doctrine to these issues is that states in such cases should be prepared to have their conduct assessed by, in this particular issue, the UN Committee against Torture or, if they are not a party to the relevant UN convention, should apply the findings of the Committee analogously. By adopting this approach, states which have negotiated an 'elastic relationship' to certain human rights for themselves are in a defensive position, knowing that in the last instance they are not the ones who can judge the room they created for themselves.

But part of the problem is, of course, that many states are not willing to accept external control by bodies of independent experts. Even the Netherlands is not amused by external criticisms, or when it is overruled by international supervisory bodies such as the European Court of Human Rights, in which, according to its Constitution, international law plays a primary role and, in which, people under its jurisdiction are allowed to file complaints before international and European supervisory bodies in cases of alleged human rights violations. A significant proportion of the member states of the UN are not party to any human rights conventions at all, while, furthermore, far too few states have the courage to also become party to those (parts of the) conventions and/or protocols thereto which provide for rights to complain (giving individuals – and sometimes others – international *locus standi*), and which would give the ratification acts a serious extra dimension. See it as extra (quasi-)legal teeth, alongside the periodical reporting obligations and the like. But as said, many states are rarely willing to accept outside criticism, let alone criticism by independent experts. Further to that, many of them even protest if a peer review as developed by, for instance, the UN Human Rights Council comes too close. (Just think of the Universal Periodic Review, within which three states 'have a look' at the human rights practice of another UN member, followed by comments/recommendations by the Council as a whole.) *Let that be warning number three.*

National vs. international

Apart from this, it has to be noted that even if states are party to conventions and formally have to accept judgments and views of international supervisory bodies – letting aside here some weaknesses of the UN and regional supervisory mechanisms as such – they (often) do have a "margin of appreciation" (again: universality is not necessarily uniformity). For instance, the right to fair trial is undoubtedly one of the universal human rights, but the paths to it may be very different. By way of extremes, one can observe states with a complete absence of an independent judiciary, and states that actually have a very sophisticated legal system developed over many years. For both, the right to a fair trial is a "common standard of achievement", something they have to realise and live up to, but the roads leading to it are clearly different. As to the margin of appreciation notion, it can be added more in general that some states are very young and have many other concerns, in addition to strictly human rights concerns, while other states are trying to put an end to a left-wing or right-wing dictatorial past and cannot do so from one day to the next. Other states again have intrinsically political tensions that are at loggerheads with a number of fundamental ideas behind human rights. For example, in Islamic states, religion and state power are extensions of each other. Nevertheless, these states are expected to commit to freedom of religion, the core question being to my mind how tolerant they are towards other religions and to what extent they try to restrain their Muslim citizens from taking action against other (non-)believers. In such a case, the slogan that universality does not imply uniformity still applies, but also reaches its limits; it is no longer a matter of actively striving to achieve the higher goal, which in this case is the full recognition of the freedom of religion, but of effectively removing the sharp edges of a government policy aimed at privileging a particular religion. This is as relevant in today's world, as it has ever been.

So, while it would be great to separate discussions on human practices from all kinds of discussions on political, religious, economic issues, the reality is that they often *are* linked, desirable or not. In an ideal world, discussions on human rights issues should maybe be above daily politics, but the fact is that they are often part of it, and that is doesn't make sense to pretend otherwise. It would lead to blueprints made at desks and disconnected to outdoor, hard realities.

That reality encapsulates the fact that states do a lot of window-dressing in the field of human rights, by inserting human rights standards in constitutions and by ratifying human rights conventions while adding numerous reservations and understandings, often on very a fundamental level, even against the "object and purpose" of the relevant convention (as the Vienna Convention on the Law of Treaties orders to avoid). A case in point is the ratification of human rights conventions by Islamic states, which often insist that the conventions should not contravene Sharia-law. One can think of the position of women. Some Muslim states, for instance, have added interpretative declarations and reservations to their ratification of the Convention on the Elimination of Discrimination against Women. An example is the perceived incompatibility of the Sharia with Article 16 of CEDAW, which requires that states "take all appropriate measures to eliminate discrimination against women in all matters relating to marriage and family relations". The number of states that have entered reservations to Article 16, in whole or in part, is so high that the CEDAW Committee has voiced its serious concern.

Other examples of links between human rights debates and political systems, relate to communist-driven systems; think of weighing the (collective) general interest versus the rights of the individual.

Further to all this, it should be kept in mind that sovereign states tend to have a central government, which is not always (fully) in charge as far as international legal affairs is concerned. One can think of either states like Nigeria with its complex structure of ethnic communities or a state like the USA with its federal composition and its complex relation to international legal obligations, as has become clear again in the *Avena* case before the International Court of Justice, concerning the application of international (human rights) law in the state of Texas.[35] *Consider this warning number four.*

So, four warnings against easy answers in response to the universality of human rights. In sum: 1) the huge variety and number of human rights; 2) legal and quasi-legal answers not being as convincing as they look; 3) states urged to accept human rights terminology ('standards') but hesitant, to say the least, towards outside interference (implementation *vs.* supervision); 4) frictions between international legal obligations and national (constitutional) legal characteristics.

The 1948 UDHR words are extremely relevant and well-chosen; in the course of time only a few basic concepts and issues have been added. One can argue that 65 years later: 1) states that violate human rights are, overall, in a more defensive position than in the late 1940s – in that period the *raison d'état* and its complement (the right to violate rights in order to survive as a state) had a much broader content than is the case these days (consider for instance the Pinochet case or the Statute of the International Criminal Court); 2) the UN and a range of regional organisations have developed a variety of human rights protective mechanisms; 3) we are better equipped to differentiate between parts of the debate purely belonging to the political domain and those issues that can be conducted in terms of interests transcending the level of state sovereignty.

---

35 See my: "*Avena* as a Challenge to The Federal American Legal System", *The Hague Justice Portal*, December 2008 (also in French: "Avena ou le système juridique fédéral américain à l'épreuve").

The way forward

Let's start again with the UDHR's "common standard of achievement". The UDHR formulates the destination, as well as, to a large extent, mankind's destiny, and leaves the reader with the core question of how to reach the terminal station (or as close as possible). One can also easily observe that this is a long, never-ending way to go. But one should nevertheless not speak of stagnation; this would suggest the possibility of making a factual comparison between the late 1940s and the beginning of the new Millennium, which is in fact not possible, at least not in a methodologically solid way. For instance: how about weighing poverty and environmental degradation in human rights terms? How about measuring the effects of the use of technologically advanced weapons upon human rights? How about comparing the human rights effects of interstate wars to such effects caused by civil wars? And on another level: how about dealing with the fact that due to the Internet, etc., we now know much more than we did 65 years ago?

The issue of 'the way forward' is central to the 2008 Universality of Human Rights report, by the Advisory Council on International Affairs. The core word in the report is without a doubt 'universalisation' – it strongly emphasises the notion that reaching a sound human rights practice first of all asks for a process-like approach, instead of (or alongside) one in which states are told that human rights *are* universal and that it is *simply* up to them to fulfil their obligations. In 65 years it has become clear that the latter approach is sometimes fruitful, but also has obvious shortcomings. This was and is, in general and in a non-enumerative way, the case during/within the Cold War and its after-thoughts and effects; the (partly ended as well as within the remnants of the) period of Latin-American authoritarian regimes; the ever existing phenomenon of fragile states; the divide in levels of development between states, not necessarily North-South, with poverty as its central characteristic, but also in relation to the level of maturity of political and legal institutions; the growing self-confidence of the BRICS-states; the Islam/non-Islam split.

In the words of the Advisory Council, 'universalisation' can reduce the gap between principles and practice, while it covers a number of separate actions and processes that should take place within a given cultural, religious, social and political context. The Council mentions: a) Increasing knowledge and awareness of human rights, in governmental and non-governmental circles, and among the different ethnicities (for example indigenous peoples and national minorities and their leaders) of which States are composed; b) popular acceptance of human rights as a relevant way of looking at certain issues; c) the implementation and legal enforcement of human rights norms; d) their mobilisation in addressing social concerns; and e) the actual realisation of human rights by all economic, political and legal means [*i.e.*, not by legal means only]. The Council adds: "When it comes to knowledge and awareness of human rights, for instance, attention can be drawn to the importance of human rights education (both in schools and through, for instance, radio and television programmes) and of translating information on rights into the language(s) of the country concerned. The existence of a general knowledge of legal rights and procedures among the population also creates an enabling environment for increasing awareness of human rights". And where the acceptance of rights claims is concerned "policies can focus on searching for and underlining the commonalities between human rights principles and those in the dominant cultural traditions of the country concerned", while "with respect to the implementation and legal enforcement of human rights norms, the relevant issues include the role of domestic constitutional and administrative law, the independence of the judiciary, and access to justice. The mobilisation process depends on the willingness and the ability of both lawyers and NGOs to 'frame' concerns in terms of rights violations."

This is a bottom-up approach, which in the end focuses upon exactly the same outcome as the external, top-down approach: holding those who are politically and legally responsible for upholding human rights, and who are often in a position to progressively realise them, responsible for their wrongdoings, confront them with their human rights obligations and show them a way forward. It might sound soft in the ears of some, especially those who believe that social behaviour can be changed by force, but the Advisory Council builds on the notion that there is no alternative if one wants to reach sustainable steps. In the words of the Council, "the universalisation of rights feeds into their acceptance as universal, and the other way around".

The relevance and risks of taking cultural contexts into consideration

In discussing the way forward, the Council also observes that as a result of the trickle-down effect of international human rights law in national legal systems, cultural exceptions are in practice put forward only to a limited degree. And when they are, they are mainly voiced by local communities (as opposed to the state that has ratified the relevant human rights instrument), or by states if they serve the interests of the political or religious establishment. It is often more a matter of internal legal orders, than of states willing to use the terminology of 'cultural exceptions', at least as long as it concerns discussions about human rights practices within the context of international treaty law. But even in political debates they are heard less than about twenty years ago.

The Advisory Council observes that many African states no longer support harmful traditional practices such as female genital mutilation/circumcision, domestic violence and child marriage – at least not on the official, international level. This is in line with the relevant human rights instruments, such as the Convention on the Elimination of All Forms of Discrimination against Women (CEDAW) and the Convention on the Rights of the Child (CRC). Further to this, these practices have also been explicitly banned by pan-African conventions. For example, the recent Protocol to the African Charter on Human and Peoples' Rights on the Rights of Women in Africa provides that the states party to the Protocol "shall prohibit and condemn all forms of harmful practices which negatively affect the human rights of women and which are contrary to recognized international standards" (Article 5).

But what about reality at the lower, non-official levels? It is interesting to look at these issues from the perspective of interacting legal orders (see the 'fourth warning') and make that a productive rather than a blocking argument. To begin with, and remaining in the African continent, one could look at, for instance, Article 27 (1) of the African Charter on Human and Peoples' Rights: "Every individual shall have duties towards his family and society, the State and other legally recognised communities and the international community"; individuals thus belong to a variety of circles, each of them with their own rules. One can also look at a range of African constitutions, such as the Chapter on Traditional Leaders of the 1996 South-African Constitution, Article 211:

1. The institution, status and role of traditional leadership, according to customary law, are recognised, subject to the Constitution.
2. A traditional authority that observes a system of customary law may function subject to any applicable legislation and customs, which includes amendments to, or repeal of, that legislation or those customs.
3. The courts must apply customary law when that law is applicable, subject to the Constitution and any legislation that specifically deals with customary law.[36]

Such articles can be judged in many ways. The positive connotation relates to the importance of, at the end, doing a tailor-made job, in order to create support at the grassroots level for all kinds of important measures. The other, negative way of reading them, however, is emphasising the danger that powerful traditional leaders would in no way respect the (individual human) rights of 'their' people. Suppose the traditional leaders are forbidding 'their subordinates' to enjoy internationally and constitutionally recognised human rights, such as the right to freedom of expression (e.g., criticising the leader for his lavish lifestyle), or the right to be free from discrimination (e.g., in the context of customary succession laws); what happens then?

The South-African legal system, for example, is clear on this. The 1996 South-African Constitution contains a Bill of Rights (Articles 7-39) related to a huge variety of civil, cultural, economic, political and social rights, including "the rights to have [one's] dignity respected and protected" (Article 10) and "the right to fair labour

---

36 Note that the 1996 Convention speaks of "customary law" while its 1993 (interim) predecessor still spoke of "indigenous law". Customary law, however, is meant to include indigenous law, thereby avoiding the need to identify which traditional communities are indigenous and which are not.

practices" (Article 23 (1)). And while it also says that the South African Courts "must apply customary law when that law is applicable..." (Article 211 (3)), the Constitution is clear on 'the order of things': "The Bill of Rights does not deny the existence of any other rights or freedoms that are recognised or conferred by common law, customary law or legislation, *to the extent that they are consistent with the Bill*" (Article 39 (3), Italics added). That sounds clear and not open to many interpretations. In practice, however, the South-African Constitutional Court is struggling with, and therefore elaborating upon and contributing to, a better understanding of the issue of the relation between international, national and indigenous law. Two particular issues, of a diverging nature, are relevant for many other African and non-African states.

The *first* relates to the need to interpret indigenous law 'as it is'. The South African Constitutional Court time and again underlines that indigenous/customary law "should be accommodated, not merely tolerated".[37] In the eyes of the Court, this means that South African indigenous/customary law must be interpreted according to its own meaning and in its own context and setting. So, according to the South African Constitutional Court, it must be recognised "that customary law places much store in consensus-seeking" and "naturally provides for family and clan meetings which offer excellent opportunities for the prevention and resolution of disputes and disagreements", while furthermore, "they provide a setting which contributes to the unity of family structures and the fostering of co-operation, a sense of responsibility in and of belonging to its members, as well as the nurturing of healthy communitarian traditions such as *ubuntu*. These valuable aspects of customary law more than

---

37 All quotes taken from the Judgment of 15 October 2004 as to the combined cases CCT 49/03, Nonkululeko Letta Bhe, the Women's Legal Centre Trust et al. vs. Magistrate Khayelitsha, the President of the Republic of South Africa, the Minister for Justice and Constitutional Development et al.; CCT 69/03, Charlotte Shibi vs. Mantabeni Freddy Sithole, the Minister for Justice and Constitutional Development et al.; and CCT 50/03, South African Human Rights Commission and Women's Legal Centre Trust vs. the President of the Republic of South Africa, the Minister for Justice and Constitutional Development et al.

justify its protection by the Constitution." The concept of *ubuntu* – literally, "a person is a person through other people" – is said by the Constitutional Court to be a dominant value in African traditional culture, encapsulating communality and the interdependence of the members of a community. It is a culture which "regulates the exercise of rights by the emphasis it lays on sharing and co-responsibility and the mutual enjoyment of rights".[38] According to one judge "it is this system of reciprocal duties and obligations that ensured that every family member had access to basic necessities of life such as food, clothing, shelter and healthcare", while according to him and the ten other Judges of the Court "as with all law, the constitutional validity of rules and principles of customary law depend on their consistency with the Constitution and the Bill of Rights", thus linking their view of traditional legal issues to the Constitution and its emphasis on the priority of international (human rights) law.

In another Judgment,[39] the South African Constitutional Court further elaborates upon the need to keep in mind the specific characteristics and values of traditional legal systems. According to the Court, "cultural identity is one of the most important parts of a person's identity precisely because it flows from belonging to a community and not from personal choice or achievement", and "belonging involves more than simple association; it includes participation and expression of the community's practices and traditions, hence

---

38 In more detail, as worded in a partially dissenting judgment by Judge Ngcobo, added to the 2004 Judgment: "*Ubuntu* (...), expresses itself in *umuntu ngumuntu ngabantu*, describing the significance of group solidarity on survival issues so central to the survival of communities. While it envelops the key values of group solidarity, compassion, respect, human dignity, conformity to basic norms and collective unity, in its fundamental sense it denotes humanity and morality. Its spirit emphasises respect for human dignity, marking a shift from confrontation to conciliation. (...) the need for *ubuntu* expresses the ethos of an instinctive capacity for and enjoyment of love towards our fellow men and women; the joy and the fulfilment involved in recognizing their innate humanity; the reciprocity this generates in interaction within the collective community; the richness of the creative emotions which it engenders and the moral energies which it releases both in the givers and the society which they serve and are served by."

39 Judgment of 5 October 2007, in the case CCT 51/06, MEC for Education: Kwazulu-Natal, Thulani Cele: School Liaison Officer et al. vs. Navaneethum Pillay.

to human dignity", and "dignity and identity are inseparably linked as one's sense of self-worth is defined by one's identity". It is further observed by the Court that "the protection of voluntary as well as obligatory practices also conforms to the Constitution's commitment to affirming diversity" and that "differentiating between mandatory and voluntary practices does not celebrate or affirm diversity, it simply permits it". Furthermore, the Court observes that "South Africans come in all shapes and sizes" and that "the development of an active rather than a purely formal sense of enjoying a common citizenship depends on recognising and accepting people with all their differences, as they are". This sounds correct, but at the same time it should not be romanticised, to not even mention the problems many communities, and especially the vulnerable people within them, are confronted with. And what about the individual rights of those who do not want to be 'locked in' in the collective, community-driven aspirations of the chief or other head(s) of the community, while they are not willing or in a position to leave that community?

The *second* issue in relation to customary, indigenous law is the notion of living indigenous law. For example, the 2004 South African Constitutional Court case related to the rule of primogeniture (the rights of the first-born) in indigenous South African law. In the words of the Court, the general rule is "that only a male who is related to the deceased qualifies as intestate heir", meaning that "in a monogamous family, the eldest son of the family head is his heir. If the deceased is not survived by any male descendants, his father succeeds him. If his father also does not survive him, an heir is sought among the father's male descendants related to him through the male line." And, "The exclusion of women from heirship and consequently from being able to inherit property was in keeping with a system dominated by a deeply embedded patriarchy which reserved for women a position of subservience and subordination and in which they were regarded as perpetual minors under the tutelage of the fathers, husbands, or the head of the extended family."

In discussing such issues, the South-African Constitutional Court also notes, however, that "indigenous law is not a fixed body of formally classified and easily ascertainable rules" and that "by its very nature it evolves as the people who live by its norms change their patterns of life." What needs to be emphasised, according to the Court, is that "because of the dynamic nature of society, official customary law as it exists in the text books and in the Act is generally a poor reflection, if not a distortion of the true customary law. True customary law will be that which recognises and acknowledges the changes which continually take place". Therefore, according to the Court, "a critical issue in any constitutional litigation about customary law will be the question whether a particular rule is a mythical stereotype, which has become ossified in the official code, or whether it continues to enjoy social currency." The issue then of course is that some have an interest in keeping the law the way it is, while others are 'knocking on the door', often inspired by human rights based words and concepts.

In addition, the Court observes that "the difficulty lies not so much in the acceptance of the notion of 'living' customary law, as distinct from official customary law, but in determining its content and testing it, as the Court should, against the provisions of the Bill of Rights". That brings us again into the domain of international human rights law, in this case concerning the non-discrimination of women. In the concluding words of a partly dissenting judge: "With human dignity as the lodestar, it becomes clear that treating people as worthy of equal respect in relation to their cultural practices requires more than mere tolerance of sincerely held beliefs with regard to cultural practices". Nuanced and correct, it is clearly a way forward towards introducing a core concept of international human rights law (non-discrimination) into a local legal domain.

In doing so, the Court also deals with the classical issue of duties of the individual *vis-à-vis* the community. Unlike the UN human rights conventions, the African Charter on Human and Peoples' Rights, for example, includes a chapter on the duties of the individual, duties owed not only to the state, but also to the family, to society, etc. (see above). It goes without saying that in carrying out these duties respect for the rights of the individual as defined by international human rights instruments should not be compromised, and the South-African cases-law provides for a way of cautiously and carefully dealing with the sensitive part of that issue, in the end giving priority to individual rights if the individuals wish so.

The South-African examples finally make clear, again, that the discussions about the universality of human rights not only occur in, let's say, the context of states and international law, but also, and even sometimes more, *within* separate sovereign states. That is something which is often forgotten, mainly because in traditional international law the focus is upon state responsibility, in a way in which states are responsible for whatever internal affairs, and because there might be an overestimation of what central governments might be willing or able to do. This is not to say that they should *not* be addressed; on the contrary. It asks, however, for much more pinpointed action.

That issue is complicated by, as well as finds fruitful ground in, the fact that many peoples worldwide claim the right to self-determination, *i.e.*, the right to mind their own business; in most cases internally (forms of autonomy), sometimes externally (secession). The right to self-determination is a right of which the International Court of Justice has stated that it is to be seen as a right *erga omnes*, while it is generally considered to belong to the abovementioned category of peremptory standards of international law *(ius cogens)*. The subjects of the right are not the states, but the manifold peoples within their borders. Keep in mind that as of now, the UN is composed of 192 sovereign member states, together containing some 5000 peoples/communities. The South-African case-law, for instance, makes clear that the right to self-determination is often invoked, but can also be limited as soon as the way it is executed conflicts with individual human rights claims. In this respect, the South-African system is one of the most progressive ones on the African continent, and it might help setting the stage for other states as well.

Outside the African continent, it can be observed that especially Asian states have been, and sometimes still are, challenging the universality of human rights, although even there the terminology has changed compared to about twenty years ago. Some Asian states have been using the concept of 'Asian values', especially in the early 1990s, in response to the more forceful export of 'Western ideas' that followed the end of the Cold War.[40] Singapore and Malaysia were

---

40 This section, taken from the 2008 report by the Advisory Council on International Affairs, is based upon work undertaken by Byung Sook de Vries, Ph. D. student at Tilburg University.

by then and sometimes still are the main proponents of these values, though other Asian states, such as China, Japan, South-Korea, Indonesia and India, have largely adopted the same stance. In their view, 'Asian values' stem from sources that include Taoism and Confucianism, the latter taking a different view of morality than the rights-based morality of human rights. It is more virtue-based and centres not on being an individual holder of rights, but on becoming 'a person of excellence' – a concept in which modesty plays a significant role – and on living in harmony with other members of the community. Writers trying to formulate 'Asian values' that are valid throughout Asia focus on the following: respect for hierarchy and authority; the primacy of the family and social consensus over conflict; the higher priority given to law, social order, and security than to individual civil and political rights, in the interests of economic and social development; the precedence of communal welfare over individual human rights; and an emphasis on self-discipline. Further to that, the Association of Southeast Asian Nations (ASEAN) is now tentatively exploring ways of developing a human rights system that combines compliance with international human rights standards and cooperation with international human rights mechanisms on the one hand, and respect for 'Asian values' on the other.

Here again it is important to keep in mind the dynamic nature of cultures, which as to the Asian world can be illustrated with examples such as the eradication of foot binding in China and of widow burning in India. In both cases, as the Advisory Council of International Affairs observes, the involvement of people indigenous to the cultures in question proved vital in framing the campaign leading to eradication within the appropriate cultural context. Those in favour of the practices were engaged in discussions and the justifications put forward for these practices proved not to be insurmountable, regardless of whether they were based on religion, tradition, marriageability or beauty.

The examples show a way forward, again working with the notions of 'universalisation' and 'processes', taking time aspects and the changeability of views into consideration, and inspiring the discussants with universal human rights terminology. Having said that, the basic thing is, of course, to open up societies for new, in this case, human rights inspired views. Freedom of expression, information and communication, the right to education, the right to political participation, and concepts such as tailor-made access to justice, may allow cultures to change from within. This is, by and large, a chicken-and-egg situation, in relation to which the previously discussed top-down approach can definitely play a role, alongside the bottom-up one expressed here. Both can help to break that vicious circle, in an interaction to be chosen from case to case.

To conclude

Human rights have come a long way, and are often seen as one of *the* success stories in the field of international law and international relations since WWII. Despite all controversies on a conceptual and practical level and despite the need to operate in a way that combines ideals to multiple senses of reality, there is no doubt that we are in the midst of processes of constitutionalisation and humanisation of the international economic and political order, with human rights values leading the way.

The core word is 'universalisation', constantly looking for a process approach with an open eye for obstacles. Making human rights universal, means to contextualise within the margins set at the international level, with a special emphasis on peremptory standards of international human rights law, and with the use of all available instruments where possible and indicated, from silent diplomacy to assessments by international supervisory bodies, and whatever other action that might have a realistic chance to be successful. That might include actions such as 'country resolutions' adopted by the UN Human Rights Council or even economic sanctions, although such approaches rarely lead to durable solutions. The latter relates to the fact that they are coercive and often top-down only. The alternative is adding a bottom-up approach, as presented here, and to fundamentally reconsider the effectiveness of the mechanisms used so far.

In such lines of action, there is a huge role for the civil society (NGOs, local leaders, companies, trade unions), in order to make the message tailor-made and (more) likely to be effective in the long run. Such civil society actions should not be conducted by representatives with legal training only, but also by people with a background in, for instance, anthropology, history, political science, theology and economics. This is vital, in order to make the discussions start from the right assumptions *and* to guarantee that the actions are contextualised as much as possible, and thus have a better chance to change the daily lives of people all over the world.

Summary

In the 65 years or so since the Universal Declaration of Human Rights was adopted in 1948, there have been many legal developments in modern human rights law resulting in the emergence of, among other things, the UN human rights treaty system and the Universal Periodic Review process conducted by the Human Rights Council. As a result of these accomplishments, human rights are often seen as one of the success stories in the field of international law and international relations since WWII. When the Universal Declaration of Human Rights was drafted, it was by and large seen as a self-evident framework for managing the relationship between state, individuals (and communities), the core goal of the Declaration being the wish to express what 'human dignity' is all about. Nowadays though, many political systems around the world are – either still or again – presenting a different view of human rights, including setting totally different priorities in the broad field covered these days by the term 'human rights'.

Van Genugten issued four warnings concerning the supposed universality of human rights: (1) The sheer numbers of UN human rights conventions and other human rights instruments, adopted since 1948, are as such not decisive to state that *the* human rights are universally applicable. Each of the instruments deserves close scrutiny, before that statement can be made. (2) universality is not uniformity – within the frameworks set states have space to 'do it their own way'; in addition, the (quasi-) legal input of states in a variety of debates is often not as clear cut and convincing as it looks at first sight; (3) many states are urged to accept human rights terminology ('standards') but are not willing to accept external control and criticism by external bodies or independent experts; (4) there are frictions between international legal obligations and national (constitutional) legal characteristics of states.

With these four warnings in mind, Van Genugten addressed 'the way forward': we should aim for a process-like approach. The buzz-word should be 'universalisation' rather than 'universality' ('human rights *are* universal'). A bottom-up approach is needed to confront those who are politically and legally responsible for upholding human rights with their obligations and to show them a way forward. It is important to include here perceptions of local communities, as cultural exceptions are mainly voiced by local communities as opposed to states that have ratified human rights instruments. Thus, the discussions on the universality of human rights occur not only between states and international law, but especially also within sovereign states, between national governments and local communities who may practice certain cultural rituals which conflict with universal human rights norms. All that has to be – and can be – done without falling into the trap of cultural relativism. Civil society organisations can play an important role in communicating these local perceptions and in contextualising some of these international human rights norms.

Discussion

Question by moderator Lars van Troost (Amnesty International):
Is there truly agreement about the destination and where we want to go to with Human Rights? And should Human Rights be the basic universal norms at any time?

Response by Willem van Genugten:
I believe there is a worldwide consensus on what is called the 'per-emptory standards'; standards on torture, genocide, racial discrimi-nation, and the like. Apart from that, many human rights are recog-nised, but take care: sometimes only the core words are accepted, not the way they are elaborated upon by supervisory bodies. In addition, still many states are not a party to relevant conventions, or made numerous reservations while ratifying them. So, there are many ele-ments of rights left that are essentially not yet accepted worldwide. These cases require negotiations or (quasi)legal decision-making to reach further consensus, agreement, real support. Just because docu-ments *say* a norm is universal, that doesn't mean it actually *is*. It is

also essential to consider local communities at the grassroots level; discussions at this level can decisively contribute to the building of a coherent approach and of meaningful and sustainable support.

Question by Lars van Troost:

So you would say at this moment, the only real universal norms we have are the peremptory norms, because that is quite a difference? Those are only eight or nine norms if compared to nearly 90 Human Rights documents that the UN is talking about and that you referred to in the beginning of your speech.

Response by Willem van Genugten:

First I would make a difference between the instruments as such and the manifold norms incorporated into them. Apart from that, it is important to underline again that the core of many norms is accepted, at least on paper, but not for instance the way the norms have been refined by UN supervisory bodies. Let me take the example of the right to a fair trial. Most countries in the world agree that this right should be granted – but the discussion nevertheless continues about what exactly a 'fair trial' is. We may worldwide agree on certain aspects of it, but by far not all. So all elements must be identified and defined before we will find a meaningful consensus amongst states.

In the end you are right, if we want to know what is *really* accepted universally by states, without any hesitation, then the answer is: not that much yet. In many cases it is a case of 'keep working towards further acceptance'.

Question by Lars van Troost:

What does that then mean for international committees, such as the Human Rights committee when it has to decide on concrete cases and it has to work from the conventions?

Response by Willem van Genugten:

We should keep in mind that we do have international treaty law alongside political bodies. If a state becomes party to a treaty, that state is bound by treaty law and, in principle, by the views and 'General Comments' of the relevant committees. If a state decides to become a party to, for instance, the treaties on women's rights, the rights of the child or the rights of migrant workers, then that state basically agrees to accept the authority of the relevant supervisory bodies, some controversies left aside here.

On the other hand, we have the United Nations Human Rights Council as a political and peer review body. Some of the standards that the Council can base itself on are globally accepted, there is a consensus. But, many cases involve discussion, as no consensus exists, be it not on the standards as such then on the way in which they are and should be implemented in policy documents and practiced on the ground. Also the wish to fully except the outcome of the Universal Periodic Review varies enormously amongst states. So in the political field, the disagreement is overall much stronger than in the treaty field. And luckily enough, on average about 150 or 160 of the 193 UN member states are party to the relevant treaties. They are by and large bound by these committees of independent experts. At that point you can also escape to a great extent the discussion on universality, because it is up to committees to say what they think.

Question by Lars van Troost:
But is there no growing reluctance to be bound to international treaties?

Response by Willem van Genugten:
First of all, I would say that States are still making too many reservations while ratifying treaties, thus trying to escape the fact the treaties might really change something in their internal legal order. Apart from that, it can be observed that States are in general complying with the order to provide their periodical reports, albeit often with some delays of a few years – but too many of them do not offer the option of access to individual complaint procedures, which is overall a real tool for international scrutiny.

Question from the audience:
Will it be possible in the future for common values and divided norms to be accepted in the world?

Response by Willem van Genugten:

In the first place, lest we forget, there are many norms that are more or less accepted globally: such as the ban on forced or child labour, to mention a few other examples in addition to the ones I mentioned before. The list may not be as short as we sometimes think. But again: support for the freedom of speech, for instance, on paper is a) not similar to full acceptance of the 'sub-norms' attached to it, nor b) necessarily equal to practicing the norms, to say it euphemistically.

Then, what I wanted to warn against in my lecture is that often the debate on the universality of human rights is conducted far too easily. We pretend at times that we can find the definition of 'universality' in a law textbook, and then act surprised when we realise how much discussion is still ongoing in so many countries.

I also underlined that the words as such do matter, but, more importantly, that we have to focus on the process of universalisation: how can we go about changing practices in the end? This is the role of politicians and NGOs, silent diplomacy or applying sanctions, companies, lawyers, anthropologists, theologians, etc. In my lecture I touched upon local communities: it is important to explore what local communities – leaders as well as members – think and do, to understand their ways, their wishes, their motives; to ask the individuals belonging to these ethnic communities to what extent, and in which ways, international human rights might be different from their local habits and rules. Successively, they can be challenged to bring legal cases to local, regional and national courts in order to, step after step, develop a route that makes indigenous or other forms of 'traditional law' conform with international human rights law, while not forgetting the richness of such traditional laws as well.

In the meantime we still of course have issues that cannot be ignored anyhow; cases that demand immediate action. We have many examples, but if it is about structurally changing things, this is to my mind the one and only way to do it.

Question from the audience:

What do you think about the possible tension between economic development and human rights?

Response by Willem van Genugten:

The shortest answer might be that it makes sense to reformulate prosperity words into human right terminology. Prosperity then might be defined as the right of food and good healthcare and the right to live a life worthy of human beings – and then we come close to human rights terminology. This is the easy answer and you will likely not be satisfied by that, but prosperity is not confined to the field of economics – it can also be used in the context of human rights law.

But this is an interesting and relevant question, because time and again many states justify the violation of human rights by claiming a lack of development. They blame their underdevelopment for their inability to live up to human rights demands. But human rights do not only concern the freedom of religion, freedom of expression or access to justice; they also refer to food, shelter, healthcare and so forth. When states do not have the prosperity to provide for the second category, they tend to neglect the first as well. Luckily there are many less developed states, such as some African ones, that are still trying to do their very best to live up to specific human rights standards, despite their poverty levels.

Another issue is that if a state is communist-driven it is definitely not going to be willing to give priority to civil liberties above economic development. Examples are Cuba, China, and North-Korea. It is their top-down, state-driven view upon individual rights that prevents them from giving civilians access to human rights terminology.

All in all, I would say, economic development is in most cases good for human rights – but, a lack of it is often used as an excuse to not even try.

Question from the audience:

How do you make sure that global values are being applied at a micro level?

Response by Willem van Genugten:

This is an extremely important issue. Otherwise, there is this so-called disconnect between what one thinks in a place such as New York or Geneva, and what is happening in rural areas somewhere in mid-China, mid-Nigeria. I, personally, have a strong belief in female leadership on the local level. In many communities you see a lot of males ruling the community, unwilling to share their power. Others in the community might hold different views, on for example, prosperity – they may rephrase prosperity in terms of food, health, survival and so on. This is often where females, grassroots level, local and international NGOs come in.

The world has numerous NGOs, some say 70,000 or more. Some are only active in Geneva and New York, but many are active at the grassroots level. It is their job to get the information and knowledge to local people, through schools and local news programmes, radio and television, and other social circles, in order to make people aware of international human rights law – of their specific rights. The side-effect of all that is empowering the people, making them believe and experience that in the end they can do it themselves. One example: many (male) leaders are not willing to change the practice of female genital mutilation. But as soon as you start educating young women and as soon as you start to bring in arguments they can use and bring them into contact with the human rights discourse, they can finally challenge their local leaders and can tell them that their views are power-based instead of oriented upon a human rights approach, in this case forbidding traditional practises that relate to the right to health or even to practices that qualify as 'torture or other forms of inhumane treatment'.

So education and grassroots level NGOs are extremely important – and so too is the role of women, because they often have a very good way at looking at issues, much better than many people who believe in keeping power the way it has been for centuries.

Question from the audience:
Have you seen any examples of this?

Response by Willem van Genugten:
Yes, I saw this happen in cases of foot-binding in India and in several South-African cases I touched upon in my lecture. I have visited South-Africa many times, for teaching and research, and each time during my classes or projects we discuss local issues, down to earth, to fully understand the differences between what is said by leaders and what is said by local knowledgeable people. You can learn so much from them – they are saying very different things. Now, I am

neither an anthropologist nor an economist. I am a lawyer and phi-losopher, but I like to work with these other disciplines in order to have that connection to what is going in 'the outside world'. In these situations, anthropologists might even have better equipment than lawyers, although I prefer to speak about them in terms of comple-mentarity. And from a legal perspective, this is about 'law in context'; not 'black letter law' only, but rather focusing upon the question *why* it doesn't function the way is it said to function on paper.

Question from the audience:
What happens to states that have signed a treaty, but which do not comply with the rules?

Response by Willem van Genugten:
Well, sometimes states ratify a treaty simply as window-dressing. Although we have the Vienna Treaty on the Law of Treaties, forbid-ding reservations to be made that contradict with the core of the treaty that is being ratified, reservations are nevertheless made all the time. The United States, for example, became party to the International Covent on Civil and Political Rights, but it tabled an extremely long list of reservations and understandings, in the end making clear that the treaty was adding nothing, not even a comma so to say, to what was already arranged for in the US Constitution. Normally speaking, other states should have protested, but they were just happy that the US was on board, and so they accepted it.

When you look at which states have ratified a particular treaty, it means not too much, until you also have considered their list of reser-vations and the question whether or not they have accepted the addi-tional complaint procedures. The next step is whether they live up to the observations and recommendations of the treaty bodies. If not, the cure is pressure by words – put them on the imaginary black lists, give extra arguments to NGOs, in order to create the type of pressure that makes governments move in the direction of respect for human rights. In addi-tion, there are more compulsory instruments in 'the international toolkit', such as (smart) sanctions and even military interventions, authorised by the UN Security Council or not, but these measures should not be used too easily nor should their effects or long-term outcomes be overestimated.

Question from the audience:

If you look at the history of human rights ratification, is there anything can you say about objections made by other states with regards to reservations?

Response by Willem van Genugten:

There was a time, particularly during the 1960s, 1970s, 1980s, when there was much talk about the non-acceptance of reservations. This period of time saw the initiation of many human rights conventions, and the joining of many states – and there was a lot of talk about avoiding reservations. Our own ministry of Foreign Affairs and the European Commission even discussed the creation of special branches to deal with reservations made with regards to international treaties, but almost nothing has ever since happened as a result, that is to say on a systematic and structural level. Everybody agrees on paper that states should be refused access to a treaty if they list too many reservations on core elements, essentially making the ratification obsolete, but the next step, the final step to refuse states becoming a party to a specific treaty, is almost never set. Countries like France, India, and the US simply say: "this is our business, whether we become a party or not, this is our business and no other states, let alone committees of independent experts, can block this."

Question from the audience:

How far would you go in not discussing human rights issues in China?

Response by Willem van Genugten:

As to China, I would work along two lines: 1) The dialogue should always be conducted within the context of the standards of international human rights law. For instance, when the minister of Foreign Affairs engages with his Chinese colleague, he should come well-equipped with high level knowledge of existing international human rights law; 2) It is important to listen and to know the history of China and to see trends in its development. See what I said about that approach in my lecture. However, listening to one another is good, but does not mean that you have to accept everything you hear – at that point you would be in the ambit of cultural relativism.

In the end both lines have to come together: understand local particularities, have a serious dialogue – what is now often called a dialogue is rather an exchange of views – but also make clear what the end goal is: universality of human rights in practice.

Question from the audience:
How would you respond if I say it is academically okay, but politically perhaps not the right moment to conduct these dialogues?

Response by Willem van Genugten:
I think it is academically not okay, and it is politically never the right moment. And you still have to do it. If you talk about forced labour camps in China, then the Chinese government will always say it is not the right moment, but you have to do it. And you can do so, because it is clear that forced labour is forbidden and that this is a peremptory standard of international law. It might be uneasy to say this to the Chinese, but that as such does not matter; you can have hesitations on whether it will be effective, but you have to do it. Academics should not be a free flow of brain; that is too easy. In addition, we cannot start discussions time and again from scratch.

Question from the audience:
What about the Millennium Development Goals?

Response by Willem van Genugten:
If we talk of nine billion people living on our planet 40 years from now, many of them will definitely live in poverty, also living in states not willing or able to do something about it. I was glad when the Millennium Development Goals were compiled, especially when they were formulated using human rights terminology, be it only partly. Some of them are doing well, some are not. For example, poverty alleviation (MDG 1) is doing relatively well, although we have to look at it again after the economic crisis. And keep in mind that the Millennium Development Goal on poverty alleviation only concerns the halving of poverty levels; nobody should really be satisfied with this. And whether we call it the MDG 2.0, or whether we have other forms of international commitments, it won't matter as long as we

see it as a real commitment for the international community as such.

My favourite MDG is number 8, which is about creating the infrastructure for long-term, sustainable development, amongst others by giving developing countries better access to worldwide markets, etc. In that context, as well as in relation to all other MDGs, there also is a huge role to be played by private companies. The MDGs do basically reflect a duty for states, it is *their* promise, but they can and should not try do it alone.

SID NL Annual Conference 2011
Global values in a changing world: challenging universality

Every year, the Netherlands Chapter of the Society for International development (SID) rounds off its annual lecture series with a conference in The Hague. The closing conference of the lecture series 'Global Values in a Changing World: Synergy of State and Society in a Globalised World' took place on Wednesday 14 September 2011 in cooperation with Amnesty International, PwC, NCDO and the Worldconnectors. The focus of the conference was a discussion on the concept of universality, and included speakers representing different approaches.

During the first decades after the Universal Declaration of Human Rights was signed in 1948, the concept of universality seemed to be taken for granted. It was subscribed to by governments and most people took it as a given reality. However, the concept is nowadays increasingly disputed, and the relativity of global values has come to the fore. Interestingly, this stands in contrast to the simultaneous and on-going process of globalisation. Interconnectedness and exchanges between people and the sharing of ideas and cultures, is becoming more and more a reality. At the same time, this has also led to discussions about the frameworks of universal norms and rights. In the Netherlands, under the influence of recent political debates, human rights are increasingly framed as a product of the European identity; as the fruit of European enlightenment, an inherent part of European culture and identity. This includes the implicit notion that 'we' have human rights and 'they' – the Chinese, the Islam world and Africans – don't. In addition, it implies a duty and role for 'us' to export these rights and duties; to transform them and to teach others so that we may achieve the universality of the human rights.

However, such a forced manner of attempting to prove the universality of human rights, means ignoring the endogenous nature of human rights throughout the world: that people in different corners of the world feel the value of human rights from within. The discussion on universality is therefore an important one, because in a globalised world we are continuously looking for pillars that underpin our living together in this globalised and increasingly smaller global village. Simultaneously, it is important to appreciate the cultural diversity of people. This dichotomy is the biggest challenge within the discourse of global values and human rights: it is important to bring these two tendencies – universality and cultural diversity – closer together.

The universality of values: a historical perspective

Jack Donnelly

What I am going to talk about isn't actually what it says on the schedule; I am an American so I don't follow orders very well. I have worked on issues of universality in the field of human rights for more than 30 years and today I will present to you all a particular perspective. I hope to show you how the concept of universality of human rights is rooted in a particular time and place.

Unfortunately, much discussion on universality involves people talking past each other; this is we have different senses of the term and apply it in different ways. What I hope to do is to perform a conceptual cleaning-up. I will make three main points that will hopefully frame the issue in such a way that we will at least be able to identify those issues we can agree to disagree about.

Firstly, universality and relativity are often presented as opposites. In fact, though, the primary sense of universality is fully compatible with considerable relativity. And if this is indeed the case, then the issue becomes not whether something is relative or universal, but how something that is universal in one important sense can also be relative in another, no less important, sense.

Secondly, the fundamental values of the late modern Europe, such as human rights and development, are universal in at least three important ways. I refer to them as: 'international legal universality', 'overlapping consensus universality', and 'function universality'.

Thirdly, when discussing the universality of high order values and practices, such as human rights and development – or even the right to freedom of speech or the right to work – it's important to distinguish between degrees of generality and specificity. I find it useful to think of a layered situation in which we move from very general formulations, which are relatively universal, towards specific issues of implementation, which depend much more centrally on the particular circumstances.

So, back to the first point, which really deals with the issue of definition. The first definition of 'universal' in the Oxford English Dictionary is "extending over, comprehending or including the whole of something." In this sense, universal is actually relative to a particular class or a group; it applies to a particular domain. For example, universal healthcare, universal primary education and universal suffrage involve making healthcare, primary education and voting rights available to all citizens, nationals or residents of a country – not to everyone on the globe, let alone anywhere in the universe, if there are others out there. What about a universal remote control? One of those wonderful tools neither controls all possible entertainment devices nor will it work everywhere in the universe, except in the movies of course, when the hero is required to save the world! In fact many American universal remotes won't even work in Europe. In this sense of the word, universality refers to the domain over which we are claiming values or principals or practices or devices.

The second definition puts it that universal is "of or pertaining to the universe in general or all things in it, existing everywhere or in all things." In this sense, little if anything in an empirical world is universal. The Oxford English Dictionary thus immediately adds that this definition is "chiefly poetic or rhetorical", to which I think we should probably add "or philosophical or theological". And so, if values such as human rights and development are universal values in this "everywhere in the universe" sense of the word, or even "in all times and all the places on this planet", I doubt many people would subscribe to or support such a view – even on philosophical grounds. Perhaps certain religious fundamentalists, but not very many other people. It is certainly not a position that I would support. Rather, I think that arguments of universality take the contemporary world as the frame of reference. Human rights and development, I want to argue, are relatively universal for us, now. And by us, I mean virtually everyone on this planet now and in the foreseeable future.

I think that there are three kinds of supporting evidence for this claim, which I will discuss as three forms of relative universality, and which brings me to my second point. Human rights and development have what we can call international legal universality. The core international treaties on human rights include the Covenants on Civil and Political Rights (ICCPR) and on Economic, Social and Cultural Rights (ICESCR), the Conventions concerning Racial Discrimination (CERD), Discrimination Against Women (CEDAW), Torture (CAT), and the Rights of the Child (CRC). We have an average ratification rate of 88% for these treaties, reflecting a striking degree of endorsement of human rights and development as universal values in the contemporary world. States do not commit lightly; they may not do it with as much commitment as those of us in this room would like, but they do not take it lightly. It is unusual for a body of treaties to have this level of endorsement. And that endorsement tells us something. In fact, those of us who have been doing this for a while have seen the context in which human rights advocacy takes place transformed by this process of international legal endorsement.

Back in the seventies and early eighties I would have to defend the idea, or existence, of human rights. Now we can focus our attention on questions of implementation in most countries of the world. Maybe not North Korea, not Burma, maybe not even China, but in most of the world this endorsement by states has altered the context of local and transnational and international advocacy in a way that it is of real practical value. States' ratifications makes life easier for advocates, as they no longer have to argue about what the values are, they just have to argue about whether the practices adhere to these values. This international legal universality may perhaps be restricted to an elite interstate level, but it is nevertheless important.

This bring us to the second kind of universality; what I call overlapping consensus universality. Those of you who have studied political theory will recognise this notion from John Rawls, the American political philosopher who makes a distinction between what he calls 'comprehensive doctrines' – the sort of overarching or foundational, philosophical, religious or illogical perspectives in a world of views – and, what Rawls calls, 'political conceptions of justice' – constitutional agreements about the basic terms of political legitimacy. Rawls developed this concept for Western liberal democracies, where people with very different comprehensive doctrines – utilitarian and religious fundamentalists, Marxist and Kantians, atheists and believers, adherents of all different kinds of comprehensive doctrines – have, in fact, managed to reach an overlapping consensus on a political conception of justice that we usually talk of in terms of liberal democracy. What I want to suggest to you is that at the international level something very much like this has happened with values like human rights and development.

People from very different and even irreconcilable comprehensive doctrines today agree on human rights not as a foundational philosophical doctrine but as a political conception of justice – a standard of political legitimacy in the contemporary world. Since the end of WWII, and especially over the past two decades, an international overlapping consensus on the body of internationally recognised human rights, has in fact emerged. More and more proponents, of more and more comprehensive doctrines, from more and more regions of the world, have come to see in human rights a political expression of their deepest values. In the contemporary world Christians, Muslims, Jews, Buddhists, Confucianists, atheists, Kantians, utilitarianists, Thomists, Marxists, social constructivists, postmodernists and many others, have, *for their own many different reasons*, come to participate in an overlapping consensus in the body of international human rights.

I emphasise "for their own many different reasons". We do not have to agree on foundational doctrines in order to agree on universal values at the level of political practice. An implication of this argument is that human rights have no single philosophical or religious foundation, and looking for one would make no sense. Only a philosopher or theologian would engage in that and today probably not very many put in that effort. They now have multiple foundations and this is not a bad thing; it is actually a good thing that you don't have to buy into any particular philosophical theory or religious doctrine in order to support human rights. Human rights are rooted in a number of different foundations – both in the Western world, where we typically ignore foundational philosophical disagreements, and in the rest of the world, where these foundational disagreements do not get in the way of a partial overlapping consensus on human rights. I think this an extremely important characteristic of the contemporary world.

These two forms of universality are actually relatively uncontroversial and ultimately matters of empirical description. 'International legal universality' is supported by a large number of ratifications, and 'overlapping consensus universality' is grounded in people's behaviour, documented through surveys for example – these are empirical descriptions of the world.

There is a third type of universality, which I call 'functional universality'. The basic argument I want to make here is that human rights and development have become overriding social and political goals and practices because the rise of modern markets and modern states has created certain kinds of standard threats to human dignity, which have created the need for human rights and development across the globe. In other words, our contemporary world, in which modern centralised bureaucratic states and modern markets have the capacity to penetrate the lives of people in ways that were unimaginable a hundred years ago, presents certain kinds of problems that people face in protecting not only their personal dignity, but also the dignity of their families and communities. Human rights are a tested set of practices that protect an egalitarian conception of human dignity against the standard threats posed by modern states.

People across the globe have tried all kinds of ways to protect themselves against the dangers posed by states; they have tried communism, and religious fundamentalism, they have even tried various kinds of syncretic approaches, which were popular in Africa in the 1960s and 1970s. Through a process of elimination, human rights have proved themselves to be the best set of practices we have available. In other societies and in other times, a life of dignity was possible without having to define these values and practices. Even in the West you will not find evidence of this set of ideas more than a couple of hundred years back. The idea that every human being has certain rights and that he can claim against state and society, simply because he is a human being, is a relatively new idea. Or, perhaps the category of human being was restricted to a very small slice of the species homo sapiens. The idea that all of us are human, every member of the species is human, is perhaps what is new.

In other times and other places we had conceptions of human dignity and threats to that dignity that did not require human rights. The overlapping consensus we now witness reflects the fact that people across the globe are facing the same kinds of problems from states and markets and they are drawing on different philosophical, religious and cultural traditions in order to justify the same set of practices that happened to develop first in the West. Not because they were in any way Western.

Look at the West in 1500, the beginning of modern Europe. Was that not the most unsuitable place for the idea of equal human dignity to develop? You couldn't imagine a worse place (and time). It was about to enter into a hundred years of religious warfare, and to revive the practice of slavery as it was beginning to conquer the world. A place that was developing the doctrine of the divine rights of Kings, a place in which a tiny minority of birth ruled over the rest of population. And yet this world was transformed, in part through human rights, into the contemporary West with its liberal democratic (and social democratic) welfare states.

Now on to my third point – an issue of levels of generality and the correlation with universality and relativity. I want to argue that at a very high level of generality everyone has the right to work. This is the level at which there is a considerable degree of universality – and the Universal Declaration usually is formulated at such a high level of generality. But we also need to consider two further levels. The first is what I call the level of conception; for example, the concepts involved in the protection against 'torture', the right to 'social security', the right to 'healthcare.' The concepts are universal. People endorse the concepts at this high level of generality. But then comes the second level, of conceptions, which can vary (within limits set by the concept). And then at an even lower level of generality, which I call the level of implementation, particular kinds of practices exist to put a given conception into everyday practice.

So let's say that in Singapore they have particular conception of freedom of press. They actually do endorse freedom of press and they have a particular local conception of what freedom of press means. Singaporeans talk about out-of-bounds markers, and if you are Singaporean you know where the markers are. Everybody knows what they can or should not be saying. This is a form of self-control, a form of a locally accepted idea. You can actually say anything you want; you may lose your job, you may be prosecuted for libel, but you won't be thrown in jail (anymore). That is a conception of freedom of press that I, as an American, do not find adequate. But we do actually agree on the idea of free press. We disagree, however, about the broad limits of that idea and experience even more disagreement when we get down to specific implementation. This is where universality and relativity come together.

I would suggest that there is actually a reasonable degree of consensus even at the level of conceptions; that there are usually few widely endorsed conceptions of particular human rights concepts. But there are real and important differences when it comes to the level of implementation. What may be adequate for one country may be utterly inadequate for others. If we link this idea (disagreement at the level of implementation) with the concept of overlapping consensus, we see that when it comes to particular issues of political debate there is considerable space for very important disagreements about priorities, limits, expenditures of resources, strategies to going forward, and about the best kinds of arguments for practices that support human rights. The particulars of implementations are deeply local – in the Netherlands no less than in Niger. What is universal for us today are the overarching values. The trick is to maintain the commitment to universal values, whilst operating at local levels, at which particularities are so important.

One last point; I want to suggest that these particularities are much less connected with culture than most people usually think. If it were up to me, we would no longer talk about culture and human rights. After all other explanations have been exhausted we fall back on 'culture', because somehow that will explain away any behaviour; we say "they are different", but we mean "they are weird". Furthermore, in the contemporary world the differences are not so much between East and West or North and South, but between people who are more or less enmeshed in the modern world of markets and states. When you are embedded in markets you have no trouble understanding why development is considered the most important value and why economic and social rights are so important, regardless of what books your grandparents read, or who they worshipped.

There are of course cultural differences at the level of implementation, but these cultural differences do not correspond to geography. We have culture wars in the West and particularly in the United

246

States. I swear that George Bush is of a different culture than I am, and we are both happy about that. Culture is not where the relativity comes from. If I were an advocate trying to convince people not to beat their wives, I would of course rely on the local beliefs in order to make that argument. But that doesn't mean necessarily that we have cultural differences, it's just that we have different ways of coming to the same values – in the same way that Westerners have different ways of coming to the same values and practices.

Such appeals to broad cultural differences are dangerous because they end up not just dividing but demeaning people. They end up with the argument that "well because they are Africans, they can't possibly want the same things that we want". But remember that the terms African or Asian are Western notions – no one in Asia considered themselves Asian until the Western term was applied. In fact, because they face the same kinds of problems, it would actually be surprising if, as human beings, they didn't want the same kinds of practices that we do. I have yet to experience that, and I think that very few of us who deal with this issue have actually experienced people who, upon facing problems posed by modern states, wouldn't want to enjoy internationally recognised human rights.

This may mean, though, that people living in isolated communities are actually living in a world in which they have fundamentally different values and in which the practices of human rights might not make sense. And it might also mean that sometime in the future we will be living in a different world again, in which the practices of human rights won't make sense. But for us at this moment, meaning almost all of us on this planet, human rights are universal values that are fully compatible with respect for local traditions and that allow for considerable differences in implementation.

Universality of values in practice: dealing with new global realities

Meghna Abraham

At Amnesty International we strongly believe in the universality of human rights, and Jack has just given a very good analysis of the different trends that have occurred in recent history. One point of his that I completely agree with is the broad and different levels of the universality of human rights. I am going to use two notable examples here: the USA, in relation to social economic and cultural rights, and China in relation to civilian and political rights.

Both states have fundamentally challenged the human rights treaties. The US has, for example, signed and ratified the Covenant on Civil and Political Rights (yet not the protocol that would allow US citizens to seek compensation for violations committed by the US government), but it has notably not yet ratified the Covenant on Economic, Social and Cultural Rights, and has failed to ratify the Conventions on the Rights of the Child and to Eliminate Discrimination against Women. China, conversely, has ratified the ICESCR but not the ICCPR. It has also ratified the CRC and CEDAW.

Another issue to keep in mind, is to consider the nature of engagement of states at an international level. The rhetoric, and the level of engagement of states, on international human rights has completely changed. Whether you look at human rights, or any other multilateral discussions, almost all states now use rhetoric – the language of human rights and development – and not just at the international, but also at the domestic level. So, as an example, China's constitution does talk about human rights; in fact, the Chinese criminal court was modified to include certain fundamental protections in terms of human rights. Just recently, the Chinese introduced a new set of urban regulations focusing on expropriation of land. So, as we see human rights laws being accepted on a global level, I think the discussion shouldn't be on universality, but on implementation.

I find that debates on universality unfortunately mask gaps or challenges in terms of implementation. So what we see is that states are not fundamentally disagreeing on human rights, but challenges do occur when it comes to the actual implementation of those human rights and the problems that arise in the current global reality. So let's be careful to not use broad conceptual debates about universality to mask the scope involved of implementing that human right on a national scale. Again, look at the USA and China; for all their differences, their response to human rights is similar in many ways – they both react by accepting the human rights, but with the condition that much weight is given to their preferences, social conditions and social diversity. The USA insists that its democratic system will from time to time involve reconsidering these agreements; China, although not calling on democracy, agrees that if they are to be held accountable, they wish to be granted a wide margin of discretion in terms of implementation.

Let's look at the issue of 'forced eviction' in China. China accepts the 'social, economic and cultural rights', and the fundamental part of the right to adequate housing and protection against forced eviction. Yet, are the people really protected against forced eviction? Can they actually claim remedies after being evicted by the Chinese government from their homes, whether in a rural place or in an urban context, because of reconstructions of the old parts of the city, or because of the building of a new mega structure, or because land has been sold off to developers?

To be able to claim remedies you need a system within which lawyers can defend clients without the fear of being locked up themselves. We are all familiar with the case of Zahn Hang Chung, the Chinese lawyer who actively represented hundreds of families that had been forcibly evicted, and who was eventually charged with supplying state secrets to foreign entities, because he faxed information on forced eviction cases in Shanghai to an international NGO. As a result, he lost his practice, his license to practise law and can no longer obtain permission to travel. On a number of occasions he has been placed under house arrest. Now, very few lawyers in China are still willing to take on these cases. So, in practice, what's the use of China ratifying the ICESCR if it will not freely permit the implementation of it? In addition, people in China have become so frustrated with their inability to protest the situation, as protests get shut down by government forces immediately, that now we have cases of people killing themselves as a last resort of protest.

The American example is related to healthcare. It's estimated that more than two women die every day in the US from implications related to childbirth and pregnancy. Half these deaths could be prevented if maternal healthcare was made accessible, available and of good quality. For those who can afford it, the US offers one of the best healthcare systems in the world. But for large sections of the population healthcare is too expensive, insurance is unavailable, information is inaccessible, etc. These people tend to belong to minority communities: African American, Hispanic, Native American. Strangely, America believes strongly that there should not be any discrimination in its country – yet believing in equal rights for women, such as equal rights to freedom and non-discrimination, should include equal access to healthcare. So, and this is relevant to both China and the USA, you cannot fully recognise and uphold some rights whilst disregarding others. Most human rights are intrinsically linked to others.

So to bring it back to the debate here, I would say there are two levels of universality. First is the level of implementation. Second is that all rights in a set are interconnected and should not be separated – it is not a 'pick and mix'. And I don't think that the challenges to the universality of human rights are only coming from 'exotic' cultures, in Asia or Africa. It is not that the West has exported their idea of human rights, and that some are being contested by 'others' – at least that has been our experience at Amnesty.

There are some acts we thought we had agreed to no longer engage in; that there exists, for example, a universal agreement against the use of torture. But we know that in our 'war on terrorism' governments consistently break this promise. And in Italy and France, right now, Roma communities have been identified as a threat, and are therefore being forcibly moved to new areas, out of camps where they have lived for 30 or 40 years – camps that were originally established by the government. So governments are, including Western ones, pushing the limits of human rights implementation all the time. But where does it start – where will it end? All rights will be questioned:

civil, political, economic, social, cultural, gender, discrimination, and so on. If all states want leeway based on their preferences – how much leeway can be granted, before the treaties lose their meaning? The point here is that we have to be very clear, up front, about how much space states are given to manoeuvre within their domestic context.

Understandably, states coming out of conflict situations and that are in transition will need more time to come to terms with the treaties – discussions will have to take place about how to implement the rights in practice. This will indeed be more complicated and take longer than in states with established legal systems, but at no point should it, even in conflict situations, be acceptable to pose the question "will we be applying protection against torture?" The point is, if we open up any of these for debate, we will not be able to stop what becomes debatable, and then we will effectively be fundamentally changing the international human rights system.

So the real challenge to universality is implementation. I don't think it's fair, or reasonable, anymore to say that the world is divided into states that do, and others that don't, respect human rights. That is a crude and arbitrary classification. The truth is, there are outliers on either side. And even in states considered to be 'best' at upholding and protecting human rights, we see violations – and unfortunately, these are more often than not committed against the poorest and most vulnerable. Poverty and discrimination are normally found hand in hand.

For example, Slovenia claims to provide 100% of its citizens with drinking water – but in fact Roma communities are denied this right. And, basically any country in western Europe denies undocumented migrants their labour rights. So I think the bigger issue for us, in terms of universal applicability and implementation of human rights, is to question which groups of people, in various contexts in the world, are facing the challenges in terms of the realisation of human rights. It's a fairly obvious point, but something that I think often gets lost. Human rights movements, or the human rights community as a whole, has not dealt with this issue sufficiently.

If we have this universal legal framework, why are certain groups of people not being able to access these rights? What are the barriers they face? The reasons do vary from state to state, but when it comes down to conflict, an age-old discussion arises again, and we start to redefine 'who is human'. For example, during situations concerning security, certain individuals may be singled out as a threat, and are consequently believed to not deserve equal protection of rights. In other cases, someone with a 'wrong' sexual orientation will be denied equal rights, as they too are seen as a threat. And in practice, people who don't have a certain social economic status or indigenous status or minority status, will often be denied the ability to capture their rights; and political rhetoric will paint them as the 'problem' or as the 'other'.

Another big challenge we face today, in our current global reality, is the multiplicity of actors with an influence on human rights. In some situations you will see that there are individuals with more power than government; or what about the power of companies in this globalised world? Companies have a responsibility to uphold human rights, but so too do governments have the responsibility to control these actors. But we all know of the influence of major international financial institutions in developing countries and their ability and tendency to control public policy. So what are the obligations of states in these situations? We can call this issue 'human rights beyond borders' – and it is a contested terrain.

Is the implementation of human rights truly universal? Do, for example, the obligations of the Netherlands extend beyond borders to ensure that companies, with headquarters or a substantial base in the Netherlands, uphold human rights in the countries of operation? Because the reality is that companies make use of loopholes in other countries all the time. And unfortunately in our attempt to give states the appropriate room to play with, we perhaps forget the actual people affected by the ways in which human rights are actually upheld, defended and violated. We perhaps forget to consider the existing monitoring systems in place. We need to consider how people can claim their rights in practice. So for me I would say the biggest challenge in terms of universality is applicability – not the universality of the values contained in the human rights treaties.

Discussion

Comment from the audience:
When looking at challenges to human rights, we should reconsider the way we handle our economics, because the present economic structures will have disastrous consequences. They put human rights under tremendous pressure. Secondly, and Kofi Annan has also brought this to discussion, our priorities are absurd: we spend 1.7 trillion dollars on military expenditures and not even 7% for the real challenges – issues that threaten the existence of many billions of people.

Question from the audience:
I'm very interested in the combination of both the individual approach and the global approach – or relative versus universal approach. For me there should be one universal exception to this relativity, for those people who want to talk about their human rights on whatever level. Human rights must remain up for discussion, or else there is neither universality nor relativity. I would like to have both your comments on this.

Response by Jack Donnelly:
I think you are exactly right. When you start restricting what people can say you run into a serious problem. If people are given the freedom to say what they want, that is an indication that many significant changes have been made in a society. Restricting the discussion of human rights is in fact an indication that the rights themselves are restricted.

Response by Meghna Abraham:
I am interested in what you called an "exception to the relativity argument". For people to be able to talk about human rights, you need freedom of expression, information, and association. So again we see the interconnectedness of rights – and you see the disparity; there is no point in accepting the right to health, if you deny people the right to free information. How can people make a considered decision about their healthcare if they do not have access to healthcare information. So I think I agree with you. You can't really talk about labour

rights if you don't have the freedom of association; if you don't have trade unions then labour rights can become difficult to enforce.

On the issue of handling economics, I think one of the challenges that we see in our work is the disconnect between different areas of public policy and international law. In other words – we look at economics as a separate entity, we regard international trade as separate from human rights, and that's the problem. Human rights should be the framework for economics, for international trade, for public policy.

And on the issue of our absurd priorities, we absolutely couldn't agree more. We see huge challenges when looking at types and levels of resources that are engaged to address, but also to monitor, the issues we have been discussing here. We talk about the state being held accountable, but who conducts the monitoring of this accountability? There is a significant disconnect. Look at poverty policies; rarely do they really consider poverty in terms of human rights. Money is thrown at the problem, but little monitoring takes place – and can those most disadvantaged groups and communities really even access the resources directed towards them?

Question from the audience:
The EU has an instrument called the 'European Instrument for Democracy and Human Rights'. I would like to ask the speakers please to comment on the link between democracy and human rights. Is there a real link? Can democracy help to implement human rights?

Response by Jack Donnelly:
I am not a fan of democracy. Two things first: what does democracy mean? If democracy means rule by the people, I don't want it; I don't want people ruling, because people regularly want to do very nasty things to other people. In my own country, for example, the problem is democratic rule, not constitutional rights. Human rights are in fact the set of constraints on what democracies are allowed to do. The most important thing is to set the ground rules about what the free decision of the majority should be allowed to regulate. When you have the right set of ground rules determining which things are out of bounds and which things must be decided by the state, regardless of

254

what the majority of the population wants, then democracy functions very well.

I think in fact we don't really believe in democracy, not in the classic sense. What we believe in are certain kinds of liberal values; it is the adjective 'liberal' in liberal democracy that does most of the work. Democratic decision making is a second order principle to deal with those things that are not regulated by fundamental rights. Whether we understand those fundamental rights as human rights, as constitutional rights, or as legal rights, it's the framework of rights that is the most important and which sets the limits; that's where our focus should be. So when we get to the point at which we are talking about democracy – which democracy? People's democracy? The Bolivarian revolution? Chavez is democratic. If you want to ask is Venezuela democratic, yes it is democratic, and that's part of the problem. Because they are not committed to the idea that there are a set of basic rights that set the framework within which democracy can operate.

Question from the audience:

I first have one short comment on the analysis of Donnelly. I fully agree with this analysis of universality over the past decade. The concept of universality is increasingly contested at the level of implementation, but not at other levels. I think I can repeat the words of the 1993 World Conference on Human Rights, that the universality of human rights is now beyond question and that belief has been further increased in the past years.

I also have a question, relating to what I missed in Mr. Donnelly's analysis. If you look at the history of the development of human rights, you see an increasing acceptance of accountability by states, both at the domestic and the international level. Is that part of Mr. Donnelly's concept of overlapping consensus universality?

Response by Jack Donnelly:

That is a tough case. I think it is true that the accountability mechanism has, particularly during the last 20 or 30 years, gained significantly more power. I am not an international lawyer who deals with this accountability mechanism all the time, but I don't think that that is where the action is. The real action is in local accountability;

international accountability mechanisms are primarily useful to the extent that they lend feedback to the local mechanisms, so that local advocates can use the reports and the findings of your committee. We should be very careful that we don't overestimate the actual significance of these mechanisms. We can operate locally, we can operate at the transnational and multilateral levels, but we should see those as a really small part of the process that is fundamentally about local mechanisms of accountability. I am not criticising in any way the work that you focus on, but I think that in the big picture the really important changes are local kinds of accountability.

Different approaches towards universality

Panel discussion

David Forsythe

My remarks follow on some themes from this morning, about the difference between general agreement in the abstract and the problem of implementation. It will also address the question of accountability for human rights violations. What I want to talk about is the UN Security Council and criminal law, particularly international criminal courts. I want to suggest that despite the general agreement, if states are unwilling to implement what they have agreed to and particularly if they are unwilling to apply the norms to themselves, then the general agreement doesn't mean very much.

I would like to discuss the five permanent members (P5) of the UNSC (China, UK, USA, France, and Russia), and their policies on international criminal justice since 1993, when the first international criminal court was started: the Tribunal for the former Yugoslavia (ICTY). I start with the assertion that there is a general agreement that those who are responsible for gross violations of human rights should legally be held accountable. You can see this principle in various treaties – I am talking about genocide, crimes against humanity, war crimes – and the R2P doctrine that includes ethnic cleansing as well. I think that, as long as you keep it an abstract discussion, entirely theoretical, there is a universal agreement that those responsible for these heinous crimes should be held accountable in a court of law. If you look at events since 1993, it looks like progress is moving ahead very nicely with the ICTY, the ICTR (Rwanda), the ICC (International Criminal Court) – you also have the courts for Sierra Leone, Cambodia, Lebanon; you have the Pinochet case, reaffirming the principle of universal jurisdiction, and in general, states have accepted the obligation to try, or extradite for trial, those responsible for gross violations of human rights. So in certain parts of academe one talks about the legalisation of international relations, which includes, as an important part, more adjudication.

Against this introduction I want to look at the record of the UN Security Council. First of all, the UNSC has helped develop multiple international legal norms within international criminal justice. So, in principle, at the abstract level, the UNSC is on board on behalf of international criminal law. The Security Council has called on states to implement these norms and has sometimes supervised the process, following up to see who is doing what. The Security Council has, however, carved out exceptions for certain states, and personnel of certain states who, for example in participating in UN peace keeping operations or field security missions, are exempt from the threat of criminal prosecution. The Security Council has created, but sometimes not, when responding to situations, *ad hoc* criminal courts. The Security Council has created, but sometimes not, special criminal courts. The UN Security Council has both recognised and ignored the ICC, in certain situations. And the Security Council, in my judgment, has left a thoroughly confused record of when to prosecute for gross violations of human rights and when to endorse amnesties and impunities as a better approach to human dignity. So if you will, there is a rich but complex record when one looks at the UN Security Council and criminal law, particularly utilisation of criminal courts.

My argument is fundamentally that this record is the result of the P5. This is not to denigrate the role of other elected members, but basically things transpire or do not because of the P5. Noticeably, most of the initiatives on behalf of international criminal justice come from the three constitutional democracies in the group. They are not just electoral democracies, but liberal or constitutional democracies: UK, France and United States. The US of course has tried to exempt itself from the ICC, unlike the UK and France, which have ratified the Rome Statute. And here you meet the problem of double standards. I think there are two general reasons why the US has exempted itself, or has tried to. One is an emotional approach and one is an analytical approach. By emotional I mean nationalistic; the feeling that the US is so brave and so good, that it should not have to answer to any other international body – and. with the exception of the World Trade Organization, I know of no other organisation that the US belongs to that has the authority to pass binding judgment on US policy. For all other memberships the US applies its veto – *de jure* (e.g., UNSC) or *de facto* (e.g., NATO).

The analytical approach comes from what I call, in not very scholarly terms, the 'Dick Cheney school' – the claim that international relations is a very nasty place, and you may have to make very nasty decisions, and you may have to torture, and you may have to commit war crimes, and therefore the US does not want to have to answer to the ICC about the use of force.

It is quite interesting to see that China often either abstains or votes in favour of resolutions that would bring into play the ICC. And this policy comes from an authoritarian, or perhaps semi-totalitarian state, that has on its record the Tiananmen Massacre, which continues to repress any dissent, and which was quite nervous during the Arab Spring about what all of this would mean for China. Nevertheless, China often either abstains or votes in favour, as it is consistently calculating whether a veto will either damage relations with the US and the West or with developing countries. For example, recently China voted 'Yes' to refer matters out of Libya to the ICC. I think China waited to see the position of the Arab League before jumping on board. I think China takes a very instrumentalist, analytical, narrow, nationalist approach to these decisions – thus not committing to international criminal law *per se*, but basing decisions purely on their current relations with developing countries and the West. (Recently China's policy regarding Syria has been an exception to this pattern.)

This is not terribly different from where the administration of George W. Bush wound up when it abstained on the resolution referring matters out of Sudan to the ICC. Despite a long effort to kill the ICC, the Bush administration allowed the use of the ICC because it was out of other feasible options, in its view. It did not know what to do about Sudan, but was under heavy domestic pressure. There were a number of religious NGOs interested in Darfur and Southern Sudan, a kind of Christian, evangelical politicised movement. And then of course, the Obama administration voted for the resolution concerning Libya. I think this is what happens, particularly in the cases of US, China and Russia. If the norms and situations don't apply to them, they are perfectly willing to have international criminal justice for others. They are perfectly willing to have the ICC come off the shelf and be activated as long as it's not their nationals involved.

Like many academics I can talk at some length on this topic, but I won't. Because it's not just China, the US and Russia. Look at the UK and the ICTY; the British voted for the court, and then they tried to kill it. The British position was complicated as they believed more in diplomacy for the western Balkans than in legal proceedings. In other words, they considered the situation and decided they might want to negotiate with Milosevic, in an attempt to bring the atrocities to a halt, perhaps even strike a deal, and wouldn't want the court to get in their way.

So there are various discourses about advancing human dignity: 1) there is the language of human rights, which emphasises law and courts; 2) the discourse on human security, which tends to bypass law; 3) the discourse on complex humanitarian emergency, which also tends to bypass emphasis on law and courts. So there are various discourses that propose to advance human dignity, but certainly one of these is the legal discourse on human rights and humanitarian law, which increasingly involves criminal courts. The Security Council is drawn into these discourses and its resolutions have to choose among them.

Seth Kaplan

I find the idea of universality to be very appealing and I agree with most of the points that it encompasses, but I often find the dialogue of human rights to be oppressive and overbearing. While I can agree with many of the points made by the previous speakers, I think it is important to recognise that certain parts of the way human rights are framed in the West need to be understood as a product of its unique history, specifically the role of Christianity in the Western world. Religion lends many great values to the wider world and should be appreciated for this, but the way the human rights agenda has been developed and argued all too often ends up only showing the Western world's view. Although human rights is not a Western concept by nature, and is not necessarily unique to the West, I think everyone would agree that the way it is presented at times comes across as somewhat evangelical, especially to non-Westerners. For instance, many of the items on the agenda can be seen by Africans and Asians as demands to get rid of old traditions and become one of us. As a result, even though human rights may have great value, the way it is communicated and promoted can be very off-putting for non-Western people. That's my first point; I think it is very important for Western people to understand a non-western perspective.

My second point is that I do believe that all human beings have the great majority of the values set out in the human rights agenda. This is true no matter where you come from, from which religion, and with which traditions. There is a fundamental nature of what it is to be human. Whatever disagreements we have, they are relatively minor. However, they are not completely unimportant. Unfortunately, disagreeing on one point out of ten can sometimes make agreement on the other nine seem insufficient. Again that is the evangelical approach to human rights. Too often, campaigners end up assuming that any opposition to one point is opposition to the whole agenda. Our tone and our insistence on a universal approach often means that we achieve less than we might otherwise.

My third point concerns the degree with which some of these human rights ought to matter in various contexts. Take the freedom of speech. If you are in a post-conflict, ethnically and religiously divided fragile state, there is less room for freedom of speech than when you are in a country with strong institutions able to provide strong protections for the rule of law. I can scream all I want in Times Square and I don't have to worry about the consequences. But when in Kigali (the capital of Rwanda) I ought to be more careful about what I say. I would say that even in Europe you have less freedom of speech than in the USA for certain topics, especially since WWII. This is not only true in Germany, but in many countries. There is always a balance between the promotion of social stability versus the promotion of various freedoms. The question is what is the balance; it depends on the place and the time. Certainly post-9/11, the USA has some valid reasons to consider terrorism a threat, and so there might be a little more need for security, rather than absolute freedoms.

There is going to be a difference of opinion between countries when we consider the needs of a society versus those of an individual, especially over the long-term. Context and history does matter, and different societies may place the needs of the group over the long-term over at least some of the needs of an individual in the short-term, in a way we would not in the West. This should not be seen as a bad thing. There needs to be acceptance of differences.

My fourth point is a comment on the development field, not the human rights field. This discussion today is very important, but I would say for the many billions of poor people in the world somewhat irrelevant. Most of the 3 or 4 billion poor or near poor have never met a lawyer in their lives, have never known a policeman they could trust, have never seen or been to court, or if they have been in court, it wasn't one that they trusted or one that treated them as equals. This concerns not only minorities but poor people in general. The development and human rights fields have missed and underemphasised capacity building of institutions that can protect the basic rights of poor people all over the world. Rule of law programmes that can improve the capacity of states to protect the rights of people are a very small part of the budgets and agendas of human rights and development organisations. The great majority of countries have signed treaties by now, and the great majority of leaders agree with the broad human rights agenda, yet it is all somewhat irrelevant for the poor. Too many people around the world lack access to their rights, not because their governments have not signed treaties or there are disagreements at some level, but because their states are incapable of protecting their rights, for reasons such as corruption and cronyism, for example. There should be a much greater emphasis on capacity building in poor countries on both the development and human rights agendas.

Tom Zwart

It is clear that the discussion should not be about whether we have universal values or not, but about how to translate them at the local level of implementation. And that is exactly what we are focussing on in our research group in Utrecht. We try to find ways to ensure more effective implementation of these universal values. I believe that in essence we have tied one hand behind our back in this respect. Requirements for implementation have not been specifically defined. It has been left up to the states themselves to decide how to implement their international human rights obligations. It is a discretion-ary power. The only thing that we know is that at the end of the day, they have to meet these international standards. So what we do in the West quite naturally is that we tend to focus on law and rights. We see law, legislation and rights as the perfect tools to implement inter-national human rights obligations. If you look at the guidelines for state reports, the court documents and the specific guidelines, every third word is 'law, rights, legislation'.

But the treaties do not require that all states use law, rights, and legislation when implementing their obligations. It's a discretionary power. That is why I believe that we are tying one hand behind our back; so why not look at other ways to implement human rights? States in Asia or Africa will likely agree that they are indeed imple-menting their obligations, but they might not be doing so with the help of law, legislation and rights. And why should they? Nowhere does it say they have to; it is not required, and perhaps they would prefer to make use of other social institutions than law.

Which is why our research group is looking at existing social institutions that are being used by states to implement human rights, and there are many. The social institutions being used may perhaps not be obvious to a lawyer, but they are very obvious to anthropolo-gists and sociologists. The problems arise when we challenge these states – they dig in their heels. Instead of challenging them we should applaud them and compliment them. Does that mean that we have to agree, or think that everything being done is fine? No of course it is not. Even in China at the political level, people are ready to admit that not everything is perfect, as their National Human Rights Action Plans make clear.

This 'receptor approach', which we are developing in Utrecht, has two phases. The first is the 'matching phase'. While working together with people (academics) from that particular country, we look for the social institutions that match these international human rights obli-gations. Let me give you two examples. The first is female circumci-sion; much good work has been done in that area – legislation has been adopted in many African countries – yet still the practice flour-ishes. So what do you do? Well, take the organisation called Tostan; it is a local organisation active in Senegal, led by an American called

Molly Melching. She decided that although legislation is an important first step, in order to make sure that female circumcision is truly ended as a practice, you have to tie in to local social institutions. By studying and relying on the social institution of marriage and founding a family, Tostan has been able to guide the communities towards an abandonment of FGM practices. The female circumcision rate in Senegal, as a result of their one campaign, has dropped considerably. That is what we also have in mind for our receptor approach. Law can only get you so far, but not all the way.

Another example is HIV/AIDS. The World Bank developed an ABC programme in Africa to combat the spread of HIV/AIDS: Abstinence, Being faithful and using Condoms. But everyone who knows Africa even just a little, will know this programme will never work. Abstinence means no children; no children means you die. Being faithful is not a reasonable request for an African man; they will admit to that themselves. Condoms are a vote of non-confidence in a marriage or relationship; so they will not be used. The ABC programme is not working. But if you look at some local social institutions, you will see some promising developments. I can give you one example: women in Malawi. Malawi is the worst-hit country in Africa. Everybody knows sex is a taboo topic of discussion in Africa, but in Malawi the women talk about it; with their husbands, but also with their husbands' girlfriends. Malawi women ask their husbands' sexual partners to be careful, to be aware that they can infect others with certain behaviour. Malawi women also use the threat of divorce. Divorce is a taboo in Africa, but the Malawi women use it as an effective means to combat HIV/AIDS.

Now most of these countries are not human rights paradises. So usually when you find the local social institution, they do not yet meet international norms. This gap must be bridged in what we call the 'amplification phase'; we start by looking for home-grown remedies. I will give you an example. There is a project in South Africa called 'The Hope project'. It is a wonderful project. It was set up by my colleagues at the university of Cape Town. Now, we already know that there are some very good drugs available that can, at least, limit the symptoms of HIV/AIDS, and can guarantee a longer life. However, the black community, in which HIV/AIDS is rampant, does not have access to these drugs. Not because they don't have the money, but because they do not visit the doctors who administer these drugs. They instead go to traditional healers. So obviously, if we want to reach the black communities suffering from HIV/AIDS then we have to do so through the traditional healers. The project has now recruited a number of traditional healers willing to be trained in biomedicine, albeit to a limited extent, so that they can diagnose HIV/AIDS and administer the appropriate drugs. This is a good example of what we can do during the 'amplification phase'.

Meghna Abraham

It is very clear that the international human rights legal framework, or even human rights as a concept, is about communities being able to use this framework either as a moral or as a legal tool, with which they can frame their claims at a local or national level. Seth raised the question about the scope of disagreement. It gets a little bit easier when you look at international treaties. Once we are working with a framework in which states have accepted certain agreements, it's a little bit easier to understand the reason why human rights are pushing for the ratification of international treaties. As David pointed out, there is a big gap between accepting something and implementing something – and if implementation does not follow acceptance then really, what is the value of the acceptance? But when a state has signed up to a treaty, there is at least a concrete framework for discussion. Yes, there should be a scope for implementation – and yes, the system has yet to provide that space. What perhaps shouldn't be, in my view, up for discussion is that only certain rights apply. Because then the danger arises that the majority rules – and there are many instances in which we really do not want to follow the majority rule!

But then picking up on an earlier made point; I agree that law is not the only means, but I think law is the first step (of many), and quite an essential step. Just to give an example; in any country, if you want to hold a local powerful person accountable for forced evictions, you cannot do this without a legal framework in place. It may not by itself be enough, but without it victims have very little room to challenge practices, which are clearly illegal according to international law. That is for us at Amnesty the key issue. At the end of the day, if you look at human rights both as a framework for policy and also as a guarantee for people when their rights are violated, the question remains, how do you ensure that people can claim their rights? There may perhaps be a level of discretion for states on how they use the law, but in fact there are certain conditions for which law is absolutely essential. It is clear that if you want to address discrimination, law is only one tool – you are not going to change public opinion through the law, but you need both. For example, the issue of HIV/AIDS raised earlier; it is a great approach to look at the traditional healers, but if the Treatment Action Campaign had not been able to use the legal system in South Africa in a very strategic way to actually gain access to life saving anti- or retroviral drugs, then the second steps would have been a non-issue.

On the point of poverty; I would suggest that the national human rights legal framework is in fact absolutely essential for people living in poverty, although I do agree with Seth, in that poor people have little or no access to police or the judicial system, and thus what good is a legal framework. So, yes it's a neglected area; human rights movements or institutions have not focused sufficiently on who the victims are and what the barriers are in accessing justice.

Discussion

Comments by Seth Kaplan:
I am very interested to Tom's approach. I generally support the idea that human rights are best promoted when they are embedded and when they grow out of a society's indigenous cultural values. If values are imposed upon somebody (or experienced that way), they are more likely to be resisted than if they come from within. I don't think anybody would disagree with that, but of course the methods to achieve this may be contested. The basic idea should be accepted.

I want to mention the ICC. The ICC is a great idea on paper, but I find any system of law that cannot be applied equally to everyone all the time somewhat, to be honest, repugnant. Can the ICC apply the law to everyone equally? And if not, then who decides to whom that law is applied? And if it is applied to only certain parties at certain times, is that a universal system of law? No it is not.

Comments by Tom Zwart:

To return to the point made by Meghna. Of course I fully agree that law is a very important social institution for implementing human rights; I don't think that there is any disagreement about that. The only point that I am making is that until now, lawyers have monopolised the debates. Lawyers see the law as the only means to do that. That is not right. So I agree with you that the Treatment Action Campaign was essential – their results mean that young women in South Africa now have access to drugs helping them to prevent HIV/AIDS passing on to their children. But unfortunately the South African population doesn't only have young women wanting to protect their children; there are many grown-ups with HIV/AIDS as well and their laws might not work that well for them. So I would say let's stop focusing exclusively on law, and let's consider whether other social institutions can assist as well. It may turn out that law is eventually the crux, but let's not disregard the possibility for other tools. In this way, I don't think we really disagree at all on this point.

Comments by David Forsythe:

I will skip the important subject of what is going on at the national or sub-national levels, and focus instead on the international relations, for which I have two comments.

One is that the problem about a quest for universal standards versus dirty political deals is not new. I will give you two historical examples from the 1940s. First, the creation of the UN and the UNSC, because once the UNSC was installed, according to the UN charter, none of the P5 can ever be charged with aggression and held accountable under the international law through the UNSC, because they have the Veto. In 1945 it was determined that the League of Nations had been too idealistic, with every state having a veto; so they constructed the UNSC – but the only way to get the USA and Russia on board was to grant them the veto power. This was the striking of an imperfect bargain, just to try to make an improvement on the League of Nations. The second historical example is Roosevelt's Yalta deal with the Soviets. You give them Eastern Europe, because they already have it anyway, but you hope for a change in Soviet policy overtime, so you do the deal at Yalta and sacrifice the Eastern

Europe to Soviet control and you hope that it maintains a working partnership between the US and Soviet Union. That's the deal that was done. So again you have another example of hoping for good things globally, but in the meantime you have to recognise power-politics and do a deal that is controversial.

The second point is on criminal justice and double standards. One of the most important laws is the law of unintended consequences. Once the US created the ICTY, it wound up with something like the ICC – when you set something in motion you can't always maintain control. In fact what happened was that the US created Nuremberg and Tokyo, that's what really started it. Churchill and Stalin just wanted to shoot them all, but the Americans demanded legal trials. So they insisted on Nuremberg and Tokyo, and they led to the ICTY, and that led to the ICC – which they didn't want! I don't know whether it is right or wrong, but international relations is full of these dirty deals, and like the French Revolution, they evolve in ways you don't expect. And who knows whether in fact, with these current double standards on international criminal justice, we will indeed have something better 20 or 50 years from now. After all, despite their multitude of nasty raids in Berlin, the Soviets sat in judgment of Germans in Nuremburg – and yet, with that nasty process, we wound up where we are now in terms of international criminal justice, which is probably an improvement over 1945. So maybe you can go from something very terrible to something good.

Question from the audience:
I think what Mr. Zwart said on states being able to choose for themselves the legal remedies they want to use and it not being an international obligation, is incorrect. The Universal Declaration clearly states that there should be an effective remedy by competent national tribunals. The ICCPR says: remedies by the legal system of the states develop the possibilities of judicial remedy, it includes particularly the adoption of legislator of masses. So that is not an optional choice, the state is obliged to provide at least for legislative judicial remedy. My question is, to Mr. Zwart, what would you do if you were to go to an African country to promote the non-discrimination of, let's say homosexuals, and were unable to identify a local receptor?

Response by Tom Zwart:

There is a general consensus among public international lawyers that human rights treaties allow states to choose their own means of implementation, the means they see fit. I agree with you that there are some provisions that directly prescribe using legal means, which is also an argument *a contrario* to support the fact that they would otherwise be free to choose any means. I am not going to have an academic debate now about the exact wording of the Universal Declaration, that would bore everyone here, but I find your second question important: what if you don't find a receptor? Well our experiences are still ongoing, but so far our research findings are very promising. Usually you will find a receptor – but if the receptor is inadequate, or if indeed there is no receptor, then the state will have to bring about reforms. You will use home-grown remedies as much as possible, but if there aren't any, then social engineering becomes inevitable. When we sign up partners for the project, this is what they commit themselves to. They have to accept a number of core principals; first of all, we are not cultural relativists, we are universalists. So everybody who signs up to the project acknowledges that every state has to fully, diligently and faithfully implement its treaty obligations, full stop. No state can unilaterally invoke cultural excuses to forsake obligations under the international human rights treaties. It is of course challenging. Sometimes you don't find receptors; but interestingly, since this is an approach based on respect and mutuality, even in the Chinese situation, the Chinese keep coming up with all kinds of potential receptors, because the Chinese, as we all know, are very proud of their own culture, history and social institutions; the work is in this way made very easy for us. But there will be challenges ahead. I would say, give us the opportunity to do the research and let's see how far we can go.

Question from the audience for Seth Kaplan:

You said you doubt the legitimacy of the ICC because it fails a No Double Standards test. My question is, since failing that test, which is basically the characteristic element of international law, whether your argument goes for the whole international law or just for ICC?

I would say it's a question of degree and perception. Legislation that is applied most of the time – say 88% of the time – has much more validity than that applied rarely. The ICC eventually might be as important worldwide as the treaties that are enacted or applied in 88% of the countries and situations. But it now deals with perhaps 1% of the possible cases; in how many countries and how many parts of the world are there cases that are just not up for debate? When the ICC starts covering larger percentages, I will start to find it a lot more legitimate.

Question from the audience:

I just wanted to point out a little contradiction I've heard here. In a previous comment someone questioned whether we could even describe the perfect system of human rights. I would say that also counts for the ICC; it is not a perfect system, but I think even the USA is happy that it exists, because it helps them to deal with certain situations they don't know how to deal with. I am also very happy with the research being conducted by Mr. Zwart, because I do think that we in the West tend to have very legalistic ways of viewing how to organise society and that we try to implement that system onto others, even though there are many ways of organising society – we just don't see it because it not our way.

My other point is that the West has its responsibilities, and should be held more accountable. The US, for example, only really pays attention to the WTO – but the WTO does not take much notice of human rights. There are so many examples of free trade agreements that violate human rights. But if we were to have import taxes on soya beans, we could produce the proteins in Europe ourselves; instead we have forced evictions of farmers and indigenous people all over the poor world because of the production of soya beans. So I would suggest that the Netherlands and the EU should be required to investigate if and how free trade agreements violate human rights. Where, by whom and how would we best do this?

Response by Meghna Abraham:

This is a very interesting point, and it has been picked up already by Olivier de Schutter, the United Nations Special Rapporteur on the Right to Food, after his mission to the WTO. He looked at the complaints concerning human rights standards with regards to, in particular, agreements on agriculture. I think the issue here is, to some extent, and across many governments, that 'disconnect' I mentioned earlier; you have one set of government officials who are dealing with trade and you have another who are dealing with human rights law, standards and policy. The result is that trade agreements are completely disconnected from what governments are required to do in terms of human rights. How to fix this? This will require considerable political will and considerable pressure from various governments. I think de Schutter's report offers excellent recommendations, albeit within the context of the UN human rights council. But I think what would be very interesting, and a lot of activists are doing this, is to take this part of the debate back to the WTO. There has been a push for the WTO to adapt its agreements, bringing them in line with human rights laws; but there has been only limited progress. There is a much bigger push that needs to take place, and basically governments have to start insisting on an end to the disconnect.

Response by Tom Zwart:

I would say the law is a very important way of implementing obligations. What the states have to come up with under our approach is either law or something that matches the effect of law, something as good as law, which guarantees the rights – because there is no watering down of the standards. We are universalist so we stick to the standards, and you have to come up with the means of implementation as good as law would be in the West. So I don't think there is any discussion among us on that one.

Response by Seth Kaplan:

I think the answer to many of these questions is: it depends on the issue. Rwanda in the middle of a genocide is an easier case to make than Iraq in 2003. But the issues are not black and white, and it depends upon all shades of gray. So I don't have an answer to your question, actually. The reality of the world is that if you suppose one size fits all, you will be making a mistake in many cases. I can't give a universal answer to a universal question because the world and its situations are very diverse. We should recognise them and we need to apply specific solutions to specific examples.

Comment by David Forsythe:
I just want to comment on my reaction when watching how president Obama handled the Libya situation. Americans could not possibly stand aside and watch Gaddafi slaughter his civilians. Obama used that argument to try to build support, but he also use multilateralism, talking about how wishy-washy Europeans were in their reliance on NATO. I think he tried to use both universal values and American traditions to build support, whether it was the right or the wrong thing to do. By the way, Syria is completely different. The American policy on Syria is quite different and Obama would certainly agree that you have to deal with different situations in different ways. Again whether that is right or wrong, is not for me to say.

Challenging universality: conclusions and summary

Final remarks by Lionel Veer

By way of conclusion I was asked to reflect on the question: "Is the Dutch government willing to challenge universality and do we think that a global debate on values should lead to a debate on universality?" The short answer to this question is "no".

The Dutch government recently presented a policy paper on human rights to Parliament. In this paper it is clearly stated that the universality and indivisibility of human rights continue to be the basis of our policies. Human rights reflect the fundamental values on which democracy and rule of law are based.

But it is alright to reflect on the question concerning universality of human rights. Today's debate has shown that, more than 60 years after the signing of the Universal Declaration of Human Rights, the global situation of human rights is still far from perfect. Nevertheless, I think the focus has shifted from the promotion of the concept of human rights and standard setting to implementation of human rights. Unfortunately not all countries have signed and ratified all human rights treaties, but if all countries would put in practice what they have signed up for the world would be much better place.

In the context of standard setting there can be no debate on universality, but universality does not mean uniformity. Human rights are universal, but that does not mean that every country has to assure these rights to its citizens the same way. What matters is that these rights are guaranteed in practical terms. Improving the human rights situation in a country is first and foremost the responsibility of the country and its citizens themselves. Improvements have to come from within the country and have to fit in and build on the countries own development.

The international community can and must remind countries with a poor human right record that they should improve this. Sometimes pressure and naming and shaming is necessary, but most of the time it is better to look for less confrontational ways to get the message across and contribute to a better human rights situation. I believe it is more effective to have a dialogue between states on human rights, then for states to start 'finger pointing'.

In our new human rights strategy the focus is also on effectiveness. Helping the effective implementation of human rights, and helping states who fail to implement their obligations under the human rights treaties they have ratified, is important to the Netherlands government. *How* they want to implement and guarantee human rights for their citizens is up to themselves to decide, most important is *that* they implement these rights.

In reaction to Tom Zwart's presentation on the so called receptor approach, much is said about the rights-based approach as a preferred model for implementing human rights and the tension between the universality of human rights and cultural relativism. I think this debate is important, but we should be careful not to lose ourselves in a debate for the sake of the debate. I like to think of the receptor approach as a tool for improving human rights. In our human rights policy we like to use all tools available and the receptor approach adds another interesting tool to our toolbox.

Traditional diplomacy was focussed on government to government contacts, but in the years I have worked in diplomacy there has been an important change. Increasingly, diplomats, or at least Dutch diplomats, established contacts with non-government institutions, NGOs, civil society groups and unofficial opinion leaders. This implies that we have learned to look at the broader picture, the society in a broader sense, and with an open eye for the culture and traditions of the country concerned.

In the context of development cooperation this has proved to be more effective, and I believe that it also helps efficiency in the context of improving human rights. Effective implementation of human rights means that things will change and in our policy paper we stress that human right defenders are important agents of change. In countries where human rights are not respected, you need courageous human rights defenders and activists to bring about positive change. The Dutch government supports human rights defenders in many countries where governments neglect or violate the human rights of their citizens. Not all governments are happy with this and say we are interfering in internal matters. In a way they are right, in the name of human rights a certain degree of influencing or even interfering is allowed. The ultimate consequence of this is what we now call R2P, the right to protect. Looking at the military intervention taking place in Libya, we see how far the international community is willing to go in the name of human rights.

Without a general acceptance of the universality of human rights, without a high level of consensus that human rights, as written in the Universal Declaration and the important treaties on Human Rights, are the basis of rule of law and good governance, this development form promoting the concept of human rights to implementation and R2P would have been impossible.

I think it is good to act when human rights are violated, but it is also good to reflect on the underlying values that justify these actions. Therefore today's meeting and the interesting debate on the universality of human rights has been significant.

Concluding words by Eduard Nazarski

Concluding the conference, I would like to start with two more or less instantaneous reactions I had to what I heard this morning. Reflecting on a comment by someone from the audience – perhaps for another perspective, we should try to think about the connection between the global values we are discussing now and personal or interpersonal values as we live up to the standards we are trying to defend or promote. My second reaction was to the receptor approach. I was in Senegal, to observe and interact with Amnesty colleagues, who are advocating against female mutilation. I am the first to acknowledge that it is extremely important to look at national context and local context in order to approach human rights. But I have also seen, in Senegal for example, how human rights can be an extremely powerful concept for people living in extreme poverty, or surrounded by violence. From a position of sheer hopelessness, the idea and concept of human rights is capable of suddenly giving them the power to stand up for their rights and to organise themselves against violators of rights, or individuals who harm others.

I would also like to share with you a thought about the way the debate on human rights is conducted in our country, and in our world. In this context I would like to refer to a discussion that was raised after a number of Dutch authors were asked by Amnesty to wear a particular badge during their visit to China. The badge was one representing an empty chair – a chair that should have been occupied by Liu Xiaobo, who wasn't permitted to go to Oslo in order to receive his Nobel price.

So what does it mean to advocate and promote human rights? I will focus on China, even though Amnesty has not been able to enter the country, as we nevertheless have some good contacts with human rights defenders there. I see in the Netherlands, and elsewhere in the world, that we are witnessing a time of geopolitical changes. China and some another countries are rising in terms of economic and geopolitical power. The US and the rest of the Western world are in decline. New players are rising in the world system and this phenomenon is often referred to as the rise of the rest. In the case of China, the general idea seems to be not just that a new player is rising, but also a so-called 'game changer'. As if a new player has entered the field and has declared "I am going to play with you and these are the rules". One of the uncertainties nowadays in international relations seems to be the way in which China wants to change the game. Which existing rules and norms will China accept in the future. Which rules and norms will it be seeking to change in the same future? What will China challenge?

China will make serious efforts to limit the ambit of international human rights and related monetary mechanism. In terms of this conference China may well challenge universality. And of course this is the outlook that politicians and policy-makers share about human rights in relation to the rise of China and decline of the West. It would be ill advised not to prepare for this occasion. How should the West, Europe and the EU, and individual European states or politicians prepare for such a potential challenge to the game – especially in the arena of international human rights?

I see, in general, three different approaches. Some people state that international human rights might not be valid in China. We heard this morning about universality and the 88%. We heard how international reporting and accountability mechanisms have grown, but still there are people who believe that things are different in China. I experienced this when talking to members of the International Olympics Committee from the Netherlands, where someone said, "in China things might be different". I am also referring to the conversation I had with the Chinese ambassador to the Netherlands, who very simply said to me, "you must acknowledge that some of the emphasis you put on political rights and human rights in general is a very Western concept and China is very different from your country". So 88% of the countries have acknowledged that the international human rights are important, and the six core treaties have been signed, although maybe not always implemented. Yet in the political and public debate people still say, "well China is different and you have to acknowledge that".

The second approach is a different one. In this approach people think that, as China has validated human rights, it should live up to its promises and implement the rights. People like Liu Xiaobo and defenders of human rights who are in prison, should be freed immediately. The question arises as to what the best approach is to convince the government and the ruling party in China of the validity of human rights. This comes to the second part of the discussion this morning. We said we have universality and the pragmatic approach of implementing those universalities. Human rights defenders are agents of change from within, and we see a lot of very courageous people in China trying to stand up for human rights. These people are often in danger; they are in the position to be selective – to decide what they think is acceptable and what is not, in terms of speaking out publicly. It is vital for them to have some international and public support for the work they are doing.

I know from the experiences of Amnesty International that international pressure does help in many cases, but there is a third approach – besides the discussions on universality or the effectiveness or the implementation and the best ways to put universality into practice. Not everyone is prepared to risk angering governments or ruling parties for the sake of human rights and therefore they will not effectively or actively promote and protect human rights. I see it in businesses in China. They discuss universality and implementation, but at the same time a huge economic interest is at stake. It's crucial these days to acknowledge this situation as it influences the debate.

I think we should keep this discussion and debate very clear. Issues of political expediency should not be hiding behind intellectual debates on universality and universalisation. If political expediency of human rights is an issue, let's discuss that issue. Let's not dress it up as something else. Debates about global and universal values, global mechanisms to promote and protect them will continue, and I am pretty sure SID NL will be there in the future to stimulate and facilitate further debate.

Conference summary[41]

René Grotenhuis, president of the Dutch chapter of SID NL opens the conference 'Global Values in a Changing World: Challenging Universality', the closing event of the lecture series hosted by SID at the VU University in the 2010-2011 academic year.

Session I - The universality of values

*Opening Speech by Jack Donnelly, professor at the Josef Korbel School of International Studies, University of Denver.*Donnelly has worked on issues of universality in the field of human rights for more than thirty years. What he has learned about human rights relates, he says, also to discussions about sustainable human development, a concept that substantially overlaps with human rights. Professor Donnelly puts forward three main arguments. The first is that, although universality and relativity are often presented as opposites that cannot be reconciled, universality is in fact compatible with a considerable degree of relativity. Secondly, Donnelly argues that fundamental values of late modernity, such as human rights and development, are universal in at least three important senses (international legal universality, overlap-

---

41   Report by Roeland Muskens, Wereld in Woorden - Global Research and Reporting.

ping consensus universality, and functional universality), but that in two senses (namely ontological universality and anthropological or historical universality) they are not. His third argument is that it is important to distinguish degrees of universality or specificity.

Donnelly presents several different definitions of the concept 'universal' that lead him to conclude that universality is limited. The Oxford English Dictionary provides the following definition: "Extending over, comprehending, or including the whole of something." This means, argues Donnelly, that universal is defined as relative to a 'something' that is encompassed. The second definition is that universal, means: "applies across all of a particular domain." For example: universal healthcare, universal primary education, and universal suffrage. Donnelly argues that these universalities obviously do not cover everyone on the globe (let alone anywhere in the universe). A third definition of 'universal' is: "Of, or pertaining to, the universe in general or all things in it; existing or occurring everywhere or in all things." Also in this sense universal is by no means really 'universal'. Donnelly therefore prefers to use the term 'relative universality' when speaking about human rights.

Nevertheless, human rights can be considered universal in the sense that they are deeply rooted in international legal consensus. The six core international human rights treaties have an average ratification rate of 88%. This legal consensus allows human rights advocates to take action when people's rights are violated.

Secondly, human rights are also universal in the sense that they are subject to 'overlapping consensus universality'; an international overlapping consensus on the body of internationally recognised human rights has emerged among proponents of very different political, philosophical or religious doctrines. Despite their differences, and for their own very different reasons, they have come to see in human rights a political expression of their deepest values. The implication of this argument, Donnelly says, is that human rights have no single philosophical or religious foundation. Rather, they have multiple foundations.

The third argument for universality is that human rights have become overriding social and political goals and practices as a result of the rise of modern states and modern markets. The latter have created threats to human dignity, which in turn has created the strong need for human rights (and for development).

The concept of human rights is relatively new, Donnelly states. The notion that someone can exercise rights simply because he or she is a human being is only a couple of hundred years old. Threats to these rights exist everywhere, regardless of the political systems.

The phrasing of the specific human rights in the different core treaties is remarkably simple. For example: everyone has a right to work, or the right to freedom of speech. On the level of the implementation of these 'universal' rights, however, there are huge differences. In Singapore, for example, the conception of 'freedom of the press' means that journalists know what they can write and what is no-go. Self-control is locally accepted. You can in fact write what you wish, but the consequence may well be that you lose your job. So there is consensus about the broad conception of human rights and its related values, but the implementation differs greatly. This fits within the conception of overlapping consensus. Professor Donnelly argues that local differences and particularities are hardly culturally defined. The differences are not between East and West, or North and South. The differences are between regions that are more or less enmeshed between markets and states. The more a society is enmeshed between markets and states, the more its members will view human rights as universal. Nevertheless, except perhaps for some completely isolated communities, human rights are universally important to protect individuals.

Keynote speech by Meghna Abraham, head of the Economic, Social and Cultural Rights Team at the International Secretariat at Amnesty International: 'Universality of Values in Practice: dealing with new global realities'

Meghna Abraham starts by stating that Amnesty International firmly believes in the universality of human rights. She agrees with Jack Donnelly that at the first level of the universality debate, which was the broad understanding or principled recognition of rights, there had been significant advances and most governments had accepted human rights. However, at the levels of interpretation and implementation, there continue to be significant challenges. For example, taking the examples of US and China who had historically opposed certain categories of rights – economic, social and cultural rights, and civil and political rights respectively – both governments have now advanced their position. Both are signatories to the respective treaties, even if they are not parties, making it hard for them to repudiate these rights all together. China increasingly uses the rhetoric of human rights and has numerous references to human rights within its constitution. The US government has now taken what it describes as a 'holistic approach to human rights'. The real debate, Abraham argues, concerns the area of implementation. Broad debates around universality often masks problems with divergent views around the scope or exact content of rights and gaps in implementation and it is important to be clear about exactly where the divergences and problems lie.

At a practical level, debates that prioritise or reject some rights over others are often hard to sustain. One example is forced evictions in China. China is party to the International Covenant on Economic, Social and Cultural Rights, which requires it to ensure that all persons are protected against forced evictions. In practice, however, it is extremely difficult for victims of forced eviction to claim such protection when their rights to freedom of expression, peaceful assembly and protest are not recognised and when lawyers who take on cases regarding forced evictions are being arbitrarily detained and repressed. These rights are inherently linked and cannot be separated out in practice.

This is not unique to China. The US has a relatively high rate of maternal mortality, which is caused by the fact that women with low incomes face a number of barriers in accessing healthcare. In a recent report Amnesty International highlighted how within US gender, race, ethnicity, immigration status, indigenous status or income level can affect a woman's access to healthcare and the quality of healthcare she receives. Again in practice, it is difficult to separate out women's rights to life and non-discrimination from the recognition and realisation of their right to health.

The universal human rights framework is not being challenged just on the basis of culture or 'Asian values', but is increasingly come under attack from governments all over the world that want to carve out exceptions or reduce the scope of protections in a particular context. Some examples of this include the attack on the absolute prohibition on torture in the 'war on terror', or attempts to justify discriminatory treatment of the Roma in Europe on security or other grounds. If we begin to allow the universality of non-human rights to be questioned, we risk opening up the entire framework.

In terms of current challenges, the greatest challenge is how to ensure the universal applicability and implementation of human rights. Though there are different challenges in different countries, there are also commonalities. You cannot simply separate out countries that respect human rights and those who do not. Abraham argues that in fact what she saw in her own and Amnesty International's work is that groups of people who face the greatest challenges in realisation of their human rights, are typically people living in poverty and those who face discrimination, whether it is people from LGBT communities, ethnic minorities, people from particular castes, and/or irregular migrants. She states that there had been insufficient attention paid by the human rights community to the links between poverty and human rights. Another challenge that is of growing concern to Amnesty International is ensuring the accountability of new actors on the stage of human rights. In a decentralised system, how does one hold a powerful mayor accountable for human rights violations? Private companies and international financial institutions also increasingly exercise power in the area of human rights. This also links up to challenges around recognition of extra-territorial obligations of states. In order to ensure that human rights are truly universal, we would also need to look into, for example, the obligation of the Netherlands, to ensure that Dutch companies do not abuse human rights in other countries.

Q&A between Jack Donnelly, Meghna Abraham and the audience, led by Andrew Makkinga
One member of the audience raises two challenges that were not touched upon by the speakers. The first is the matter of the economy. The current economic system will lead to huge problems of sustainability, which will have serious repercussions for human rights. Secondly the speaker questions the current priority setting by policy makers, where billions are spent on military expenditure and much

less on serious global challenges. Another member of the audience thinks that regarding the relativity of human rights an exception should be made for the freedom to speak about human rights themselves.

Jack Donnelly replies that when people can freely talk about human rights, it shows that a lot has been accomplished. Freedom to talk about human rights is, therefore, not a strategy but rather a result. Meghna Abraham adds that the right to information is universal, because without information it is impossible to exercise your rights. Abraham agrees that there is a disconnect between economic policies and human rights. Human rights should shape a framework for economic policies. But currently both matters are completely disconnected and priority setting has gone askew.

Another question from the audience concerns the link between democracy and human rights. Jack Donnelly provokingly states that he is not a big fan of democracy if indeed democracy means rule of the people. Simply because people often want terrible things done onto others. Human rights are, on the contrary, a limitation of democracy. If a democracy is capable of executing its citizens, Donnelly argues, it should be curtailed. That is what human rights are about.

One member of the audience emphasises that there is growing accountability of states regarding their human rights records. Is this part of the overlapping consensus? Jack Donnelly agrees that accountability by states has greatly improved. On the other hand, he feels that this is not where 'the action' is. The real issue at stake is local accountability, not state accountability. Current systems of accountability are important, but they are not enough.

Session II – Panel and discussion: different approaches towards universality

Panel members are Seth Kaplan (Alpha International Consulting), Tom Zwart (School of Human Rights Research), David Forsythe (University of Nebraska-Lincoln) and Meghna Abraham.

Seth Kaplan kicks off the panel discussion by stating that the subtitle of today's conference is '*Challenging* Universality', where in fact the goal of the conference seems to be '*promoting* universality'. According to Kaplan, the way the West tries to promote human rights is offensive for many people in other parts of the globe. The problem is not the agenda as much as the manner of promotion. Kaplan compares it to the spreading of Christianity by missionaries in Africa. In fact, human rights are widely shared. There is agreement on 90% of the package. Perhaps we should first be happier with the 90% we have agreement upon. A demand for perfection is often the enemy of the good. There must be some room for disagreement.

In countries with much social stability, for instance, there is usually more room for free speech than in countries with social unrest. On Times Square one can just about say anything, whereas in a place like Kigali, certain opinions are perceived as damaging to the social fabric of society. As a matter of fact, Kaplan adds, since 9/11 in the US too there is less tolerance for free speech than before. This should be a matter of debate, Kaplan stresses.

If members of the human rights community really want to help the poor, it should be much more focused on building the capacity within states to enforce the basic rules of law instead of simply pushing an agenda that has little relevance for the great majority of people in the developing world. For billions of people on the globe, the discussion about human rights is hardly interesting. These people have never seen a lawyer, they have never been able to trust a police officer, and they have never set foot in a courtroom. Unfortunately, strengthening institutions crucial to improving the rule of law has had a very low priority, both for human rights organisations as well as for development agencies. Rule of law is only a very small part of the development agenda and of budgets, concludes Kaplan.

Tom Zwart stresses that the main challenge regarding human rights is indeed implementation. His study group at Utrecht University focuses on just that: the implementation of universal values. Governments enjoy a large degree of freedom in the implementation of the human rights they have agreed upon through the ratification of treaties. The treaties do not include guidelines on how to implement these rights. In the West, the focus is on the rule of law and on legislation. One of the research topics of the School of Human Rights Research is to look for other ways of implementing notions of human rights. For example: matching institutions. Local institutions have succeeded in lowering female circumcision in Senegal by 70%. In South Africa, the HOPE programme targets black South Africans who won't use modern anti-Aids medications and who instead prefer to consult a traditional healer. The HOPE programme trains traditional healers in recognising symptoms of HIV/Aids and encourages them to prescribe modern anti-Aids medication to their patients. Tom Zwart stresses that in many cases it is just not effective to try and impose western systems onto local, traditional circumstances.

David Forsythe talks about the progress that has been made regarding international justice. There is some agreement on universality: people who commit acts of genocide must be persecuted and punished. On a theoretical and abstract level, there is agreement on this. And based on this general agreement, progress has been made especially in the establishment of several international criminal courts, with which most states cooperate.

The UN Security Council has a mixed record regarding international justice. It often calls upon member states to uphold human rights, but in some cases the Council has specified exceptions to the general rule of international law. For example, the ruling that international peacekeeping soldiers cannot be brought before international criminal courts.

The US has always exempted itself from the International Criminal Court. It has done so, explains professor Forsythe, for two reasons. The first reason is emotional and nationalistic; the US deems itself too good to be subject to prosecution by the ICC. The second reason is more analytical and/or political; international relations are nasty, and sometimes it is necessary to do nasty things. China's role in the Security Council is remarkable. China either abstains from casting its vote, or it votes in favour of international law. China's behaviour is calculated and instrumentalist. It does not want to risk disturbing its relations with either the US or with the developing nations. For example, China voted in favour of handing over the Libya case to the ICC. Obama too agreed to a role for the ICC in this case. In the case of Sudan, even the Bush administration agreed to a role for international law, albeit under pressure from domestic religious groups. In short, the US and China are quite willing to agree to international law when the culprit is a country other than their own.

Meghna Abraham concludes that the vital issue is that a legal framework regarding human rights must have practical meaning on a local level. It is relatively easy to talk about and agree on treaties; implementation is the real bottleneck. Not open to debate, Abraham repeats, should be the fact that all rights are applicable to all people everywhere. Law is not the only instrument in upholding people's rights, but it is vital. If you want to hold a local mayor accountable for forced evictions you can only do so on the basis of a legal framework, rooted in international rules and regulations.

Discussion among panel-members and audience

Seth Kaplan agrees with Tom Zwart on the importance of local culture in upholding human rights. Kaplan is less enthusiastic about the ICC and the way the international community selectively hands over cases to this criminal court. A law that does not apply to everyone is repugnant, says Kaplan. Finally, he stresses that he did not mean to say that human rights are irrelevant for billions of poor people, but that the *debate* on human rights is irrelevant to them. Tom Zwart agrees that the law is important in upholding human rights, but he argues that lawyers have wrongly hijacked the debate on human rights. The focus should not just be on the law, but also on other instruments.

According to David Forsythe the problem of universal standards versus dirty deals is not new. In international relations it is sometimes sensible to accept a less than perfect situation, because this may lead to improvements in the future. The veto-right of the five permanent members of the Security Council gives them virtual impunity. This veto right was a *sine qua non* for the birth of the Council. In history there are many such cases. For example, the Nuremberg Trial was far from perfect; it was a case of victor's justice. But 50 years later, Nuremberg led to the establishment of the ICC. The ICC was faulted because the US refused to participate, but since its establishment the US increasingly allows a role for the ICC. The practice of international relations is full of double standards and dirty deals, Forsythe stresses. But sometimes these lead to something good.

One member of the audience stresses that states do have an obligation to provide a legal framework for human rights. The permissiveness that Tom Zwart implies is incorrect. Tom Zwart concedes that there are certain obligations for states regarding their legal framework, but emphasises that states do have a substantial discretionary freedom to shape their national laws and regulations regarding human rights. It is important to also search for 'home-grown remedies' for human rights advocacy. For instance, it is impossible to deal with homophobic practices in Africa without involving people at grassroots level.

Another question relates to the dubious position of the ICC, which is seen to apply double standards. Isn't that common practice for the whole of international law? Kaplan dislikes the ICC because it does not apply to everyone equally. Whereas 88% of states have ratified the human rights treaties (and therefore at least try to implement their rules), less than 1% of relevant cases ever reaches the ICC. Who decides? No system that reaches so few people so discriminately can be considered the rule of law. On the contrary, it can too easily become the rule of politics.

Meghna Abraham highlights the work of the Special Rapporteur on the Right to Food on this issue. The heart of the matter is, says Abraham, that there is a disconnect, even within the same government, between people in the ministries focusing on human rights and others who are engaged in international trade law. Abraham highlighted the importance of ensuring that international trade agreements were consistent with states' human rights obligations.

Closing: implications for Dutch foreign policy

Lionel Veer, Ambassador for Human Rights, Dutch Ministry of Foreign Affairs. 'The Universality of Values: Drawing Conclusions for Dutch Human Rights Policy'.
Ambassador Veer starts off by stating that the Netherlands firmly subscribes to the notion of the universality of human rights. At the same time, he realises that a shift is taking place from emphasis on the 'standards' towards emphasis on the 'implementation' of human

rights. The standards are undisputed, but implementation is less straightforward. The Dutch government is always concerned with the effectiveness of its policies. The progress in upholding human rights must come from society itself. It is very context specific. Not only talk about universality, but also focus on change for the better.

According to Ambassador Veer, human rights law is not like, for example, the law of gravity; the latter is to understand gravity around the world, but the first is to change the worldwide human rights situation. These laws must be seen as agents for change. We live in a society based on the rule of law. Citizens are supposed to uphold and answer to the laws of society. Citizens give up part of their freedom in exchange for protection from the state. Human rights are about the relation between the state and the people. The state is there for the people; not the other way around. These ideas come from the era of Enlightenment. This is what French philosopher Rousseau called the 'social contract'. Interestingly he was influenced by the works of Confucius. Many scholars at that time looked at China as an example. So in its origins human rights are not only Western. The 88% of countries that have ratified the human rights treaties can be seen as having agreed to a kind of social contract.

A recent development is that states are willing to intervene in other states when human rights are violated, which comes with the concept of R2P (Responsibility to Protect). Non-state actors increasingly play a role in this. The Dutch government focuses on human rights defenders, because it believes that change must come from within, which requires local agents of change.

The Netherlands cannot take on all challenges regarding human rights, Veer stresses. Universality is not disputed, but selectivity is inevitable. We cannot do everything, but doing nothing is not an option. Effectiveness is one of the major defining elements of Dutch human rights policies.

Eduard Nazarski, director of Amnesty International in the Netherlands. In his closing words, Eduard Nazarski responds to the argument made by Tom Zwart to focus on local solutions to human rights violations. Nazarski agrees that it is important to look at the local context. Yet on his travels to Uganda and Kenya, Nazarski witnessed the enormous importance of international human rights as a weapon for marginalised people. Laws are essential, says Nazarski.

Some say that human rights are not valid in China. China sees itself as different. Others stress that human rights are universal. But the issue is how to convince the Chinese authorities of that universality. According to Nazarski, human rights activists play a vital role in changing the Chinese attitude towards human rights. Human rights activists are change agents, who merit international support. A third position is that China is simply too powerful to raise fundamental questions about human rights. In this view there can be some discussion on the universality of these rights, but discussions should not hamper business opportunities. Nazarski analyses that China is not merely a new player on the international stage, but that it is a 'game changer'. This realisation throws up many uncertainties: what will the position of China be? In what direction will the country head? Will China challenge the existing human rights framework? Several answers are possible.

Contributors

Meghna Abraham has been the head of the Economic, Social and Cultural Rights Team at the International Secretariat at Amnesty International since 2009. She started working at Amnesty International in 2007 as the Economic, Social and Cultural Rights Policy Coordinator. Prior to this, Meghna has worked at the Centre for Child and the Law, National Law School of India University; Human Rights Centre, University of Essex; World Organisation Against Torture; Centre on Housing Rights and Evictions; and the International Service for Human Rights. She has also acted as a consultant with the Office of the High Commissioner for Human Rights and other NGOs and also taught at a number of universities. She holds a BA, LLB (Hons.) degree from the National Law School of India University and the BCL and M.Phil in Law degrees from the University of Oxford.

Patricia Almeida Ashley is adjunct Professor at the Department of Geoenvironmental Analysis of the Institute of Geosciences, Universidade Federal Fluminense (UFF/IGEO/GAG, Niteroi, Brazil) and holder of the Prince Claus Chair in Development and Equity at the International Institute of Social Studies of Erasmus University Rotterdam, the Netherlands. She was appointed in 2009 for her interdisciplinary approach to Socially Responsible Entrepreneurship (SRE) and her knowledge of the relationship between SRE and important social issues. She is leader of the research group Rede EConsCiencia – Education, Policies and Technologies in Consciousness, Social and Environmental Citizenship and Ecodevelopment: http://redeeconsciencia.blogspot.com. She has also been Member of the Commission on Sustainable Development and Energy at International Chamber of Commerce.

David Booth is a Research Fellow at the Overseas Development Institute in London, where he directs an international research consortium, the Africa Power & Politics Programme (www.institutions-africa.org). Previously Professor of Development Studies at the University of Wales Swansea, he was trained in sociology, has edited two multidisciplinary development studies journals and has done research and policy advisory work in several countries of Latin America and sub-Saharan Africa. His current interests centre on institutional diversity in African governance and the implications for international development strategies.

Paul Collier, CBE, is a Professor of Economics and Director for the Centre for the Study of African Economies at the University of Oxford. From 1998 until 2003 he was the director of the Development Research Group of the World Bank. He is the author of three books: "The Bottom Billion: why the poorest countries are failing and what can be done about it", published in 2007; "Wars, Guns and Votes: democracy in dangerous places", published in March 2009; and his most recent book, "The Plundered Planet: how to reconcile prosperity with nature", which was published in May of 2010. His research covers the causes and consequences of civil war, the effects of aid and the problems of democracy in low-income and natural-resources rich societies.

Jack Donnelly is the Andrew W. Mellon Professor at the Josef Korbel School of International Studies, University of Denver. Human rights is his principal scholarly interest ever since he wrote his dissertation for his PhD on the development of the concept of human rights. Most of his writings have been in the broad, multidisciplinary field of human rights and they include three books: 'The Concept of Human Rights', 'Universal Human Rights in Theory and Practice' (second edition, 2003), and 'International Human Rights' (third edition, 2006). He also wrote a series of articles on human rights and cultural relativism, which advance a strong argument for a relatively universalistic approach to implementing internationally recognised human rights.

Gary Dymski is Professor of economics at the University of California, Riverside, and since April 2012 affiliated with the Economics Division, at the Leeds University Business School. He received his B.A. in urban studies from the University of Pennsylvania in 1975, and an MPA from Syracuse University in 1977. He worked as economic analyst for the Legal Services Organization of Indiana from 1977 to 1979, and from 1979 to 1981 was staff director and fiscal advisor for the Democratic Caucus in the Indiana State Senate. Gary received his PhD in economics from the University of Massachusetts, Amherst in 1987. He was a research fellow in economic studies at the Brookings Institution in 1985-86, and then taught economics at the University of Southern California from 1986 to 1991 before joining the UCR faculty.

David Forsythe is professor at the University of Nebraska-Lincoln and Charles J. Mach Distinguished Professor, Emeritus, as of May 2010. In 2008 he held the Fulbright Distinguished Chair in Human Rights and International Studies at the Danish Institute of International Studies, Copenhagen. In 2007 he was the Gladstein Visiting Professor, Human Rights Institute, University of Connecticut. He received the Distinguished Scholar Award, American Political Science Association, Human Rights Section, 2007. He received the Quincy Wright Career Achievement Award, International Studies Association, Midwest Section, 2003. He is the General Editor of 'The Encyclopedia of Human Rights', five volumes, Oxford University Press, 2009. His book, 'Human Rights in International Relations' (Cambridge), will go into a third edition. His co-authored book, 'The United Nations and Changing World Politics' (Westview) is in its sixth edition.

Willem van Genugten is Professor of International Law at Tilburg University and Dean of The Hague Institute for Global Justice. He is also Visiting Professor at the University of Minnesota, USA and Extraordinary Professor of International Law at the North-West University, South Africa. He holds the position of Chair of the standing Commission on Human Rights of the Dutch government, and is vice-chair of the Dutch Advisory Council on International Affairs, of which the Commission is a part. He is Editor of the 'Netherlands'

School of Human Rights Research Series', and Editor-in-Chief of the 'Netherlands Yearbook of International Law'.

Afke de Groot is coordinator of the Netherlands Chapter of the Society for International Development (SID). She holds a MSc in Cultural Anthropology from the University of Amsterdam. Before joining SID she worked as a researcher at the Institute for Research on Working Children (IREWOC). She was also country coordinator Nepal and India for Amnesty International Netherlands.

René Grotenhuis is President of Society of International Development Netherlands' Chapter and Chief Executive Officer of the Catholic development organisation Cordaid. He has acquired a wealth of knowledge and experience in the field of development co-operation, initially as a policy officer and later as a member of the Executive Board of several Dutch development organisations (until 1998). Since his appointment as the Chief Executive Officer of Cordaid (2003), he has become one of the key players in the Dutch development debate, partly due to the fact that he has recently written a variety of publications on development issues. From 2008-2011 he was the president of CIDSE, the European network of Catholic development agencies.

Hein de Haas is Senior Research Fellow at the International Migration Institute (IMI) of the James Martin 21st Century School and the Department of International Development at the University of Oxford. His research focuses on the linkages between migration and broader processes of human development and globalisation, primarily from the perspective of migrant-sending societies. He did extensive fieldwork in the Middle East and North Africa and, particularly, Morocco. He has a PhD in social sciences (Radboud University of Nijmegen, the Netherlands), an undergraduate degree in cultural anthropology and an MA (cum laude) in human and environmental geography (University of Amsterdam). He acted as consultant or advisor to governments and international organisations including the UK Government Office of Science, EU, UNDP, UNRISD, IOM and Oxfam.

Seth Kaplan is senior fellow at New York University and managing partner of Alpha International Consulting, which helps corporations tailor their strategies and operations to fit the challenging conditions found in developing countries. He is also a foreign policy analyst and the author of 'Fixing Fragile States: A New Paradigm for Development' (2008). This book critiques current Western policies in fragile states and lays out a new approach to overcoming the problems they face – an approach that gives due weight to socio-political conditions, governance systems, human-resource constraints and investment environments. His articles on countries as varied as the Democratic Republic of Congo, Bolivia and China have appeared in a wide variety of journals and newspapers.

Inge Kaul is adjunct professor at the Hertie School of Governance, Berlin, Germany and advisor to various governmental, multilateral and non-profit organisations on issues of international cooperation finance, public-private partnerships and global-issue diplomacy. She was the first director of UNDP's Human Development Report Office, a position, which she held from 1989 to 1994, and director of UNDP's Office of Development Studies from 1995 to 2005. She is the author of numerous publications on international public economics and finance and the lead editor of 'Providing Global Public Goods; Managing Globalization' (Oxford University Press, New York, 2003) and 'The New Public Finance; Responding to Global Challenges' (Oxford University Press, New York, 2006). Her current research focuses on institutional issues of global public goods provision, especially UN system reform and the future of multilateralism.

Kate Nash is Professor of Sociology at Goldsmiths, University of London, where she is also co-Director of the Centre for the Study of Global Media and Democracy; and Faculty Fellow at the Center for Cultural Sociology, Yale University. She recently published 'The Cultural Politics of Human Rights' (Cambridge University Press 2009) and the second edition of 'Contemporary Political Sociology' (Wiley-Blackwell 2010). She is currently writing 'The Sociology of Human Rights' (Cambridge University Press).

294

Eduard Nazarski has been the Director of Amnesty International Netherlands since 2006. In this capacity, he is responsible for overall management, representation and international policy. His fields of expertise are human rights, refugee policy and civil society. Before working with Amnesty, he worked at VluchtelingenWerk Nederland, where he worked for 9 years in various functions. He has been member of the board of the European Council on Refugees (ECRE) since 1997. From 2005 to 2009, he was chair of the ECRE. Eduard Nazarski studied Anthropology at Nijmegen University (1982) and obtained an MBA degree in 2000.

Lionel Veer is Ambassador for Human Rights at the Dutch Ministry of Foreign Affairs. He studied Philosophy at the University of Amsterdam and after working for this University he started to work for the Ministry of Foreign Affairs and has not left since 1984. He has held several positions in the Netherlands and at Dutch Embassies in Cameroon, Dublin, Zagreb and Paris. He has been Director of the Movement of Persons, Migration and Alien Affairs Department.

Shi Yinhong is Professor of International Relations and Director of Center on American Studies at Renmin University of China. He received his PhD in International History in Nanjing University in 1988. His previous positions include Professor of International History at Nanjing University (1993-1998), Professor of International Relations at International Relations Academy in Nanjing (1998-2001), Visiting Professor of Public Policy for teaching at the University of Michigan(2004, 2005, 2008), and Visiting Professor of Modern China Studies for Teaching at Aichi University in Nagoya (2004). He was President of American History Research Association of China (1996-2002). His research interests are history and ideas of international relations, strategic studies, and foreign policies of China and the United States.

Tom Zwart is professor of human rights at the Faculty of Law, Economics and Governance of Utrecht University. He is also the director of the Netherlands School of Human Rights Research, established by the five leading Dutch universities, which consists of around 200 researchers from diverse disciplines. He specialises in the Asian and African approach towards human rights, the relation between international criminal law and local peace and justice initiatives, and human rights and traditional values. Zwart has been a visiting scholar at a number of universities around the world including Australian National University, Cambridge University, Chinese People's Public Security University, Sciences-Po (Paris), Sydney University, Tsinghua University, Washington University (St. Louis), and Zhejiang University. He has advised national and international governmental bodies on human rights, including the EU, the Council of Europe and the UN Human Rights Council. Prior to taking up his position at Utrecht, Zwart served as head of the European and Legal Affairs Department of the Dutch Home Office, and as senior counsel to the Dutch Deputy Prime Minister.

Sonja Zweegers has a MSc in Anthropology from Amsterdam University. She worked as Publications Coordinator at the Institute for Research on Working Children (IREWOC), and is currently the Managing Editor of The Newsletter, the quarterly publication of the International Institute for Asian Studies (IIAS), Leiden, the Netherlands.